The Father's Heart

His Delight, Your Destiny

Dave Carroll

The Father's Heart: His Delight, Your Destiny
© 2013 Dave Carroll

Published by Village House Press
Englewood, OH

ISBN: 978-1-940243-08-5
Library of Congress Control Number: 2013948534

*For Mom and Dad, whose love and lives
have given me a lifelong glimpse
into the heart of the Father*

Acknowledgments

I have always wanted to write a book. For the past decade, I have lived with a nagging feeling that I should probably write a book. Then I finally got to the stage where I knew that I *must* write a book...this book. Anything less at this point would have been disobedience. This is more than just a book to me. It's the heart of my ministry and my reason for living, poured out in the form of words on a page. But this was far from a solo effort, so I need to say thanks to some special people who had irreplaceable roles in making this whole thing possible. When the Lord uses the truth in this book to transform lives, a big chunk of the "well done" belongs to them!

To my editors. Not the professional staff of a major publishing company, but people who know my heart and have generously given their love, their gifts, and their time:

My mom, Darlene Carroll, who tirelessly put her nearly forty years of teaching experience to good use—finding errors in typing, punctuation, subject-verb agreement, etc. and reminding me of a whole host of grammar rules that I had forgotten even existed.

My daughter, Hannah, who thinks like her daddy and who is already a better writer than her daddy, assets which made her invaluable in organizing the big picture flow of my thoughts and ideas and in helping me choose the right words and phrases to communicate the message clearly and effectively. Time and time again, I would look at her suggestions and say, "Yes! That is exactly what I really wanted to say!"

My friend, Marisa Lapish, who edited with her heart, diving into the material from the standpoint of someone who wants to use it to minister the love of the Father to others. Thanks for your constant affirmation and encouragement in the midst of the writing process.

To my pastors in Ohio, Mark Spansel and Jeff Pierce, whose friendship and kindred spirits assure me that maybe I'm not crazy; that it's OK to be human; that the heart of the Father is still the heart of the gospel, the heart of effective ministry, and the heart of everything that is good in life. You guys are awesome.

To my wife Jen, whose endless patience with me is a continual reflection of the Father's love. Thank you for lovingly encouraging me to write, for relentlessly reminding me that the Lord has called me to write, and for so often sacrificially setting aside your desire to be with me in order to create time and space for me to write. Thanks for allowing my spontaneity to invade your orderly world, for creating a home environment where we can share the Father's love with many, for always believing in me, always praying for me, and always loving me.

To my kids, Hannah, Elizabeth, Joshua, and Sarah, who fill my life daily with irrefutable evidence that God loves me. Thank you for honoring me by not interrupting when the "Daddy is creating a book" sign was on my door, and by giving me quiet whenever Mommy would say, "Shh! Daddy is trying to write." Thank you for the joy and privilege of being your father, for a lifetime of great teaching illustrations, and for the way you so naturally share in our ministry, opening your hearts and lives to whoever comes our way. I'm so proud of you, my beloved children in whom I am well-pleased.

To our many spiritual sons and daughters in Uganda. It has been our joy to share our lives with you over the course of these past sixteen years. When I look at the pain and brokenness that is all around me, it can be overwhelming, and sometimes I am tempted to just give up. But when I think about where many of you came from, and when I look at the beauty of the Father's love at work in you today, you become living billboards that remind me of the reason I exist. And it inspires me to keep going.

To those who have graciously allowed me to share their personal testimonies of the Father's transforming love in their lives. May He use your stories in this book to write a new chapter of love, life, healing, and freedom in the hearts and lives of many people throughout Uganda and all over the world.

Contents

Before You Begin

I once heard a preacher tell a story about a woman who was sitting under a tree, reading the Bible. A friend passed by and asked, "What book are you reading?" She responded, "I'm not reading this book. This book is reading me."

There is more than one way to read a book. You can move through all of the chapters, put it on your shelf, and say, "That was pretty good." Or you can live in it, page by page, opening your heart to allow God to enter places where maybe you have never allowed anyone else to go, asking Him to speak to you and work deeply in you.

You have a choice. You can read this book…or you can allow God to use this book to read you. Here are a few suggestions:

Read it prayerfully. Before and after you read each chapter, take time to seek the Lord and to surrender your heart and mind to Him. Sometimes you may need to pause in the middle of a chapter to ask for wisdom, to repent, or to allow Him to bring some needed healing.

Keep a notebook with you to write thoughts and reflections. When the Holy Spirit brings something to your mind as you are reading, write it down. It will help you to remember key points, and it will give you something to pray about later.

Take the necessary time. My recommendation is that you spend at least as much time reflecting on the chapter as you spend reading it. Don't move on to the next chapter until you have taken the time to meditate on what you have read, to pray, and to allow God to work in you.

Study with a small group. This book can be used for individual study and growth, but it would be ideal if you could work through this with a small group of friends with whom you are very comfortable. Read one or two chapters and do the reflection and further study at the end. Then come together as a group at the end of the week, to share what God is doing in you and to pray for one another. You must be willing to be honest with one another, to share pain, struggles, and weaknesses. If you will do that, I believe that the Lord will do a wonderful work in your lives.

Let the truth work in you. Don't just rush to the next chapter! Give the Lord time to take what you have read and drive it deep into your heart. There are four brief sections at the end of each chapter which are designed to help you do that:

- *Key Thought.* This is an important point from the chapter to help you focus your heart and mind on the truth you have just encountered.

- *Personal Reflection/Group Discussion.* These questions will help you to examine your heart, and also to assimilate and apply what you have read. Be sure to do this on your own *before* you meet with your small group.

- *Scriptural Prescription.* The truth is good medicine for your soul. At the end of each chapter is a key Scripture for you to memorize and to meditate on. Read it at least three different times each day, so that your heart absorbs it and it becomes a regular part of your thinking.[1]

- *Further Study.* This will take you deeper into the Word, applying Scriptures that were in the chapter and studying new Scriptures related to the content of the chapter.

Introduction

Every year, during the dry season in Uganda, many farmers intentionally set their fields on fire in order to clear away remains from the previous crop, to kill weeds, and to get rid of unwanted bush in preparation for planting. I have seen it happen every season for more than fifteen years. But each time I look at the blackened acres of ash-covered ground, I still can't help but think to myself, "Is it really possible that life could ever spring from this ground again?"

Yet every year, when the first rains fall, little flecks of green begin to appear amidst the charred stubble. Signs of life where it had looked like life wasn't possible. By the middle of the season, you would never guess that this same field was barren and panting for its next breath just a few weeks ago. The soil is now healthy, and new seeds have been planted. And by the end of the season, this ground that once appeared to be dead is bursting forth with the fruit of an abundant harvest.

That's a beautiful picture of what happens when hearts that have been beaten down and reduced to ashes are flooded with a fresh out-pouring of the love of God.

Like the dry ground that thirsts for rain, people were created with an intense longing for life. Deep in the heart of every person is a hunger to love and to be loved…a hunger to know that they belong….a hunger to know that their life has meaning and purpose, to know that they're not just aimlessly turning the calendar pages one day after another, but that they're called to live for something much larger than themselves…a hunger to know that they're invited to experience infinite beauty, perfect peace, and unending faithfulness…a hunger to know that they can live in the safety of a strong embrace, an embrace that will never end. People are hungry for home.

That hunger is in you. And from the beginning of time, God's desire has been that you would find your home in Him, to know that your security, your value, and your hope come from only one source–understanding and walking in the simple truth that you are deeply loved by God.

When people really understand and embrace His love, He takes the most hopeless of people and fills them with hope. He takes lives that were shattered and makes them whole. He takes those whom society had thrown away as useless, and He makes them His most faithful sons and daughters.

So many times, I've seen the love of God invade broken lives– lives that were desperate, lives that were hopeless, lives that had lost the ability to dream[2]–and turn them into something beautiful, something budding with new life. His love is powerful.

I have seen the love of God transform lives time and time again. But as I am confronted with the pain and brokenness around me, sometimes I still can't help but think to myself, "Is it really possible for life to spring from these hearts again?"

When we think about the problems in sub-Saharan Africa, we normally think of things like poverty, AIDS, lack of access to clean drinking water, political instability, hunger, and lack of quality medical care. Don't misunderstand me. Those are all huge problems which require equally huge solutions.

Yet the truth is, they are all just symptoms of a much deeper problem, something that no amount of political restructuring, economic development, education or social reform could ever begin to solve. Those things may alleviate the symptoms, but they can't deal with the real disease.

From the fishing villages on the shores of Lake Victoria to the storied houses on the hills of Kampala, there is a deadly disease that is sweeping through our nation, afflicting people indiscriminately, regardless of race, age, gender, nationality, economic position, or social status. The condition that threatens the life of our nation more than any other is this: people have *broken hearts*. They are broken because of their own sin, broken because of the sins of others against them, and broken because they don't understand the depth of God's love for them. And broken hearts make a broken world.

There is so much uncertainty in this life. But one thing that is certain is that life will continue to come, along with its familiar companions—abuse, neglect, pain, heartache, disappointment, and death. Too often, we who profess to follow Christ are deaf to the cries of the broken-hearted. And while we sing, dance, clap our hands, and listen to another Sunday sermon filled with empty promises of health, wealth, and prosperity, the world is dying around us....

Somewhere in Karamoja, a ten-year-old girl is getting out of bed for what seems to be another normal day, having no idea that her parents are going to sell her into the hands of human traffickers for the price of a bag of charcoal.

Somewhere in Rakai district, a thirteen-year-old boy in the village wonders how his family can survive another day. There are eight children. None of them have ever gone to school. They're hungry. His little sister has malaria, and there is no money to take her to the doctor. Their mud house is falling down, but he doesn't have the time or resources to do anything about it. And they have never experienced the love and direction of a parent. Thanks to AIDS, this young boy *is* the parent, just one of the thousands of child-led families in Uganda.

Somewhere in a hostel on campus, a young lady wakes up feeling empty and dirty. She was looking for love, but she was used and quickly thrown away by yet another guy. She wonders if somewhere there is someone who could look at her, not for the beauty of her body, but for the beauty that she has within her. She wonders if there is someone who could ever love her for who she is, not for what they can get from her.

Somewhere in Luwero, a woman sits on the floor in her small house, clutching an album filled with pictures from a day that held out the hope of a happy life. But as she nurses the wounds from her husband's latest drunken rampage, that woman in the photos wearing the beautiful white dress seems like someone from a distant dream.

Somewhere in Mbale, a nine-year-old boy lies awake at night in a boarding school dormitory. More than anything, he just wants his daddy to come and say good night to him, to tell him that he loves him and that he is proud of him. But Daddy has never really been part of his life. He has always been too busy trying to become a successful businessman. Sending his son away to school at age five was the only way to be free to focus on his career. And a lonely little boy, in a room full of lonely little boys, lies in bed with a broken heart. He wonders if somewhere there might be another world where it doesn't hurt like this one does.

Don't be deceived. This isn't a disease that hits only the poor and disadvantaged. Even the Kampala philosophers who write their wisdom on the back windows of taxis tell us that: *"the rich also cry."* And they are right. I continually come face to face with people who look successful on the outside, but are starving for love and dying on the inside:

A group of pastors–men who are admired and looked to by many for the answers to life's questions–sobbing like children, as they begin to confront the wounds they have carried in their hearts since they were kids.

A young lady from a wealthy family, a girl who had everything that money could buy, weeping in our sitting room because she didn't get something that money can't buy–her father's love.

A soon-to-be university graduate, after I taught a class on Biblical parenting, asking me in despair, "Most of us come from such abusive and broken families. Is there any hope for healing in this nation?"

A successful businessman just hanging his head and telling me, "I don't even know what love is."

People in this world are hurting. "Our world is plagued with an epidemic of pain," writes Floyd McClung in *The Father Heart of God.*[3]

A friend of mine from seminary once said that if you could sum up, in one statement, everything Jesus was trying to communicate through His life and ministry, it would be this: "It's not supposed to be this way."

Hearts weren't created to be broken. People weren't meant to be lonely and rejected. Children weren't meant to be abandoned and left to try to navigate life on their own.

Jesus came preaching about life as God created it to be—a life where people love and are loved, a life where there is joy, a life where there is peace, a life where people are filled with a real and living hope. Wherever Jesus went, He demonstrated the power of that life. He loved those whom no one else would love. He touched those whom no one else would dare to touch. He healed broken bodies and broken hearts. And He left behind Him a trail of transformed lives wherever He went.

Those aren't just old stories about Jesus. That's the calling of the church, to proclaim and to demonstrate the loving power of life in the family of God. Not just in a church service, but in the world, where real people live…where people are hurting…where people are broken. He calls us to take His love to the lost, the poor, the rejected, the abandoned, and the abused.

God loves people. He wants to pour out His love into the lives of people. And He accomplishes it by working through people. That's God's method. There is no magic formula. Big prayer meetings and worship gatherings are great, but tangible, lasting transformation happens when the power of God's love works in the hearts of people, through the lives of other people in the midst of real life.

How do we change a nation? Nations will be transformed when communities are transformed. Communities will be transformed when churches are transformed. Churches will be transformed when families are transformed. And families will be transformed when individual people are transformed.[4]

It begins with His work in <u>you</u>. He wants to work through you to reproduce His *life* in the lives of others. He wants to work through you to bring *healing* to broken hearts. He wants to work through you to lead others into *freedom*. Not the freedom to do whatever they want, but the freedom to be the people that He created them to be.

Before you can be a vessel of that life, healing, and freedom, though, you have to first know it for yourself. And it is found only in the heart of the Father.

But there are so many people who don't understand His heart, even in the Church. Many of you think of Him as the religious God whom you know only from a prayer–"Our Father who art in heaven." You see Him as a distant, faraway God who made it possible for you to live forever in the next life, and who you hope will occasionally show up to do a miracle for you in this life. But otherwise, He seems to be disconnected from you and disinterested in the innermost needs of your heart. That's not the God whom Jesus came to reveal. When Jesus calls you to "come," He is inviting you to the heart of Abba, the Father who is near... the Father who the Bible says is gentle, caring, and forgiving... the Father who is strong...the Father who knows every weakness and every need, every hope and every dream, every frustration and every struggle, every failure and every victory.

He knows what makes you laugh, and He knows what makes you cry. He knows when you stand up, and He knows when you sit down. He knows what you think about when you are alone, and He knows every word you speak, even before you speak it. He is a Father who cares about you, a Father who will never abandon you, a Father who rejoices in you, and a Father who loves you.

He wants to fill your life with His *life*. He wants to pour out His love to bring *healing* into every painful corner of your heart and soul. He wants you to live in the wonderful *freedom* of a beloved son or daughter of God.

That life, healing, and freedom is found when you really understand His heart towards you. And what is in His heart towards you is almost indescribable. Brennan Manning writes:

> If you took the love of all the best mothers and fathers who have lived in the course of human history, all their goodness, kindness, patience, fidelity, wisdom, tenderness, strength, and love and united all those qualities in a single person, that person's love would only be a faint shadow of the love and mercy in the heart of God the Father addressed to you and me at this moment.[5]

Every Christian knows, in his mind, the fact that God loves him or her, yet for most professing believers it is nothing more than information. But Jesus didn't come so that we could be better informed. He came so that we could be completely transformed. And the transforming love of God can't be understood just by reading a book. It has to be revealed to you.

So before you go on to chapter 1, I want you to pause for a few minutes. I want you to open your heart honestly to the Father. Ask Him to speak to you. Ask Him to show His heart to you. Ask Him to work in you. Expect to hear His voice. Expect to find life. Expect to find healing. Expect to find freedom.

To give it is His delight....to find it is your destiny.

As you read the following poem, written by my daughter Hannah, put yourself in a posture that is ready to receive from God, a posture that Henri Nouwen describes in this way: "I have to kneel before the Father, put my ear against His chest and listen, without interruption, to the heartbeat of God."[6]

We Cry "Father"

We cry "Abba, Father." We call out to You.
Break the chains of our pain that still bind us.
We are lost in a world of shattered hope.
But You're our Father, Lord. Come find us.

We cry "Abba, Father." We call out to You.
"There's no hope. Just give up," the world told us.
We are crushed underneath an army of fear.
But You're our Father, Lord. Come hold us.

We cry "Abba, Father." We call out to You.
Do You care, somewhere there up above us?
We are trapped in a world that has thrown us away.
But You're our Father, Lord. Come love us.

And the Father says:
"Don't be afraid
For I bear your pain.
I'll give you My peace,

I'll show you the way.
I'll always be here
So My children, don't fear.
I'm your Father. And I love you."

Part I:

Finding Life
in the Father's Heart

I pray that you, being rooted and established in love, may have power, together with all the Lord's holy people, to grasp how wide and long and high and deep is the love of Christ, and to know this love that surpasses knowledge–that you may be filled to the measure of all the fullness of God.

Ephesians 3:17-19 (NIV)

Chapter 1

Life:

His Delight

I didn't find God—He found me...For religions teach man's search for God, and the gospel teaches God's search for man.[7]

E. Stanley Jones

God is love. He didn't need us. But He wanted us. And that is the most amazing thing.[8]

Rick Warren

Going Where Daddy Goes

A few years ago, I had to go out to the hardware store to get supplies for some repair work I was doing at home. As I was getting myself ready to go, I called out to my wife to tell her that I was going to leave in a few minutes. My daughter Sarah, who was four years old at the time, heard me and decided that she was going to go along.

"I want to go with Daddy!" she cried out with excitement.

As she ran from her room, she was still trying to put on her socks as she was moving, nearly falling down in the process. "I want to go with Daddy!"

She put on her coat and began to get her shoes on. "I want to go with Daddy!"

Finally, completely ready, she stood up, opened the door eagerly, and then looked back at me and asked, "Where are we going?"

She didn't even know where I was going! She didn't know if I was making a quick trip to the supermarket for some eggs or attending an all-day pastors' conference, if I was going to visit a friend in the hospital or taking my car to get it serviced.

She had no idea where I was going. But it didn't matter. She wanted to go, not because where I was going sounded exciting or beneficial to her, but simply because *I* was going there.

It's a heart issue. It's all about love. It begins with my heart towards her. She knows how much her daddy loves her and how much he delights in her. Her heart then responds to what she has received: she loves her daddy, trusts her daddy, and delights in her daddy. And out of the overflow of what is in her heart, she decides that *wherever* Daddy is going is the place where she wants to be.

That is a beautiful picture of what it means to be a child of God. You see, being a Christian isn't a matter of something we have to do. It isn't about joining a new religion, getting involved in lots of church activities, or trying really hard to live by a new set of morals.

Being a Christian is about a complete transformation of the heart, which impacts everything about the way we live. It begins in the heart of the Father who delights in us and loves us relentlessly. That love does a powerful work in our hearts. In response, our hearts and lives reflect the love we have received: we love Him, we trust Him, and we joyfully follow Him wherever He leads. Just because *He* is there. No other reason.

When Jesus calls us to Himself, He is first and foremost inviting us to come home to the heart of the Father–to find forgiveness, to find freedom, to find healing, and to find life in His love. But that's not all. The One who says, "Come to Me" also says, "Follow Me." In other words, "Go where I go. Do what I do."

John, one of the original Twelve who answered the call to follow Jesus, wrote that if we claim to belong to Jesus, if we claim that we live in Him and that He lives in us, then we ought to "walk in the same manner as He walked" (1 John 2:6).

That is a powerful statement! That means if we are genuine followers of Christ, then we will go where Jesus goes and do what Jesus does. And if we're going to walk like Jesus, it means we have to have hearts that are like His heart. What motivates you and me must be the same thing that motivated Him!!

So the question that we need to ponder prayerfully is this: "How did Jesus walk? What motivated Jesus to do the things that He did? What was in His heart?"

In John chapter 5, Jesus was entering Jerusalem with His disciples. Next to the gate of the city, there was a pool where multitudes of people who were sick, blind, and disabled would gather and wait, because the word had it that at certain times of the year an angel of the Lord would come down and stir up the waters. And whoever got into the water first would be healed.

Now it is important to note that Jesus wasn't on His way to a scheduled meeting at this place. He was going to Jerusalem for one of the Jewish religious feasts. He wasn't planning to go to this pool at all. He was going somewhere else. But a heart that is filled with the Father's love is always ready to be interrupted in order to share His love with someone who needs it.

For Jesus, ministering the love of the Father to people wasn't His profession, nor was it an event that He put on His schedule. It wasn't a task to be done. It came from within His heart, the natural overflow of who He was.

As He was entering the city, Jesus' eyes were drawn to one particular man among the multitude, a man who had been crippled by sickness for 38 years. Jesus had compassion on him, and He asked him, "Do you want to get well?"

"Of course, I want to get well!" the man answered, "But I don't have anyone to help me, so by the time I get myself moving, someone else gets to the water first."

Well, there was no reason to sit and wait for another angel to come and stir up the waters again (all of the angels work for Jesus anyway, so if He really wanted one, all He had to do was call). Jesus already had everything that the man needed, and He said to him, "Stand up, pick up your mat, and walk." And the man was healed instantly.

When the Jewish religious leaders heard what had happened, they began to persecute Jesus, because He had done these things on the Sabbath. Their hearts were blinded by their desire to keep the rules at all costs, and the rules said that you couldn't work on the Sabbath, because that day was reserved for worship of God alone.

It's ironic. They persecuted Jesus for what they thought was an act of irreverence. But what Jesus did was actually an act of pure worship. They thought they were glorifying God by trying to preserve what they considered to be the purity of the Sabbath. But in the process, they completely missed the heart of the One who made the Sabbath. By lavishly pouring out the Father's love on a broken person who was in desperate need of life, Jesus was doing the one thing that glorifies God more than anything else (on the Sabbath or any other day).

Jesus didn't back down from their challenge. He told them that this kind of work is always appropriate, even on the Sabbath. "My Father works on the Sabbath, and so I keep working, too," He told them.

Two verses later, knowing full well that they wanted to kill Him for saying that God was His Father, He clarified His actions even further: "The Son cannot do anything on His own. He only does what He sees His Father doing. Whatever the Father does, the Son also does…because the Father loves the Son."

What motivates Jesus? The Father *loves Him* perfectly and completely. So Jesus only goes where the Father goes, and He only does what the Father does.

What does that mean for us? Think about it. John tells us that if we claim to be followers of Jesus, then we will walk in the same way that Jesus walked. Jesus said that He only does exactly what He sees the Father doing.

So that means the next question we have to answer is, "What is the Father doing?" And not only do we need to understand what He is doing, but more importantly, we need to discover the goal behind all of His activity.

Why does the Father do what He does? What is in His heart? The answer to this question is the most foundational piece of truth there is, because if we are going to be the people that we were created to be, then we must know the heart and the purposes of the One who created us.

If we don't understand why we were created, then our entire lifetime will be lived like a man who is supposed to be traveling to Gulu but is following a map that leads to Masaka. No matter how well he drives, no matter how well he services his vehicle, no matter how much he enjoys the journey, he will never reach his destination. It will all be a complete waste of time…because he is going the wrong way.

There is a lot of talk these days in the church about "destiny." We talk about discovering our destiny, about achieving our desired destiny. But normally when we talk about destiny, we are only trying to answer the question, "*What* are we destined for?" We get caught up in thinking about what career we are destined for or what man or woman we are destined to marry. But very few people ever ask the question that really matters, the question that really deals with our destiny: "*WHY* are we alive?" If we don't understand that, nothing else will make sense.

Think about it. What is the point of trying to improve my relationship with my wife if I don't have a clue why I myself am even here? Why should I go to school and study when I don't even understand why God gave me a brain? Why should I get out of bed in the morning if I am not even sure why this day even exists?

Why should our people survive and continue living for another generation if we don't understand the purpose of living in *this* generation? Why should we continue breathing if we don't really understand why we were given breath at all? If we don't know why we are alive, nothing else makes sense. We need to go back to the One who made it all.

In the beginning, there was only God. At creation, there were no other opinions present. It was only Him. Paul says in Colossians 1:16 that all things–including you and me–were created not only by Him but *for* Him. In 1 Corinthians 8:6, he makes it even simpler: "we exist for Him."

It all begins in the heart of the Father. Everything that is good flows from there. "Whatever is good and perfect comes down to us from God our Father" (James 1:17, NLT).

So if we are going to understand our destiny–how we can find life, how we should live our lives, and why we should live our lives–then we have to find the answer to the big question, the one that gives meaning to all other questions. That question is this: "What does the Father do? What is the motivation of His heart?"

In the Beginning There Was…LOVE

Well, let's go back to the very beginning. Why did God even create the world? Have you ever thought about that? What was it in Him that made Him want to create people in the first place? Was He bored? Was He lonely? Was He in need of something that He didn't already have?

Not at all! From all eternity, God is and has always been perfectly happy and infinitely satisfied within Himself. Or, as my daughter Elizabeth used to say when she was little, "He really likes being God."

The Bible tells us in Psalm 16:11 that in His presence there is "fullness of joy." He isn't just occasionally joyful. Every fiber of His infinite being is bursting with joy.

In 1 John 4:8, we see that God not only has love, but "God is love." It is who He is. And in the eternal love relationship between Father, Son, and Holy Spirit, God is and always has been perfectly happy, and He enjoys Himself immensely.

Why creation then? He didn't need anything. He was satisfied beyond anything we could imagine. So why did He do it? I think it's because there is something about the nature of true love and true joy. Love and joy cannot be contained.

John Piper says that the nature of joy is to *"expand* itself."[9] It can't stay inside. It has to get out. When you have joy in you, you want to do something to show it, to invite others into your joy. You want to shout. You want to hug somebody. You want to sing. You want to dance. Actually, you don't just want to share it. You *have to* share it with others, or you'll just explode. Joy is like that.

Love is like that, too. The nature of love is to *reproduce* itself. When you are full of love, you can't just sit at home and enjoy it alone. You have to go looking for someone to share it with. Your heart compels you to do it, because you want the lives of others to be filled with the same love that fills your life. Love fills us with an endless delight, and out of the constant overflow of that delight, love will always seek to reproduce itself into the life of another person.

That is exactly what God has done. John 3:16 says that it was nothing but pure love that motivated the Father to send His Son into the world to die for our sins and to bring us life. This wasn't a quick reaction to a world that had suddenly gone bad. Ephesians 1:4-5 affirms that this was God's plan before the world even began. Before you or anyone else had done anything, either good or bad, God had already envisioned His family, a family of adopted sons and daughters. What was the motive? It says that He did it "in love."

Joy has to get out. Love has to reproduce. And when the love and joy of God overflowed in an expression of eternal delight, creation happened.

Creation itself began in the depths of the heart of God. And His immeasurable delight, which flows from His love, continues to drive Him to express His deep joy by reproducing His life in the lives of men, women, and children from among every tribe, language, and nation on earth.

His desire is for *people.* God is a Father. He wants children. And He is a good African Father…He wants LOTS of children. He yearns for them to be at home with Him so that He can make a complete deposit of His life into their lives, so that He can pour out His love on them, so that He can raise them up to be just like their Father.

He delights in Himself. He delights in His children. He wants to give them *life*...His life. That life is found in His love, and He will pursue them to the ends of the earth in order to fill their lives with the fullness of His love.

Relentless Delight

Our friend Julie told me about a time when the pursuing love of God found her and touched her in a powerful way. She was teaching Sunday School at a church on the Makerere University campus, and my daughter Elizabeth was one of her students.

Right in the middle of the lesson, Elizabeth, who was four at the time, went to Julie and said, "Julie, I have to tell you something."

Julie knew that 99% of the "urgent" comments of four-year-olds in Sunday School don't have anything to do with the lesson, so she just said, "Not now, Elizabeth."

Well, if you know my daughter Elizabeth, you know that when she really wants to say something, "not now" is not on her list of acceptable responses.

So she pleaded her case: "Julie, it's important!"

"Elizabeth, we are having Sunday School. It will have to wait."

Elizabeth was about to explode. She began to bounce up and down impatiently, pleading with a sense of extreme urgency: "But Julie...I... have...to...tell...you...NOW!"

Now Julie was annoyed. She stopped teaching, took Elizabeth aside, knelt down in front of her, and said sharply, "We are trying to have Sunday School. What do you want?"

Elizabeth just smiled, looked up into Julie's eyes, and said sweetly, "Julie, I love you so much."

Julie had things to do. Important things...even things to do for God. And she was so wrapped up in what she was doing that she almost missed the one thing that she really needed, the simple but powerful message that she was loved.

I wonder how often the Lord feels like Elizabeth did on that day. We are so busy, running around doing so many things, sometimes even busy doing things for Him. Yet in the midst of it all, He has *one* message that He is trying to communicate to us. He wants us to hear Him. He wants us to know His heart. He wants so much to break into our lives with an understanding of the simple but powerful truth that He loves us.

Sometimes life makes it so difficult to understand that it is possible that anyone could love us, let alone God. Yet He pursues us night and day, waiting to break through in those brief moments when we open our hearts to the possibility that maybe He really is who the Bible says He is....

Psalm 27:10 assures you that even if your earthly mother and father abandon you, the Lord will not abandon you. He will gather you to Himself. He will be your Father.

Psalm 121 describes Him as a Father whose care for you is so perfect that He never takes His eyes off of you. He never sleeps. He doesn't close His eyes to rest, not even for one second.

Psalm 139:17-18 says that not only does He watch over you continually, but that you are always on His mind. You are not a burden to Him—another mouth to feed, more school fees to pay, someone else to take to the doctor. You are the object of His thoughts because He is a Father who longs to give you life. These aren't just random thoughts about you, like, "I wonder what Dave is doing today?" The word translated as "thoughts" refers to God's wonderful purposes for you. It's the same word He used when He said, "For I know the *plans* that I have for you" (Jeremiah 29:11, italics added).

A loving parent is always thinking about his children: how he can provide for them, counsel them, teach them, and order everything so that they can live life to the fullest. And the writer of this Psalm says that Father God is always thinking about you, so often that if you tried to count His thoughts towards you, it would be like going to the beach and trying to count every single grain of sand. He never stops thinking about how He can work in your heart. He never stops planning how He can fill your life with His love.

As wonderful as those truths are, this next one is almost unimaginable, so amazing to me and my family that in our home it is literally written on the wall in our sitting room:

> The LORD your God is with you, He is mighty to save. He will take great delight in you, He will quiet you with His love, He will rejoice over you with singing.
>
> Zephaniah 3:17 (NIV)

Looking ahead to the day when the Lord returns, and all of God's people will finally be gathered together, fully at home with Him living in their midst, the prophet Zephaniah calls God's people to rejoice in singing because of their delight in Him. But that delight doesn't originate with His children. Our delight in Him is a response, a reflection of the delight that He has in His people, a delight that leads Him to rejoice with singing...over *us*!

Think about this. We go to church, and the worship team leads us in singing. Who are we singing about? We are singing about the Lord. Why? Because we delight in Him. In heaven, the atmosphere is filled with the voices of a billion angels who surround the throne of God in a worship service that will never end. Why? Because they delight in Him.

Zephaniah tells us, though, that the Lord does some singing of His own. He sings a song that springs from *His* delight. And do you know who He is singing about, the object of His endless rejoicing? His people...His children...you!!

I can understand this, to a small degree. I really love my children. I take great delight in them. If you give me time, I could talk nonstop about the joy that they bring me. I could tell you everything about them: the details of the day they were born, their first steps, the things they do to make me laugh, their smiles, their dreams, and their unique abilities and personalities. I could go on and on, talking about the countless special moments we have had together over the years, and how each day they continue to show me love in the most simple and beautiful ways. And each telling and retelling would cause my heart to overflow with delight.

But to think that Almighty God, who spoke the universe into existence, continually watches over *me*, continually thinks about *me*, and continually sings over *me*...because He loves and delights in *me*? It is mind-boggling. But it's true, and His desire is that you would know that truth with complete certainty in every corner of your heart and soul.

Every moment of every day, whether you recognize it or not, the Father relentlessly fills your life with messages of His love, trying to communicate it so that you can understand. Everything He does is motivated by love.

When you look at the beauty of His creation, it is the love of the Father saying, "I created this for you to enjoy." When a child smiles at you, the Father is opening your heart to receive *His* smile. When someone does something kind for you, something you didn't deserve, the Father is reminding you of the wonders of *His* grace, of *His* mercies which are new every morning.

When He does a miracle in your life, it's not just an act of power that improves your health or your standard of living. It is a signpost that points beyond your circumstances, saying, "There is a Father who loves you with an everlasting love." When you pray for someone, and it is exactly what they needed to hear, it isn't an example of your wisdom in action. It is the Father showing His love to them and to you, saying, "Don't worry. I know every detail of your life. I love you. And I am with you." When you feel His presence in a worship service, it's not just a nice feeling. It is the Father keeping His promise to you from Romans 8:16, that His Spirit will confirm in your spirit the unchangeable reality that you are His child.

He did this for me the other day, when I was in Kampala to take care of some business for the ministry. Early that morning I had been thinking about this idea of God continually filling our lives with messages of His love. And I prayed that in the midst of the day's busy schedule, the

Lord would keep my mind fixed on Him and on His heart towards me as His son.

But I began to get caught up in thinking about all the things that I had to do. And as I was walking through the aisles of ShopRite, looking at the list of items I needed to purchase, a very simple but beautiful and peaceful-looking young lady walked up to me, as if she wanted to talk to me. But when I looked up, she simply looked me in the eyes, smiled a very genuine smile and said, "Good morning." It wasn't the greeting of someone who felt obligated to say hello because you were there in front of them. It was one of those rare heartfelt greetings that says, "I am really glad to see you," the kind of greeting that makes you feel as if your existence on this earth actually matters.

As she walked away, I waited for a moment, certain that she must have had some other reason for greeting me. But then the Father spoke to me, the answer to my prayer from earlier that morning. He said, "That smile was My smile...for *you*. I love you. Don't forget."

She wasn't an employee. And she didn't seem to be shopping. I saw her walking up and down several aisles, not really looking to be interested in anything on the shelves. "Does God send angels to ShopRite?" I wondered. It seemed like a ridiculous idea at first, but then I thought, "Why not? In light of everything else He has done for me–for example, *the cross*–is it really so crazy to think that His agents of love could be roaming the aisles of our local supermarkets?"

It's not crazy at all, because His love and delight are relentless. He longs to give you life. Not because of anything you have done to deserve it, but because of His intense desire to give it. And whoever you are...no matter what you have done...no matter what kind of person you have become...no matter how many times you have come to Him for forgiveness and then stumbled and fell again...His desire for you remains the same. He wants His life to be continually birthed in you, that it would be nurtured, that it would grow, and that in Him you would find satisfaction for the deepest longings and desires of your soul.

Life. It's His delight....it's your destiny.

Key Thought:

God delights in Himself. He delights in His children. He wants to give them *life*...His life. That life is found in His love, and He will pursue them to the ends of the earth in order to fill their lives with the fullness of His love.

Personal Reflection / Group Discussion:

Had you ever really thought (before reading this chapter) about *why* God created the world? Most of us probably hadn't. But when we understand His purposes, it changes everything. The Bible says in 1 Corinthians 8:6 that "we exist for Him," and in Colossians 1:16 that we were created not only by Him, but "for Him." Your purpose for living is not to succeed or just to survive. You were created to live for the same reason that He lives. And we see that the reason He lives is to fill the world with His life and love.

- *How does that understanding affect the way that you think about your life, about your goals, about your destiny?*

God rejoices in you? God sings with delight over you? God pursues you in love, every moment of every day?

- *What happens in your heart when you hear that truth? Does something leap from deep within you and say, "Yes! I know it!" Or is that difficult for you to believe? What causes you to doubt it?*

Scriptural Prescription:

The LORD your God is with you, He is mighty to save. He will take great delight in you, He will quiet you with His love, He will rejoice over you with singing.

Zephaniah 3:17 (NIV)

Further Study:

Read Psalm 81:6-16. Look at the desire of God to give life to His people, even though they are continually rebellious. Don't get too caught up in thoughts about exactly what He would give you or how He would protect you, but look into His heart, a heart that never changes, a heart that desires only one thing–to pour His life and love into the lives of people.

Chapter 2

Compassion:

His Heartache

If you would sum up the whole character of Christ in reference
to ourselves, it might be gathered into this one sentence: 'He was
moved with compassion.'[10]

Charles H. Spurgeon

He Knows My Name

A few years ago, I was preaching at a church in a nearby village, and the
pastor was publicly introducing his family members to me before I got
up to speak. He pointed to his children, one by one, and he told me their
names: "This one is Samuel, and Sanyu, and Milly…and…"

With a confused expression on his face, he stopped and looked at
one of his sons. After a few moments, he turned to his wife and said,
"What is his name?"

"Isaac," his wife replied with visible embarrassment.

"Ah-hah," he said. "This one is Isaac."

This was not one of those instances where someone's mind just goes
blank, and he forgets something for a moment. He knew it was one of
his children, but he really did not know his own son's name!!

Sadly, many people think that God is like that, that He sees them as
part of the crowd, as one of the billions of people He created, but that

He doesn't really know them intimately or care about the specific issues of their lives.

That's definitely how we normally view the world. We bypass the uniqueness of each individual, and we put people into categories, identifying them by their religion, their tribe, their race, or their social status: that Muslim…those Catholics…that Mugisu…those Bakiga…that big businessman…those villagers.

We might look at a crowd packed into Namboole Stadium for a football match and say that we see a mass of Ugandans. But when we understand the heart of the Father, we know that when He sees the crowds, He doesn't see categories. He sees people. He looks beyond the crowd, and He sees deep into the hearts of Florence…Mukisa…Akello…Gloria…Oyat…Simon…and Bamwesigye.

Real people with real potential, with real dreams, with real needs, with real fears, and with real frustrations.

He knows each one by name. And not only does He know their names, but He knows everything about them, down to the smallest detail. The Bible says that every hair on their heads is numbered. God knows every hope and every dream, every weakness and every sin. He knows the experiences they have been through. He knows the pain they carry in their hearts. He knows it all. He calls them to be part of His family, the community of believers. But He loves them and He cares about them as individuals…as *people*.

He knows them intimately, and He wants to give them life. He wants it so much that it hurts.

Painful Love

Moses spent most of his childhood on the streets of Kampala. He was an incredibly bright kid, with a smile that was infectious (when you could get him to smile). When we first arrived at the children's home where we worked for several years, a number of staff members warned us to "watch out for that one." Well, to us, that was an invitation, and we were determined that we would get to know him and pour the love of the Father into his life in whatever way we could.

We began by giving him a job. The boys were always looking for ways to earn money, and so staff members hired them to carry water, to slash their compounds, and to weed their gardens in order to help them get a few extra shillings. We hired Moses to take care of our compound.

It was quite a struggle, to say the least. We enjoyed the opportunity to spend time with him, but let's just say he wasn't the most reliable employee that we have ever had. Sometimes he showed up, sometimes he didn't. There were so many times that we thought we should just fire him, and a couple of times we actually did. But each time, the Lord reminded us that the purpose of this employment wasn't to minister to our compound, but to minister to Moses' heart. Over and over, we could hear the Lord's words to Hosea, when He told him not to give up on his adulterous wife but to go after her and bring her back home: "Go and love again." So we kept pursuing.

After some time, we began to see the Lord softening his heart. Moses became like part of our family. He loved our children, and they loved him. He had a lot of rough edges and a lot of pain, but God was visibly at work in his life. He was constantly borrowing and reading missionary biographies. He became part of my discipleship group, and he was so hungry to understand God's word and how to communicate it to others. The first time I heard him speak in the secondary school chapel, I was so impressed that I told my wife, "I think we have a preacher in the making here."

One afternoon, he came to our house and asked me if we could talk. He wanted to go to Rakai, where he was born, to see if any of his relatives were still around. We agreed to take him, and several days later we made the long journey to a place he hadn't seen for nearly eighteen years. I was amazed that he remembered all of the twists and turns of the dirt roads leading back to the village he had last seen when he was six years old. We stopped to ask for more specific directions from a couple of bicycle repairmen, and just by looking at his face, they recognized Moses as the son of his father (and they confirmed what Moses had always suspected but didn't really know for certain until that moment—his father had died years ago).

They directed us to the home of his auntie, who was delighted to see Moses. We spent several hours with her, visiting the grave of his father, learning more about his family, and meeting a few of his relatives who were still living there. Moses was so excited. He had seen his home. He had a sense of identity. From that day on, he never stopped talking about "my people."

Eventually, the Lord called us to move on from the children's home, to go to another village and establish a missionary training centre. Things didn't go well for Moses after that.

He had some struggles, and he eventually dropped out of secondary school and moved away from the children's home. He worked just enough to survive, slaughtering a pig and selling the meat whenever he needed some money. For the most part, though, he was just hanging around in the trading centre with other young men who had nothing to do. We tried to help him find a way to earn a stable income, and we managed to connect him with a couple of really good opportunities. However, he reverted to his old work ethic, and those opportunities were quickly lost.

After some time, the Lord spoke to us clearly that we were to go and find Moses and bring him to stay with us. He loved animals, and we had about forty pigs that we were raising at the training centre. So we hired him to take care of them. Finally, he had a steady job, he was at home, and we were able to invest in his life again. Things seemed to be moving in a positive direction, and we were praying with hopeful anticipation about what the Lord had in store for him.

But we learned just how persistent years of pain and rejection can be. Even after years of being loved, the ability to really trust and receive that love can still be so fragile. A series of events unfolded which revealed this sad truth in a very short time.

One day, I came home and saw piglets running all over the land. It was chaos. I called Moses and said, "What in the world are you doing?" I didn't quite understand his explanation of what had happened, but at least we were able to round up the pigs and get them back into their shelter.

Later that day, I saw him sitting on the step in front of our store-room, and he looked so distraught. I asked him what was wrong. He said, "Uncle, you told me earlier that I have no purpose on this planet."

I had no idea what he was talking about, so I asked him to explain. He said dejectedly, "You said that I am not doing anything worthwhile in this world."

"When did I say that?"

"You said, 'what in the world are you doing?'"

"No, no, no," I tried to clarify. "That is just a phrase we use in the States to emphasize a question. I was simply asking why you were letting the pigs run all over the place."

He understood the words of my explanation…but the pain in his heart remained.

Not long after that, he decided that he was going to go and see his auntie in Rakai. His plan was to live among his relatives on the family land, and eventually to begin his own farm there. So we gave him a couple of days off, and he went and shared his plans with his relatives. Their response was devastating. "You can't come here," they said. "We don't have land for you. You are no longer part of us."

Moses came back home, looking like someone who had just lost everything. In his mind, he *had* lost everything. When he had finished telling me about his journey, he just stared at the ground with tears in his eyes. And with a look of utter desolation on his face, he declared softly, "Uncle, I don't have a family. I am nobody."

We tried and tried and tried to talk to him, to assure him that *we* would be his family, and more importantly, to assure him that *God* was his Father. But the damage had already been done. What he had been told his whole lifetime had now been confirmed in his heart. He was just a street kid. No family. Of no value. Completely alone. Can't trust anybody. Can't be trusted. In his mind, that was just who he was. Nothing more.

A few days later, my wife was sending him down to the village to buy some pork. It had been awhile since we had bought pork, so as she was getting money from her purse, she asked Moses how much we should expect to pay. He gave her the price, and just to clarify, she said, "Really? That sounds high. I thought it was lower than that." She was just surprised. But he thought she was questioning him because she didn't trust him. The next day, Moses disappeared, and we haven't seen him since. It has been nearly seven years.

Several years ago, we heard rumors that he was making charcoal somewhere far off in the forest. Sometime after that, we were told that he had been put into a drug rehabilitation centre. But after a few days, he ran away. Most likely, he went back to the forest, but we have no idea exactly where he is now.

Whenever I think about Moses, it hurts. Not because of anything he has done to me, but because of how much I love him. I want life for him. I want him to live in the freedom of the Father's love. I want Moses to really know that God is a Father who will never abandon him. I want him to know how much the Father delights in him. I want him to know that the Father is pursuing him relentlessly, and that He will not give up until He brings Moses home.

When I imagine him there in the forest with a broken heart – longing for love, but hardened to the possibility of it – the heart of the Father in me just aches. It's not a sad little feeling that says, "That's too bad. I wish it were different." It's a severe grief that penetrates to the core of my soul, a deep anguish arising out of deep love. It's a searing pain that I can feel physically from the inside, as if a large hand is reaching down my throat and trying to tear my heart out.

"To love is to hurt," I once heard it said. Sometimes that means that we loved someone but we didn't receive love in return. That kind of pain can be devastating, and we will talk about that in a few chapters.

The pain I am talking about here, though, is different. It doesn't have to do with love that you have not received, but love that you long for someone else to receive. When you love someone, your greatest desire is to see them thriving, enjoying everything that God intended for them. Yet when they reject that love, or for some reason are unable to receive it, it brings a grief that is intolerable. Not because you wanted something *from* them, but because you desperately wanted something *for* them.

Nobody understands that pain better than God Himself, who suffers heartache, not from a sense of personal injury, but from a bottomless well of compassion, a yearning for His children to find life in Him.

The Father Who Suffers With His Children

In Matthew 9:35, it says that Jesus was going through "all the cities and villages, teaching in their synagogues and proclaiming the gospel of the kingdom, and healing every kind of disease and every kind of sickness." Wherever Jesus went, the crowds were always there.

In one situation, the house where He was teaching was so crowded that the friends of a disabled man had to remove part of the roof and dig a hole in the ceiling in order to lower him inside to see Jesus. On another occasion, so many people had gathered to hear Him teach that they were literally stepping on one another. There were times when He taught and healed from morning until night, not even getting a chance to stop and get a bite to eat. When He and His disciples finally decided to get away to a quiet place for some much-needed rest, the people found out where Jesus was planning to go, and they ran ahead of Him and were there waiting for Him when He arrived.

They just kept coming, sometimes hundreds, sometimes thousands. Sick. Blind. Disabled. Demon-possessed. Poor. Hungry. Abused.

Rejected. Lonely. Stories of despair. Stories of crushed hopes and shattered dreams. It was relentless. But it didn't annoy Him that they were always following Him. It wasn't an inconvenience to Him to have to deal with all of their problems. It moved Him. It broke His heart. Whenever He saw them, Matthew says, "He felt compassion for them" (Matthew 9:36).

Normally when we use that word 'compassion,' we are just saying that we feel badly for that person. We look at their situation, and we have a sense of sympathy ("Oh, that is too bad!"). To say that Jesus had sympathy or felt sorry for the people, however, doesn't even begin to describe what was going on inside of Him.

When Matthew wrote this gospel, he didn't use any of the typical words for 'compassion' in his language, because none of them was sufficient to capture what the disciples saw in the eyes of Jesus when He came face to face with the brokenness of people. So Matthew used a word which described a pain in the intestines,[11] the kind of pain that is so unbearable that something has to be done immediately to find relief.

Our English word, "compassion," comes from a Latin word which literally means "to suffer with," to participate in the suffering of another person.[12] When Jesus looked at the crowds, He didn't just feel sorry for them. Their pain became a deep anguish in His own heart. Speaking about this word, renowned Swiss theologian Karl Barth wrote this:

> The term obviously defies adequate translation. What it means is that the suffering and sin and abandonment and peril of these men...went...right into His heart, into Himself, so that their whole plight was now His own, and as such He saw it and suffered it far more keenly than they did. It means that He took their misery upon Himself, taking it away from them and making it His own.[13]

It was so intense that it actually became His pain, and He felt it in a way that even the people themselves didn't feel. How is it possible that He could feel it even more than they did, when they themselves were the ones actually going through the suffering? It's because of the heart of the Father which was in Jesus, a heart that knows exactly what His children need, and a heart that aches with a desire for them to receive it. I know the feeling all too well.

A number of years ago, one of my daughters was suffering terribly in the midst of a battle with an anxiety disorder. It wasn't like the normal anxiety that we all have to learn to deal with. It was caused by an improper balance of certain chemicals in the brain, something that was way beyond her control.

Fear consumed her, even when she knew that those fears didn't make any sense. For example, she used to be terrified of wolves, and she would say, "I know there are no wolves in Uganda, but I am afraid of them anyway." She feared that the house would catch on fire, that there would be a hurricane, or that snakes would come up from out of the floor. A slight change in the schedule or any kind of new situation would send into her into a state of panic.

She didn't want to be that way, but she couldn't really do much to stop it. For years, she lived in an almost constant state of frustration, and the feeling of being out of control manifested itself in outbursts of anger and abusive behavior, or in tears of helplessness and desperation. On a few occasions, when she was only about four years old, we even witnessed the clear presence of demonic influence (which is heartrending to see happening to your own daughter).

She didn't fully understand what was going on. But she knew there was a big problem. She knew that she felt out of control and completely helpless. She knew that it often had an almost paralyzing impact on the whole family. Sometimes, she said that she wished she had never been born. Other times, with tears, she pleaded for answers: "Daddy, why did God make me this way? Why won't He just fix me?" She desperately longed to be free.

We talked to so many doctors and counselors. We did extensive research about her condition, trying to learn anything that we could possibly do to help her. My wife and I had long conversations almost daily, many of them lasting late into the night, talking through how we could help our daughter and how we could love her and parent her most effectively. And we spent countless hours in prayer for her.

It was so painful to watch. We wanted so much for her to be free. We wanted her to have life in all of its fullness. The heart of the Father in us agonized for our daughter. Her pain became our pain, in a way that she herself couldn't even feel. Many times, I just wept before the Lord, appealing to His Father heart: "Lord, this is my daughter. This is *Your* daughter. Please. Even if You have to give her anxiety to me, then do it. I'll take it. But please set my little girl free. I want *her* to really live."

The Father's one desire is that His children would have life— that they would know love, experience peace, be filled with hope, and walk in joy and in freedom. When they don't get it, the heart of the Father literally suffers. And what Jesus saw when He looked into the eyes of the people in the crowds caused His heart to stir with that same agonizing love.

Like Sheep Without a Shepherd

Matthew says that the people were "harassed and helpless." These are powerful words, much more profound than the English translation communicates. The first word meant to be torn apart, as if by a wild animal. The second word meant to be cast down, to be completely disheartened and discouraged.[14] Why were they like that? Because they were "like sheep without a shepherd." And for a sheep, that is a dangerous way to live.

You see, sheep weren't created to be independent animals, for a couple of major reasons. First of all, they are fairly stupid. They don't have the wisdom to guide themselves through life. They don't know how to find the fresh water and green pastures that they need in order to thrive. Phillip Keller, who grew up in Kenya, and later worked as a shepherd, writes:

Sheep are notorious creatures of habit. If left to themselves, they will follow the same trails until they become ruts; graze the same hills until they turn to desert wastes; pollute their own ground until it is corrupt with disease.[15]

Without a shepherd, sheep are absolutely lost. They have no idea where to find life. So they mindlessly follow the rest of the flock, even when the rest of the flock doesn't have any idea where it is going. A bunch of sheep will never find life on their own. They will simply continue to do the same things they have always done, even to their own destruction.

Secondly, sheep can't protect themselves. They aren't very strong. They don't have claws to fight with. Their teeth are meant for chewing grass, not for doing battle. So when they see an enemy, the only thing they can do is run (but unfortunately, not fast enough to escape). Sheep need a shepherd to guide them away from environments that are potentially filled with wild animals, and to protect them when the wild animals invade the environment the sheep are already in. Without a shepherd, sheep are likely to be torn apart, or "harassed," as Matthew put it.

God designed sheep with one thing in mind—that they would be led by a shepherd. The shepherd takes care of everything the sheep need to really live. The shepherd takes them to find food. The shepherd protects them from wild animals. And when they are cast down, the shepherd picks them up and sets them back on their feet again.

Sometimes while resting, a sheep will roll over to stretch, and in the process, its whole body shifts too far, putting the sheep on its back in an indentation in the grass. For us, that wouldn't be a problem. We could get up whenever we wanted to. But sheep are built in such a way that, once they are in that position, they aren't able to get their feet on the ground and get back up again. When this happens, shepherds say that the sheep is "cast."[16]

When stuck in that position, the sheep is unable to release gas which builds up in its stomach, eventually crushing the lungs and causing the sheep to suffocate.[17] The cast sheep is also completely vulnerable to being attacked by a wild animal (and a wild animal would love nothing more than to find a sheep helplessly lying on its back).

A sheep that is cast is in great danger. If someone doesn't roll the sheep back into a normal position or set it on its feet, it can become distressed and die within a few hours. Keller describes the scene, and what it does in the heart of the shepherd:

> A cast sheep is a very pathetic sight. Lying on its back, its feet in the air, it flays away frantically struggling to stand up, without success. Sometimes it will bleat a little for help, but generally it lies there lashing about in frightened frustration. This knowledge that any cast sheep is helpless, close to death, and vulnerable to attack makes the whole problem of cast sheep serious for the manager. Nothing seems to so arouse his constant care and diligent attention to the flock.[18]

That's what was happening in the heart of Jesus when He looked at the people in the crowds. He didn't see masses. He saw faces with names. He knew each one of their unique stories intimately…and the stories weren't happy ones.

Lost. Unable to find life. Torn apart. Cast down. Vulnerable. Frantically struggling in frightened frustration, but helpless to do anything about it. It moved Him with compassion, the heartache of the Father that yearns to give life to His children. Those stories of brokenness still move Him with compassion today.

Compassion that Moves

When we say that we feel compassion, it usually means that we feel sorry for someone in our hearts…and then we turn and walk away. But the love and compassion of Jesus can't do that. The love and compassion of Jesus always leads to action.

In Mark 1, a man with leprosy came to Jesus in the synagogue, fell on his knees, and said, "If You are willing, I know that You can make me clean." Lepers were outcasts. But Jesus didn't create people to be outcasts, and so He was "moved with compassion." He touched the man and made him clean, freeing him to once again live as a fully accepted member of society.

In Matthew 20, two blind beggars by the roadside were crying out to Jesus for help. To the people around them, they were an annoyance, so they told the men to be quiet. But to Jesus, they were sons who were created for life. He stopped and asked them what they wanted. They replied simply, "We just want to be able to see." Jesus was "moved with compassion." He touched their eyes, they regained their sight, and they began to follow Him.

In Luke 7, Jesus and His disciples were entering the city of Nain, and as they approached the gate they encountered a procession of people going to a burial. A widow had lost her only son, and in that society it meant she had lost her only way of provision and survival. Not surprisingly, Luke says that Jesus "felt compassion for her." He stopped the procession, and He told the dead man to sit up. The young man sat up and began to speak, and Jesus "gave him back to his mother." And in doing so, Jesus gave new life, not only to the young man, but to his grieving mom as well.

In Luke 15, Jesus tells a story which illustrates the heart of the Father better than any other. A boy did something unthinkable by asking for his share of the inheritance while his father was still alive. This was an offense and an insult to his father, the equivalent of saying, "Dad, I wish that you were dead....*now.*"

Legally, the father didn't have to give him anything. As long as the father was alive, everything in the estate still belonged to him. But he agreed to give the son what he asked for. The son didn't waste any time. He packed up everything he owned (he never intended to return to his father's house). And with his inheritance in hand, he rejected his family, leaving home to go and live life the way that he wanted to live.

Well, life has a way of proving that we can't manage it on our own. Eventually, the boy ran out of money, he ran out of friends, and he had no place to stay. He managed to convince a local pig farmer to allow him to work for him, in exchange for a place to sleep (but with no pay, and no food). When his hunger got to the point that the pig's food looked as good as a plate of matooke, chicken and rice, he thought to himself, "Even my father's servants get to eat every day."

So he decided to go back to his father's house, intending to offer himself as a hired hand. He was just trying to survive. Or maybe he thought that he could somehow work to repay his father for what he had taken. Whatever the reason, he began the long journey towards home. The text says that when the boy was still a long way off, his father saw him. And what was his response?

"Oh, look at that rebellious boy! I can't wait until he reaches here, so I can beat him publicly and regain my dignity."

"He thought he could run his own life. But look at him now. He's poor...he's dirty...he has no shoes...his clothes are nothing but rags. He got what he deserved."

"How does he think that he can just come home, after what he has done to his family? Doesn't he know that I could have him stoned to death? When he gets here, I am going to tell him exactly what I think about him...and then I'm going to send him away forever."

That is how many men would respond, but remember this is an illustration of the heart of God. Jesus tells us that when the man saw his son who had brought so much shame to him, he was "filled with compassion." Even though the boy was guilty, and he deserved whatever judgment the family could have chosen for him, the father didn't see a rebel. Even though the boy was a complete mess, and he was covered with shame, the father didn't see a dirty, shameful boy.

He saw *his son*. And his heart was stirred with an agonizing love, because what he saw was not the life he intended for his son. His son wasn't meant to be far away from his father, torn apart and cast down because he didn't know how to find life on his own. He was meant to be at home, finding life in his father's love. That was the father's desire all along, and now that his son had returned, His father was going to make sure that he stayed. Not as a servant, but as his son.

So the father ran to him, embraced him, and kissed him. The son began to explain that he was no longer worthy to be called his father's son…but the father didn't listen. He called his servants and said to them, "Bring my best robe, and put it on my son. Put a ring on his finger. And put new sandals on his feet!" These were all clear symbols which identified the boy as a full son of his father. And instead of summoning the people of the community for the public stoning of a rebellious young man, the father called them to come for the biggest celebration the village had ever seen. He invited them to rejoice with him, because his son had finally come back home where he belonged.

That is the heart of the Father. He is a God who delights to give life, a delight that springs from His infinite love. But people are lost. People are hurting. We have all been deceived into thinking that we can be our own god, our own savior, and our own king. And when we try to sit on the throne, where only He belongs (and the Bible says we have all done this), life has a way of tearing us apart and casting us down, leaving us without anyone to lead us to the love and life that God created us to have.

Do we deserve judgment? Absolutely, and in a big way. But we weren't created for judgment. We were created for life. And when we aren't receiving that life, it moves Him with a compassion that aches in every part of His infinite heart. Pain and heartache will not be the end of the story, though. George MacDonald says that the desire of God's heart will one day be fully accomplished:

> The God and Father of Jesus Christ could never possibly be satisfied with less than giving Himself to His own…history is a divine agony to give divine life to creatures. The outcome of that agony, the victory…will be radiant life.[19]

As long as you have breath in your lungs, He refuses to give up on you. He will pursue you to the farthest corners of the earth, and He will not rest until you are fully at home in Him. He wants to give you life. He wants it so much that it hurts. The pain is so deep because His love is so deep, love from the heart of a Father who wants only one thing for you—that you would know the depths of His love. Why? Because in His love you find peace. In His love you find joy. In His love you find freedom. In His love you find life. He longs for you to experience that life to the fullest. He longs for the world to experience it through you.

It's His delight...it's your destiny.

Key Thought:

The Father's one desire is that His children would have life—that they would know love, experience peace, be filled with hope, and walk in joy and in freedom. When they don't get it, the heart of the Father literally suffers. The pain is so deep because His love is so deep.

Personal Reflection / Group Discussion:

"To love is to hurt." The pain I am talking about here, though, is different. It doesn't have to do with love that you have not received, but love that you long for someone else to receive. When you love someone, your greatest desire is to see them thriving, enjoying everything that God intended for them. Yet when they reject that love, or for some reason are unable to receive it, it brings a grief that is intolerable. Not because you wanted something *from* them, but because you desperately wanted something *for* them.

- *Can you think of a time when you have felt this kind of pain for someone you loved?*

- *When you have failed, what is your first thought about how God is looking at you—that He longs for you or that He is disappointed in you? If God really loves you with this kind of compassionate desire, how does that change the way you view Him? How does that change the way that you understand His heart and thoughts towards you?*

Scriptural Prescription:

The LORD longs to be gracious to you, And therefore He waits on high to have compassion on you.

Isaiah 30:18

Further Study:

Read Hosea 11:1-9. Look at the fatherly love of the Lord for His people, a love that refuses to give up no matter how far they turn from Him. Listen to the heart of God, especially in verse 3 and verse 8, how His heart yearns for His children...how His heart yearns for *you*.

Chapter 3

Love:

Your Destiny

To say that I am made in the image of God is to say that love is the reason for my existence, for God is love.[20]

Thomas Merton

Freedom in Daddy's Arms

I used to play a game with my daughter Hannah when she was about five years old, to demonstrate something about putting our trust in the heart of God. I would hold her in my arms and pretend that I was going to drop her, saying, "Are you going to fall?"

She would say, "No, Daddy's strong, and he loves me!"

I would do it again: "Are you going to fall?"

"No, Daddy's strong, and he loves me!"

One Sunday, I was using this as an illustration in a sermon at church. After she told me for the second time that she knew I wouldn't drop her, I pointed to her little brother Joshua, who was only two years old at the time. I asked her, "What if Joshua was holding you? Would you trust him?"

She said emphatically, "No way! He's not strong enough!"

I pointed to a man in the congregation and asked, "What about that big guy over there? He looks strong enough. Would you trust him?"

"No," she said timidly, "because I don't know him. I don't know if he loves me."

Joshua loved her, but he wasn't strong enough. So she couldn't trust him to hold her. The other guy was definitely strong enough, but she didn't know his heart. So she couldn't trust him to hold her, either.

But when she was in my arms, she was at peace. She knew I was strong enough to hold her, and she was absolutely certain that I loved her. That certainty made her completely free. She wasn't wondering if she had behaved well enough to deserve a place in my arms. She wasn't concerned about whether or not she looked pretty enough to make me want to hold her. She wasn't trying to think of some kind of accomplishment that she could report to me in order to earn my strength and love. She knew that it had nothing to do with anything she had done. She just came, based completely on what she knew was already in my heart towards her.

When she was in my arms, she wasn't preparing herself for a fall, trying to strengthen her bones or calculating the best way to land, just in case I decided to let her go. She wasn't clinging tightly to me, in fear that I might lose my grip. She was safe, because she knew that every bit of the love and strength that I had belonged to her.

That security gave her peace in situations that would otherwise be scary: walking in the dark at night, crossing Kampala Road at the busiest time of the day, or going to a strange place where she had never been before. That peace brought a joyful freedom which enabled her to take risks: "Hang me upside down, Daddy!" "Throw me up in the air, Daddy!" She wasn't worried at all. She was confident and free...all because she was held and *loved* by Daddy.

That is the relationship that you and I are intended to have with God, that of a child who has complete confidence in both the strength and the love of his father. That confidence brings freedom, and that freedom brings the power to live the kind of life you were created to live.

Revealing the Father

The Bible uses so many different words to describe who God is: Almighty, Healer, Provider, King, Savior, our Rock and Refuge, Redeemer, and

Counselor, just to name a few. But the best description of how He relates with us, the word which best captures God's heart towards us is *"Father."* This was clearly the way that Jesus chose to reveal Him, referring to Him as Father nearly 200 times in the gospels.

God is a Father. He wants children, and as I mentioned in chapter 1, He wants lots of children. He wants His children to be just like their Father in heaven, to have their lives completely filled with His life.

His plan from the beginning was for a *family* of adopted sons and daughters who share life together, who live in the Father's presence, and who enjoy the security, the love, the joy, and the freedom of life in the Father's house. He wants to pour His life and His love into the lives of His children, and then He wants to work through them to bring even more children to Himself.

J.I. Packer, one of the most influential Christian thinkers of the 20th century, writes this:

> You sum up the whole of New Testament religion if you describe it as the knowledge of God as one's holy Father. If you want to judge how well a person understands Christianity, find out how much he makes of the thought of being God's child, and having God as his Father. If this is not the thought that prompts and controls his worship and prayers and his whole outlook on life, it means that he does not understand Christianity very well at all. For everything that Christ taught, everything that makes the New Testament new, and better than the Old, everything that is distinctively Christian is summed up in the knowledge of the Fatherhood of God.[21]

For some of you, hearing the word *"father"* brings comfort, joy, and a sense of great peace, filling your mind with images of running into big, strong arms that wrap themselves around you lovingly.

For others, *"father"* has a much different effect. The arms may have been big and strong, but they were never predictable or loving. They were abusive and scary. His arms were not at all a safe place you would want to run to. They were a dangerous place you'd rather run away from.

For others, the reaction isn't extreme in either direction. When you hear *"father,"* it elicits neither delight nor fear, but a rather bland, almost unfeeling response. Dad wasn't abusive. He was actually very kind. But he was so passive. His arms weren't a dangerous place, but they weren't exactly a place of refuge, either. The arms were loving, but they were somewhat weak. So the thought of *father* may make you feel warm and sentimental, yet at the same time, somewhat empty and neutral.

When we hear that God is our Father, it brings that same range of responses, much of it rooted in the picture of fatherhood we had growing up. And quite often, what we experienced with our earthly fathers makes it very difficult to see clearly into the heart of our heavenly Father. So when that picture has been distorted, what can we do?

We do what the New Testament calls us to do in every situation… we look to Jesus. The entire life of Jesus was a window beckoning us to come and look inside, to give us through Himself a clear and vivid picture of the Father's heart. John writes, "No one has ever seen God, but the one and only Son, who is Himself God and is in closest relationship with the Father, has made Him known" (John 1:18, NIV). The writer of Hebrews tells us that the Son is "the radiance of His glory and the exact representation of His nature" (Hebrews 1:3).

Over and again, instead of explaining everything, Jesus simply called us to Himself. When the disciples asked Him to show them the way, He didn't draw them a diagram of the plan of salvation. He simply said, "*I* am the way."

When He saw people who had been beaten down by life, He didn't recommend a good counselor or a prayer group. He gave them an invitation: "Come to <u>Me</u>, all you who are weary and weighed down with heavy burdens, and I will give you rest."

To the religious leaders in John 5:19, He said, "The Son can do nothing of Himself, unless it is something He sees the Father doing," and then a few chapters later in John 10:30, He made it even more clear when

He told them, "I and the Father are one." In John 14:8-9, when Philip asked Jesus to show them the Father, He didn't give Philip a book about the Father or point him to a web site where he could find more information about the Father. He said, "Anyone who has seen Me *has seen* the Father" (NIV, italics added).

You want to know what the Fatherhood of God looks like? Look at Jesus. He's the picture of the perfect Father.

We all long for a father like Him. And here's the beauty of it. He's not hiding. That Father longs for us, too. And He invites us to come. He isn't just inviting us to believe in a new truth…He is inviting us to *life*, to experience in reality the transforming power of the love of God and the freedom to live the way that He created us to live.

But so many people in our churches, including many pastors, and possibly including you, are not experiencing that power and freedom. They know some things about Him. They have some knowledge of His word. They pray. They are very active in the ministry of the church. They have experienced His power in various circumstances. But they haven't experienced real transformation in their character, in their marriages, in their parenting, in the way they do business, or in their relationships with others. They have felt a sense of His presence in church, but in real life where they spend most of their time, they aren't really finding Him… because they don't understand His love.

A ministry colleague once said to me, "Dave, it seems like you always preach about the love of God" (by the way, this was meant to be a rebuke, not a compliment). My response was simple: "If you can find anything else that can forgive sins, if you can find anything else that can heal pain and take away shame, if you can find anything else that can bring life and hope to lost and broken people, I would be happy to preach about it. But you won't find it."

If you miss His love, you miss everything, because the love of God is not just the most important thing in your life and in ministry…ultimately it is the only thing that is really important. Everything that is good flows from His love.

Created for Love

Too often, when we go to the Scriptures, we have a tendency to ignore those passages that clearly define what it means to follow Jesus, and we rush to more obscure passages that we can interpret in ways which seem to promise us the things that we really desire. We study God's word with such narrow vision, just searching for today's blessing, seeking comfort in a trying moment, looking for wisdom concerning an upcoming decision, or hoping for a promise of wealth and success. Those things aren't bad, in and of themselves. But unless we look at those smaller pieces in light of the big picture of God's story, our reading of God's word will end up being twisted into nothing more than a search for our personal well-being (something which, sadly, has become too common in our churches today).

If life is going to make any sense at all, we have to know what God intended for us in the first place. What is our destiny? In other words, where will I find life? How am I supposed to live? Most importantly, *why* am I supposed to live? What really matters? What is the heart of it all?

When we read the Scriptures, we have to pay close attention to Jesus and to the apostles when they say things that give a comprehensive view of what God is up to:

"If anyone wants to come after Me…"
"A man's life does not consist of…"
"But seek first…"
"To live is…"
"Whatever you do, do it all for…"

Obviously, the space on these pages is not enough to consider all of the Scriptures that we could possibly look at, but I want to examine a few key passages that make big statements about what life is all about.[22]

"Jesus, Tell Me What Really Matters"

In Matthew 22, the religious leaders were threatened by Jesus and His popularity, so they were trying to find a way to get rid of Him. They kept sending people to Him to ask Him questions about the Jewish law, hoping to trap Jesus into saying something that would give them a reason to accuse Him and have Him arrested. Two different groups of people had already come with questions to test Him, and both times Jesus amazed them with His answers, leaving them with no charges to bring against Him.

So they sent one of their experts in the law of Moses to ask Jesus a question. "Teacher," he asked in verse 36, "which is the greatest commandment in the Law?"

That's a big question. In other words, "Out of the hundreds of thousands of words in the Scriptures, what is the one thing that really matters the most?"

Jesus' answer was simple. He didn't quote any of the Old Testament Scriptures that we love to emphasize, the ones that *seem* to promise wealth, prosperity, and nonstop happiness for all of God's children. No, when it was time to state clearly what life is all about, Jesus quoted Deuteronomy 6:5, saying to him, "'Love the Lord your God with all your heart and with all your soul and with all your mind.' This is the first and greatest commandment." Then He added another, quoting from Leviticus 19:18: "And the second is like it. 'Love your neighbor as yourself.'" He finished His answer with a huge statement: "All the Law and the Prophets hang on these two commandments" (Matthew 22:36-40, NIV).

The Law and the Prophets contained the whole of the Old Testament, the only written Scriptures they had at the time. In other words, Jesus is saying that you can sum up the whole message and purpose of the word of God by this—you were created to *love God* with everything that you are and everything that you have, and you are to *love others* in the same way that you love yourself. All of the other Scriptures point to these two commandments. And the Scriptures can only be understood in light of these two commandments.

You want to know your destiny? It's simple. You were created to receive His love and to give it away[23], in worship and obedience to Him, and in practical, tangible service and generosity to others.

The Proof that God is Fully Alive in You

There is a lot of discussion as to what is the real evidence that you are filled with the presence of God. Some say that it is necessary to speak in tongues or to prophesy. Others say that faith to perform miracles is the evidence. Others say the proof is in your prosperity or in the size and fame of your ministry.

John, the beloved disciple of Jesus, was one of the leaders of the early church. In that day, there was a lot of false teaching going around, and there was one especially harmful doctrine which said that the human problem was not sin, but ignorance.[24] They taught that salvation was achieved by attaining a special secret knowledge. This led many to the conclusion that they could live however they wanted to live, with no moral restraints...as long as they had this special knowledge. This knowledge, they believed, was the mark of spiritual maturity.[25]

John responded to this teaching by writing a letter to the church. And in his letter, he made it very clear what it was that really demonstrated that the Spirit of God was fully alive in a person. Over and over again, he emphasized his points by saying, "By this we know that we are in Him..."

At the beginning of chapter 4, he is dealing with how to test whether or not those who claim to be preaching God's word are really from God. In verse 7, he makes it more general, talking about how to identify the sign of God's presence in *all* believers:

> Beloved, let us love one another, for love is from God; and everyone who loves is born of God and knows God. The one who does not love does not know God, for God is love.

> 1 John 4:7

How do we know that someone is born of God? Simple, John says: they *love*. What kind of love? John isn't talking about Sunday morning smiles and holy hugs. Verses 9-10 say that the love of God was revealed to us in the death of Christ on the cross. His love is a love that gives itself away, even if it means it has to die. That kind of love, John says, is the real evidence of God's presence in you. In case we missed it in earlier verses, he repeats it clearly one more time, in verse 16:

> We have come to know and have believed the love which God has for us. God is love, and the one who abides in love abides in God, and God abides in him.

> 1 John 4:16

What is the evidence that someone is filled with the very presence of God? That they preach with power? That they fast and pray more than everyone else? That they speak in tongues and prophesy? That they have the largest church or the most popular ministry? That they see miracles in answer to their prayers? That they have the most wealth and success?

The evidence isn't found in any of those things. God is love, and John says that the one who really demonstrates that he has the life of God dwelling fully in him is the one who *loves* in the same way that He loves.

Without It, You Have Nothing

Jesus says that receiving God's love and loving with God's love is what life is all about. The apostle John says that His love is the evidence that the presence of God is fully alive in you. Let's see what the apostle Paul has to say in 1 Corinthians 13. This is a passage which we usually only read in weddings, which is unfortunate because it is actually a very crucial chapter for us to understand. It gets to the heart of who God is and who we are called to be as His people.

The Corinthians, like all people in the Greek world at that time, placed a high value on wisdom and special knowledge. There was also a lot of division, as people were beginning to follow after great men instead of after the great God that these men talked about. They were saying, "I follow Paul," or "I follow Peter," or "I follow Apollos." There was a lot of competition between preachers, and there were many false prophets who entered the ministry seeking riches and power and status, a first-century version of today's so-called "mighty men of God." And by the way, true apostles did _NOT_ minister with these motives at all (real servants of God never do). They were driven by a different kind of ambition: "We make it our goal to please Him," Paul writes in 2 Corinthians 5:9 (NIV).

And the Corinthians loved *power*. From Paul's teaching in chapters 12-14, it is obvious that there was a lot of interest and debate on the issue of spiritual gifts, especially the power gifts such as prophecy, tongues, miracles and healings.

It was a very gifted church, but it was also a very immoral and spiritually immature church.[26] So Paul wrote to them for a number of reasons, one of them being to try to give them a right perspective on spiritual gifts and their proper use in the church. In the midst of that teaching in chapters 12-14, Paul takes some time in chapter 13 to remind the Corinthians believers about the one thing that really matters. And no matter what your belief on spiritual gifts might be, what Paul is communicating in this chapter is unmistakably clear: the identifying characteristic of true followers of Christ is *love*. Not just any love, but God's love (which Paul describes in powerful detail in 13:4-8).

Paul contrasts the love of Christ with what the Corinthians considered to be the evidence of true spirituality. He tells them that power is nothing unless we are walking in the fullness of His love. He begins with spiritual gifts. He tells them that if they are not living a life filled with the love of Christ, then all of their powerful praying and prophesying is just a bunch of noise:

> If I speak with the tongues of men and of angels, but do not have love, I have become a noisy gong or a clanging cymbal. If I have *the gift* of prophecy, and know all mysteries and all knowledge; and if I have faith, so as to remove mountains, but do not have love, I am nothing.
>
> 1 Corinthians 13:1-2

He goes on to explain that even if someone shows the most extreme devotion to Jesus and performs the most heroic acts of service and sacrifice, it is completely useless unless that person is filled with the love of God:

> And if I give all my possessions to feed the poor, and if I surrender my body to be burned, but do not have love, it profits me nothing.
>
> 1 Corinthians 13:3

In our nation today, he might add: "Even if I go to all of the overnight prayer meetings and lunch hour fellowships…if I fast three times a week…if I have a huge church and am heard on radio and TV…if I give big concerts and sell thousands of CD's…if I often fly to America to preach…if I am successful in business…if I have a university degree… if I am wealthy. Even if I have all of those things that the church and the world are so impressed with, but I don't have *LOVE*, then the truth is, I have absolutely *nothing*."

We can have powerful gifts. We can do all of the spiritual things that everyone admires so much. We can have the appearance of wisdom and God's favor in our lives. But if we aren't walking in the love of Christ, Paul says, it is all a complete waste of time. We can have it all, but if we don't have love, we have nothing at all.

Many of us would respond to this challenge by trying really hard to be more loving. But here's the problem: you *can't* make it happen on your own. Love doesn't come from your skill, or from your gifting, or from any amount of wisdom or effort. It comes from what is in your heart, the reflection of what you have already received. "We love, because He first loved us" (1 John 4:19).

About a year ago, I witnessed this truth in action when I was leading the evangelism team at a wheelchair distribution in Wobulenzi, in partnership with a ministry to the disabled which is run by a long-time friend of ours. People who needed wheelchairs would come, they would receive a new wheelchair, and then we would share the love of the Father with them and pray with them.

There was one little girl who I will never forget. Her name was Rachel. She was fourteen years old, but because of a high fever that damaged her brain when she was a baby, her body didn't develop normally. She was tiny. She couldn't use her legs. She couldn't use her arms. She couldn't speak. But she could see and hear...and she could smile.

Whenever I would speak her name, her face would break out into a big smile that seemed to light up the whole room. And she blessed me in ways that I can barely begin to describe with words. I only spent a few minutes with Rachel, but there is one thing I know for certain—God loved me immensely through that little girl. When I met her father, I understood why. He took great care of her. But he did much more than that. He treasured her. He delighted in her. He loved her. And her love was a reflection of the love of God that she had received through him.

According to the standards of what the world values, Rachel can't do much of anything. She can't go to school. She can't have a successful career. She can't do any kind of work at all.

According to what we normally value in the church, she doesn't have much to offer, either. She can't preach. She can't sing in the choir. She can't counsel. She can't serve in any kind of practical way.

But she can love. And to know and embrace the love of Christ, and to walk in that love is the most valuable asset anyone could ever have. It's not only the most important thing. As far as Jesus is concerned...as far as John is concerned...as far as the apostle Paul is concerned...it's the *only* thing that matters. Everything that is good flows from there.

That's why Paul prayed in Ephesians 3 that we would be able to understand the love of Christ, because everything depends on knowing His love.

With It, You Have Everything

For two and a half chapters, Paul has been talking about the eternal purposes of God, and about all of the resources He has given us in Christ. Now, Paul prays that we would be able to understand the truth that will release the full power of God in our lives:

For this reason I kneel before the Father, from whom every family in heaven and on earth derives its name. I pray that out of His glorious riches He may strengthen you with power through His Spirit in your inner being, so that Christ may dwell in your hearts through faith. And I pray that you, being rooted and established in love, may have power, together with all the Lord's holy people, to grasp how wide and long and high and deep is the love of Christ, and to know this love that surpasses knowledge—that you may be filled to the measure of all the fullness of God. Now to Him who is able to do immeasurably more than all we ask or imagine, according to His power that is at work within us, to Him be glory in the church and in Christ Jesus throughout all generations, for ever and ever! Amen.

Ephesians 3:14-21 (NIV)

We all know verse 20 very well, that God is the One "who is able to do immeasurably more than all we ask or imagine." We misinterpret it and claim it wrongly in prayer, thinking it means that if I pray for 5,000 shillings, He will do immeasurably more by giving me 500,000; if I ask for a second hand bicycle, He will go beyond that and give me a brand new Prado. But Paul isn't talking about big material answers to prayer. He is talking about the incredible work of God *within us,* the power to be the people that God has created us to be.

And Paul says here that if we are going to walk in the fullness of God's power, then we have got to understand one thing–*the love of God.*

While I was explaining this once, someone said to me, "Well, I already know that. I learned it in Sunday School – 'Jesus loves me, this I know.' But now I am moving on to greater revelation." Sorry, there is no greater revelation. His love is the greatest truth there is, has ever been, and will ever be. You can't move beyond it…you can only go deeper into it.

Listen, these believers at Ephesus to whom Paul was writing these things were already very mature Christians, disciples who had experienced God in powerful ways. When the church was born in Ephesus, the power of God was so real that when they took handkerchiefs that had been touched by Paul and laid them on sick people, they were healed. Many who had paid big money for their special magic books (and who made a very good living practicing magic) voluntarily brought the books to Paul and burned them…because in Jesus, they had seen the real thing!

In Ephesians 1:15, Paul tells the Ephesian believers that he can't stop thanking God for them when he hears about their great faith. In the letter to the church at Ephesus in Revelation 2, Jesus commends them for their hard work, for their commitment to sound doctrine, and for their intolerance of false prophets.

These were very mature believers. Yet the one thing that Paul prayed for, the one thing that he knew these very mature believers needed to understand, and continue to understand at deeper levels, was the *love* of Christ.

The longer I live, the more the Lord convinces me that this is true for me and for everybody I meet. As I look at the much-needed work that He continues to do in my life, and as I minister to people who are lost and hurting and broken, I realize more and more that everything depends on knowing the love of God.

You need to be reminded of it every day. You need to dig deeper into the truth of His love and grow in your understanding of His love every day. You need to allow the Holy Spirit to open up the hidden places of your heart so that His love can bring life and healing. His love is the only source of power for your life and for your ministry to others. It's a love that paid a very high price for you…a love that is always ready to welcome you…a love that will never give up on you…a love that will pursue you to the farthest corner of the earth in order to bring you back home, no matter what you have done or what kind of person you have become.

Paul is not saying that he wants you to know this in your mind, to be able to sit in a classroom and explain the love of God like you would explain mathematics or physics. He is talking about the actual experience of His love. Tim Keller says that there is a vast difference between having a rational belief that honey is sweet and having actually tasted the sweetness of honey itself.[27] Paul is praying that you would taste the love of Christ, that it would be *real* to you. He is praying that you would know His love completely – how wide it is, how long it is, how high it is, and how deep it is.

And this is the reason, he tells us in verse 19: "that you may be filled to the measure of all the fullness of God."

Think about what he is saying to us! If you are already filled to the measure of *ALL* the fullness of God, what else could you possibly need? What else is there that you could add on to make your life any fuller? Nothing!! No amount of riches could do it. No amount of fame. No amount of comfort, popularity or status. Paul said it well to the church at Colossae: "In Him you have been made complete" (Colossians 2:10).

Not "in Him *and* achievement." Not "in Him *and* status." Not "in Him *and* financial security." Not "in Him *and* religious dedication." Paul says we are complete, simply "in Him." Him alone. Nothing else required.

In 1 Corinthians 13, Paul explained that even if you have everything according to the standards and values of this world, but you don't have love, then you actually have nothing at all. Now, in Ephesians 3, he is saying that even if you have nothing according to the standards and values of this world, but you really know the love of Christ, then you have *everything!*

Listen to the heart of God in Paul's prayer in Ephesians 3 one more time, this time from the New Living Translation:

I pray that from His glorious, unlimited resources He will empower you with inner strength through His Spirit. Then Christ will make His home in your hearts as you trust in Him. Your roots will grow down into God's love and keep you strong. And may you have the power to understand, as all God's people should, how wide, how long, how high, and how deep His love is. May you experience the love of Christ, though it is too great to understand fully. Then you will be made complete with all the fullness of life and power that comes from God.

Ephesians 3:16-19 (NLT)

You were created for His love. Everything that is good flows from there. And when you really experience it, it changes everything about who you are and makes it possible for the power of God to be released in you. Not the power to get everything you want and the freedom to do whatever you want to do, but the power to live the life that God intended you to live and the freedom to be everything that God created you to be. It's a beautiful invitation….it's an even more beautiful promise.

It's His delight…it's your destiny.

Key Thought:

The relationship that you and I are intended to have with God is that of a child who has complete confidence in both the strength and the love of his father. That confidence brings freedom, and that freedom brings the power to live the kind of life you were created to live.

If you miss His love, you miss everything, because the love of God is not just the most important thing in your life and in ministry…ultimately it is the only thing that is really important. Everything that is good flows from His love.

Personal Reflection / Group Discussion:

Jesus says in Matthew 22 that the reason we exist is to receive the love of God and to give it away. John says in 1 John 4 that the proof that the Spirit of God is alive in you is that you love as He loves. Paul says in 1 Corinthians 13 that if we have everything the world is so impressed with but don't have love, then the truth is, we have nothing. But then he makes it clear in Ephesians 3 that even if we don't have anything that the world is so impressed with, but we have the love of God through Christ, then we have everything–"filled up to all the fullness of God."

- *Created for love? How does this differ from what you have always been told about life (even in church)?*

- *If it really is all about His love, then how should that change the way we live, the way we pray, the things we seek, and the way we evaluate our lives?*

Scriptural Prescription:

I pray that you, being rooted and established in love, may have power, together with all the Lord's holy people, to grasp how wide and long and high and deep is the love of Christ, and to know this love that surpasses knowledge–that you may be filled to the measure of all the fullness of God.

Ephesians 3:17-19 (NIV)

Further Study:

If we are going to understand His love, then we have to define love properly. What kind of love is God talking about? It's not a nice feeling He has towards us. It is so much more than that.

Read 1 John 4:9-10; Romans 5:8; John 3:16; 1 John 3:16; and 1 Corinthians 13:4-8, and allow the Holy Spirit to reveal to you the nature and depth of God's love.

Chapter 4

Adoption:

Your Hope

God does not merely redeem us—through adoption He brings us into the warmth, love, and gladness of His own family.[28]

Dan Cruver

Otim's Dilemma

A couple of years ago I was on my way home from Kampala after a day of meetings. As I was driving on the northern bypass between the Bukoto and Bwaise exits, I was waved down by a traffic policeman standing on the side of the road. I pulled over, and as he walked up to the car, I looked at his name badge (which I always do, in case I need to remember it later). His name was Otim.

Otim looked at my international driving permit and asked, "Which state are you from—California, New York, or Chicago?" I didn't think this was the time for a geography lesson, so I decided not to inform him that Chicago wasn't actually a state. I told him that I was from Ohio. He looked up at me and said, "You people really have big states."

Then he turned his head and looked thoughtfully off into the distance. "I want to leave Uganda, because I am alone in this world." I asked him what he meant, and he explained: "My parents died when I was young, and the rest of my relatives were killed in the insurgency in the north. I didn't have anything to do, so I decided to come to Kampala and join the police."

As he went on with his story, he kept emphasizing his aloneness. I asked him if he knew that God would never leave him, that the Bible says in Psalm 27 that even if everyone on earth decided to abandon him, God would be his Father.

He said, "I believe that God is there, but He takes too long to respond to my prayers. It is difficult."

"What is it that is difficult," I asked, trying to get a better glimpse of his heart, "the fact that *He* is God and you are not, that He insists on being in charge?"

"Yes!" Otim said emphatically, the way that you do when you are certain that someone finally understands what you are talking about. "That is exactly the problem. I want things, but He doesn't do what I want Him to do!"

It was a roadside police stop, so I didn't have enough time to unfold the beauty of the Father's heart to him, to help him see the pure satisfaction and security that is found in being His child. I only had time to briefly share with Otim the hope we have in the love of God that is found through the cross of Jesus Christ. I drove away, praying that this small bit of truth would be enough to open his heart to the possibility that maybe there is real life for him, that God would give him a tiny ray of hope that would begin to break through the dark emptiness that has filled his heart and mind for so long.

As I finished praying for Otim, my immediate thought was, "And Lord, there are millions more who are just like him." Otim's dilemma is not so uncommon. Like many people in the world, he is looking for hope, but he doesn't know where to find it. He thinks that if God would just do something to make his circumstances OK, then Otim himself would be OK. He doesn't understand that hope isn't found in what he can get from God, but in God Himself.

Otim is so much like the rest of us. He is hungry for life. He has that desire because he is human. God planted that in his heart. There is something deep within each one of us, a thirst within our spirits that longs to be satisfied and fulfilled, a burning desire to find significance and meaning in our lives. That's how God made us. That's how we're wired. The book of Ecclesiastes says that God has "placed eternity in our hearts."

We know that we were meant to connect with something much larger than ourselves. By nature, we know that God has prepared a feast, and we are invited to come and enjoy it. We were created with a hunger for life, yet like Otim we are so easily deceived as to what will actually satisfy that hunger.

We pursue the wrong solutions, because we don't really understand the problem. Otim's problem couldn't be solved by a job promotion. It couldn't be solved by getting a passport out of Uganda and a visa into America. His real problem, like that of so many people in Uganda, like so many people throughout the world, is that he is fatherless—not just physically, but in his heart, mind and soul. There is only one source of hope for Otim, and for you and me. We need to come home to the Father.

An Amazing Offer

When Jesus says, "Come," He is not primarily calling us to come and get help. He is inviting us to something much greater. He is inviting us to be reconciled to Himself, to come home and experience life and freedom in the Father's love. The gospel of Jesus Christ is intensely relational, and so often the Scriptures use the language of family, of fatherhood, and of home to describe our salvation:

> If anyone loves Me, he will keep My word; and My Father will love him, and We will come to him and make Our abode with him.
>
> John 14:23

> But as many as received Him, to them He gave the right to become children of God.
>
> John 1:12

See what great love the Father has lavished on us, that we should be called children of God! And that is what we are!

1 John 3:1 (NIV)

Home was God's design from the beginning...but we decided to look for life elsewhere. In his book, *Reclaiming Adoption*, Dan Cruver writes:

God's original intention for humanity—His original intention for us—was that we were to be His beloved sons, His cherished children. As God's image-bearers, we were created in the beginning to participate in the love that ever flows between God the Father and God the Son, and to participate in that love on the earth as our happy home. But in rebellion, God's son (*NOTE: Cruver is referring to Adam here*) left the Father's house in his heart even before he was expelled from the Father's presence physically. In Adam, we all exchanged the love of the Father for the things of the Father.[29]

We are like the two sons in the parable of the prodigal in Luke 15:11-32. The younger son asked for his inheritance in advance, because he thought he could find life outside the father's house. The older son stayed home, thinking he could find life by earning the blessings of his father with his good behavior. But both of them missed the point. They wanted the Father's blessings, but neither of them wanted the Father Himself. They were equally lost, because they didn't understand the heart of the Father. And every time we seek our fulfillment, our joy, our acceptance, our value, and our life in anything other than the love of God, we are taking another step away from the only home that we were ever meant to know.

We have been deceived, enticed to give our lives to chase after things that seem to hold out hope for us: a university degree, a successful career, marriage, money, power, sex, status, popularity, even religion. The problem is not in those things themselves. The problem is that we put our hope in them.

None of them will ever able to satisfy what our hearts are really longing for…because those things can't give us life. No matter how many of them we attain or achieve, the temporary feeling of satisfaction will always run out and leave our hearts empty, the result being what C.S. Lewis described as "a longing to be reunited with something in the universe from which we now feel cut off, to be on the inside of some door which we have always only seen from the outside."[30]

We spend a lifetime searching all over the world for something that the world can never give us. We endlessly grasp for something that is always out of our reach. Tim Keller explains it this way:

> We are all exiles, always longing for home. We are always travelling, never arriving.
> ....
> We have been living in a world that no longer fits our deepest longings.
> ....
> We never fully realize our hopes and dreams. We may work hard to try to re-create the home that we have lost, but, says the Bible, it only exists in the presence of the heavenly Father from which we have fled.[31]

The Father offered us life in His house. We rejected His offer. Look around at the condition that our world is in. Our way of doing things hasn't worked out so well, has it? Yet in spite of our rejection of Him, the good news of the gospel is that God hasn't rejected us. We have a real and living hope because He has made a way for us to come home. The Bible refers to that homecoming as our *adoption*.

Stop and consider what that actually means. We rebelled against God Himself, yet He invites us to come home as His beloved children! It would be amazing enough if God had simply accepted us in the way that the younger son in the Luke 15 story was originally proposing, that we return as servants who could work to repay the master for his mercy. When I think about who He is, and when I consider my lifelong rebellion against

Him, the fact that He is willing to allow me to be a part of His household on *any* terms at all is absolutely staggering to my heart and mind.

Even if He had only allowed me to return as a servant, that mercy alone would be more than enough to cause me to live in gratitude to Him for all of eternity. But He didn't just hire me as a servant in His household. He welcomed me into His family as a *son*. Listen to how J.I. Packer describes it:

> Adoption is a *family* idea, conceived in terms of *love*, and viewing God as *father*. In adoption, God takes us into His family and fellowship—He establishes us as His children and heirs. Closeness, affection and generosity are at the heart of the relationship. To be right with God the Judge is a great thing, but to be loved and cared for by God the Father is the greater.[32]

Commenting on Packer's words, C.J. Mahaney says:

> I love that last sentence—"To be right with God the Judge is a great thing." I just want to say it is indeed "a great thing" to be right with God the Judge through the person and work of Jesus Christ. It is "a great thing" to be forgiven of sin. It is "a great thing" to be freed from fear of future wrath. It is "a great thing" to know this day that there is no condemnation for those who are in Christ Jesus. To be right with God the Judge—that is "a great thing"! But as incomprehensible as it is, there is something greater. The greater is to be loved and cared for by God the Father. That's the *greater*.[33]

From convicted rebels to treasured sons and daughters of God Himself. It's an amazing offer. And like everything else that is good, it originated in the heart of the Father…100% of it.

Planned by the Father

To really grasp what it is that God has done for us, we need to understand that our adoption wasn't God's alternate plan, a diversion from the original design because things didn't work out the way that He expected them to. Our adoption was what He had in mind from before the beginning of time:

> He chose us in Him before the foundation of the world, that we would be holy and blameless before Him. In love He predestined us to adoption as sons through Jesus Christ to Himself.
>
> Ephesians 1:4-5

God could have used any imagery He wanted to in order to describe our salvation. He could have called it being "born again" and nothing more. But He wanted to give us a complete picture of just how incredible it is that the Father has welcomed us into His family. So, in several very key passages, including this one from Ephesians 1, He speaks through the apostle Paul using the terminology of adoption to explain our relationship with God. The idea of God *adopting* us as His sons and daughters gives us a penetrating look into the heart of the Father.

Adoption was a very key part of the Roman world during the time when Paul wrote his letters to the churches. Every day, slaves were being redeemed and being legally declared the full sons of influential men, and given the same rights as their biological children, with no distinction between the two.

There was no thought that these were second-class children. I have often heard people making a distinction between their adopted children and their "real children." There was no such thinking in the Roman world. "On the contrary," Richard Phillips writes, "it was special to have been adopted. It meant that someone important had set his love upon you and adopted you to be his son, his heir."[34]

It *is* special to be adopted. There is something unique about the heart of parents towards the child they are adopting. Biological children are wonderful (I have 4 of them, and I love them more than words can say). But it doesn't require any special love to physically produce children.

To adopt a child, however, requires a choice. There are many unplanned pregnancies, but there is no such thing as an unplanned adoption. The parents carefully consider their choice, and from the love in their hearts they look at the child and say, "We want this one to be ours."

The choice has nothing to do with anything the child has done. He can't campaign for himself to be chosen. He can't work in order to earn it. There is nothing he can do to make himself worthy of this choosing. Our Ugandan son Paul says that "the conditions for adoption are the worst conditions, situations where the child has no reason to even be alive." The child can do nothing but simply *need*. The choice to adopt is based purely on what is in the parents' hearts towards the child.

That is exactly what the Father has done for us. "Before the foundation of the world," God had already conceived the idea of a family filled with adopted sons and daughters, and it says He did it "in love." When He actually brought us into His family, there was nothing about us that deserved to be chosen. In fact, Ephesians 2:1-3 says that if we deserved anything, it was God's wrath. We were literally "dead" in our sins.

But out of the endless overflow of the same heart that envisioned it all in the first place, the Father took action and turned the plan into reality. He lifted us out of a state of complete helplessness. He paid a tremendous price in order to make the adoption official. And then He brought us *home*:

> But *because of His great love for us*, God, who is rich in mercy, made us alive with Christ even when we were dead in transgressions—it is by grace you have been saved.
>
> Ephesians 2:4 (NIV, italics added)

It all begins in the heart of the Father. He chose you. Why? Because He loved you. He made a way for you to come home. Why? Because He loves you. No other reason. It doesn't have anything to do with what you have done or haven't done. It all depends on *His* heart, on *His* love, on *His* choice. It's a gift of hope from a loving Father.

This is the hope that Otim was looking for, and it is the source of hope for everything that is wrong in the world. We need to come *home* to the Father. What He offers isn't like the cheap, temporary imitations of life offered by the world. What He offers is the real thing, perfectly and permanently good in every way.

Purchased by the Son

And it was all made possible at the cross. The cross is at the heart of everything the gospel is about. In fact, without the cross, there is no gospel. C.J. Mahaney says:

> There are those who speak about the Fatherhood of God without reference to the Cross....We cannot, we should not, and we must not, speak of the Fatherhood of God apart from the Cross.[35]

Our salvation, the invitation to come home to our adoption as sons and daughters, was not accomplished by a nice old grandfather God who just smiled at our sin and said, "Oh, it's OK. I love you anyway. Just come home." Yes, our adoption was freely offered from the heart of the Father...but He paid a high price in order to make it possible.

Our rebellion against God was serious. It required a serious solution. Our pain was deep. It required a deep and powerful dose of healing. Our debt was infinitely great. It demanded an infinitely great payment. We were slaves to sin, and He purchased us from our slavery so that we could be set free into a new life in His family. The cross is where His grace really becomes amazing, because Jesus didn't die just to make us legally not guilty in the sight of a holy God...He died to make it possible for us to run with confidence and freedom into the arms of a loving Father:

> But when the fullness of the time came, God sent forth His Son, born of a woman, born under the Law, so that He might redeem those who were under the Law, *that we might receive the adoption as sons.*
>
> Galatians 4:4-5 (italics added)

Adoption was the goal. Redemption made it possible. And that redemption was costly:

> In Him we have redemption *through His blood*, the forgiveness of sins, in accordance with the riches of God's grace that He lavished on us.
>
> Ephesians 1:7-8 (NIV, italics added)

> For you know that it was not with perishable things such as silver or gold that you were redeemed from the empty way of life handed down to you from your ancestors but *with the precious blood of Christ.*
>
> 1 Peter 1:18-19 (NIV, italics added)

Without the cross, there is no redemption. Without redemption, there is no adoption. Without adoption, there is no hope. That is why, for the apostle Paul, the cross was always right at the center of his message. If you miss the cross, you miss the gospel, and if you miss the gospel, you miss everything:

> For I delivered to you as of first importance what I also received, that Christ died for our sins.
>
> 1 Corinthians 15:3

> For I resolved to know nothing while I was with you except Jesus Christ and Him crucified.
>
> 1 Corinthians 2:2 (NIV)

> But may it never be that I would boast, except in the cross of our Lord Jesus Christ.
>
> Galatians 6:14

In his first letter to the Corinthian church, Paul had multiple issues to deal with. Yet he made certain to tell them twice that the cross wasn't just one of many things that they ought to consider, but it is at the heart of everything that matters. It is of "first importance." He resolved to "know nothing" except the cross. And to the Galatians, he wrote that the cross was so central to everything that he would *never* "boast" in anything else. He would not rejoice in anything else…he would not put his hope in anything else. Because all hope, all satisfaction, all life is found at the cross.

I want to pause here for a moment, though, to be sure that we understand the cross in the same way that Paul understood it. There's a lot of talk about the cross these days that is not at all consistent with what the Bible teaches. People are claiming the power of the blood of Jesus over their school results and pleading for His blood to cover their job interview. The bumper stickers preach their own gospel of the cross: THIS CAR COVERED BY THE BLOOD OF JESUS…THIS BUSINESS COVERED BY THE BLOOD OF JESUS.

But that's not the cross I read about in His Word. In fact, I think it is offensive to God to suggest that the perfect, eternal, sinless Son of God was mocked, spit upon, beaten, and killed in order to help you make a few extra shillings. I think it is absolutely wicked to suggest that the body of Jesus was nearly torn to pieces in order to keep your car from getting scratched. The cross is not a tool of witchcraft that we can use to manipulate God into giving us whatever we want. The cross was an act of divine love in which God met our deepest need—our need for *Him*.

Matthew 6 says that God is a Father who knows every one of our needs before we even say a word to Him, and He is faithful and He delights to meet those needs, in His time and in His way. But the cross wasn't necessary for Him to be able to heal us, to provide for us, or to deliver us from danger. Throughout the Bible, we see God performing hundreds of miracles to accomplish such things…*before* Jesus died on the cross.

At the cross, He offers so much more than the hope of finding temporary solutions to temporary problems. At the cross, He offers us *Himself*. Christ is not the way to get everything. He Himself *IS* everything! And in Him we have a hope that lasts:

And hope does not disappoint, because the love of God has been poured out within our hearts through the Holy Spirit who was given to us. For while we were still helpless, at the right time Christ died for the ungodly. For one will hardly die for a righteous man; though perhaps for the good man someone would dare even to die. But God demonstrates His own love toward us, in that while we were yet sinners, Christ died for us. Much more then, having now been justified by His blood, we shall be saved from the wrath *of God* through Him. For if while we were enemies we were reconciled to God through the death of His Son, much more, having been reconciled, we shall be saved by His life.

Romans 5:5-10

The false hope that the world offers us every day is a hope that will ultimately disappoint us. Cars can be stolen or wrecked. Even well-invested money can quickly be lost in large quantities when the economy turns sour. This year's job can disappear when the company closes next year. The man of your dreams can suddenly become your worst nightmare. Whatever "hope" the world offers is, at best, here today and gone tomorrow.

But Paul says that the hope we have in Christ does not disappoint, because it is rooted in something eternal – the LOVE of the Father. The Father who wants you *home*. The Father who will pursue you to the ends of the earth to get you there. And through the cross, that is exactly what He has done! The power of the Father's love is seen more clearly at the cross than anywhere else. He didn't wait for us to turn around and start heading for home. He didn't wait for us to clean ourselves up. The beauty of the gospel is that He made a way for us to come home when we were still helpless...ungodly...sinners...His enemies.

And if He was willing to do that for us when we were still His enemies, Paul says, how much more we can be certain that He will pour out the fullness of His love in our lives when we are His beloved children!!

At the cross, God took the worst thing that has ever happened, and turned it into the best thing that has ever happened. At the cross, I know for certain that my life is not futile....my failures are not fatal.... my death is not final.[36] He suffered the worst of everything on our behalf: all of our sin, all of our failures, all of our pain, all of our guilt, and all of our shame. He took it all onto Himself. Jesus took our broken lives and offered His perfect life in return. He did it for one reason...so that we could come home to the love of the Father. Tim Keller puts it this way:

> He came to bring the human race Home...He came and experienced the exile that we deserved. He was expelled from the presence of the Father, He was thrust into the darkness, the uttermost despair of spiritual alienation – in our place. He took upon Himself the full curse of human rebellion, cosmic homelessness, so that we could be welcomed into our true home.[37]

Promised by the Spirit

Our adoption into God's family was the Father's design from before the beginning of time. It was the Son's delight to give His life to make our adoption possible. And the Holy Spirit assures us that our adoption will one day be made complete. The Holy Spirit, Paul writes, is "a deposit guaranteeing our inheritance until the redemption of those who are God's possession" (Ephesians 1:14, NIV). And when God makes a promise, Paul says, He intends to keep it:

> For no matter how many promises God has made, they are "Yes" in Christ. And so through Him the "Amen" is spoken by us to the glory of God. Now it is God who makes both us and you stand firm in Christ. He anointed us, set His seal of ownership on us, and put His Spirit in our hearts as a deposit, *guaranteeing what is to come.*
>
> 2 Corinthians 1:20-22 (NIV, italics added)

Jesus said that He was going to prepare a place for us...that He would not leave us stranded as orphans...that He would come for us so that we may be where He is, in the presence of the Father (John 14:2-3, 18). It's a promise from God. The presence of the Spirit in us guarantees it...we *will* one day be fully and finally at home with Him.

Oh, that sounds wonderful! But here's the problem—this world we live in is still full of war, disease, death, heartache, poverty, hunger, pain, and rejection. It doesn't feel like life in the Father's house. We know the fulfillment of His promise is coming, but we're not there yet. It causes us to long for the real thing, the home we were created for, and to yearn for the full and final manifestation of our adoption:

> For we know that all creation has been groaning as in the pains of childbirth right up to the present time. And we believers also groan, even though we have the Holy Spirit within us as a fore-taste of future glory, for we long for our bodies to be released from sin and suffering. We, too, *wait with eager hope for the day when God will give us our full rights as His adopted children*, including the new bodies He has promised us. We were given this hope when we were saved. (If we already have something, we don't need to hope for it. But if we look forward to something we don't yet have, we must wait patiently and confidently.)
>
> Romans 8:22-25 (NLT, italics added)

We are free in Christ, yet we long for freedom. We are satisfied in Him, yet we are hungry for more. The believers Paul was writing to then, like the believers who read Paul's writing today, lived in the real world where life can be pretty hard, and like us they could easily slip into discouragement and bondage and despair. So what did God do? He did the same thing He does for us. He reminded them of who they are.

Earlier, in Romans 8:15, Paul reminded us that we are no longer living the insecure existence of slaves, but we have been ushered into the security of adopted sons (I will talk about this in more detail in chapter 10). The Father knew that we would often need to be reminded of the certainty of who we are today and the hope of what is to come tomorrow. And so, the Holy Spirit speaks to us continually, reminding us of a very simple but powerful reality—we have been adopted as children of God.

That reminder leads us to His love, which Paul promises at the end of Romans 8 cannot be taken away from God's adopted children by even the worst circumstances this world has to offer. You might be very familiar with this Scripture, but don't skip over it because you have seen it before. Meditate on its truth. Soak in its wonder. Let its beauty consume you:

> Who will separate us from the love of Christ? Will tribulation, or distress, or persecution, or famine, or nakedness, or peril, or sword? Just as it is written, "FOR YOUR SAKE WE ARE BEING PUT TO DEATH ALL DAY LONG; WE WERE CONSIDERED AS SHEEP TO BE SLAUGHTERED." But in all these things we overwhelmingly conquer through Him who loved us. For I am convinced that neither death, nor life, nor angels, nor principalities, nor things present, nor things to come, nor powers, nor height, nor depth, nor any other created thing, will be able to separate us from the love of God, which is in Christ Jesus our Lord.
>
> Romans 8:35-39

Out of the endless delight that God has within His heart, His one desire is to give us life, that in Him we would find satisfaction for the deepest longings and desires of our souls. When we aren't finding life, it moves Him with a compassion that aches in every part of His infinite heart. The pain is so great because His love is so great, love from the heart of a Father who wants only one thing—that His children would know the fullness of His love, that we would be filled with the beauty of His life, and that we would live in the joy and freedom of His home...forever.

Adopted as true children of God. The Father planned it. The Son purchased it. The Spirit makes us certain of it.

It's His delight...it's your destiny.

Key Thought:

It all begins in the heart of the Father. He chose you. Why? Because He loved you. He made a way for you to come home. Why? Because He loves you. At the cross, He paid an infinitely high price to make it possible. Why? Because He loves you. No other reason. It doesn't have anything to do with what you have done or haven't done. It all depends on *His* heart, on *His* love, on *His* choice. It's a gift of hope from a loving Father.

Personal Reflection / Group Discussion:

We read this quote in chapter 4: "To be right with God the Judge—that is 'a great thing'! But as incomprehensible as it is, there is something greater. The greater is to be loved and cared for by God the Father."

- *Which picture of God best describes the way you have viewed Him in your life—as Judge or as Father?*

- *What does the idea of adoption show you about God's heart? How does it give you a clearer picture of what it means to be saved? How does it help you to better understand what Jesus accomplished at the cross?*

Scriptural Prescription:

Even before He made the world, God loved us and chose us in Christ to be holy and without fault in His eyes. God decided in advance to adopt us into His own family by bringing us to Himself through Jesus Christ. This is what He wanted to do, and it gave Him great pleasure.

Ephesians 1:4-5 (NLT)

Further Study:

The false hope that the world offers us every day is a hope that will ultimately disappoint us. But Paul says that the hope we have in Christ does not disappoint, because it is rooted in something eternal—the LOVE of the Father, a Father who wants you *home*, and who will pursue you to the ends of the earth to get you there.

Read Romans 5:6-10. Reflect on the power of His love through the cross of Christ and how this secures our hope as His adopted sons and daughters.

Part II:

Experiencing Healing
in the Father's Heart

The thief comes only to steal and kill and destroy; I came that they may have life, and have it abundantly.

John 10:10

Seeing Through Broken Lenses

Several years ago, I was teaching a group of pastors at our training centre, leading them through a session on understanding the heart of the Father.

After the second session, these pastors *argued* with me for 45 minutes, trying to convince me that God doesn't love like that. They were desperately trying to find Scriptures that would enable them to hold on to their belief that our position as sons or daughters in God's family depends upon our performance, that we are always living on the edge of being cast out of His family. One pastor even borrowed imagery that I had used in my teaching, only he used it to make the opposite point that I was making. He said, "God is just like a traffic policeman, hiding around the corner, just waiting to catch us doing something wrong. And when He gets us, we are in big trouble!" I couldn't believe I was hearing this from *pastors*!

Afterwards, one pastor's wife came to me and asked to speak to me outside of the chapel. She was weeping, and she said desperately, "We really need more of this teaching. We don't understand God's love." She paused for a minute, looked down at the ground, and wiped a tear from her eye as she finished her statement: "We don't understand what love is at all."

If you asked any one of those pastors if God loves him, he would say, "Yes, Jesus loves me. The Bible tells me so." But reciting it as a fact in your mind and knowing it as a reality in your heart are two completely different things.

Sometimes the radical nature of the love of God is so hard for us to grasp. The heart of the Father we have talked about in the first four chapters is so different from what we have always been taught. It's so different from what we have experienced in our homes, in our communities, and even in our churches.

It is one thing to hear the truth. But people often really struggle to believe it, like one young lady who once told me in a counseling session,

"I know it's true that God loves me. But you make it sound so…so…
free. Nothing in this world is free. I find it hard to believe that He could
possibly love me like that."

There is a spiritual battle going on inside of our hearts and minds.
Since the Garden of Eden, the devil has been lying and scheming and
doing whatever he can do to try to keep us from seeing the heart of
God, because he knows that is where we will find life. Our enemy works
overtime to raise up strongholds, which the apostle Paul defines as mind-
sets that keep us from understanding who God is:

> For though we live in the world, we do not wage war as the
> world does. The weapons we fight with are not the weapons of
> the world. On the contrary, they have divine power to demolish
> strongholds. We demolish arguments and every pretension that
> *sets itself up against the knowledge of God*, and we take captive every
> thought to make it obedient to Christ.
>
> 2 Corinthians 10:3-5 (NIV, italics added)

Now that I am approaching fifty years old, my eyes don't work as well
as they used to. So when I want to read, I need some help. I need my
glasses. When I put them on, it's almost miraculous. On my own, I can't
see a single word. But when I look through those lenses, every word is
perfectly clear. But if someone came along and stepped on my glasses, it
would be a completely different story. I'd still be able to see through the
cracked lenses, and some of the words would be readable. But many of
the words would be distorted, and so the message of the book wouldn't
come through clearly.

That's exactly how it is when the devil succeeds at planting seeds of
deceit in your heart and mind. It's like giving you a set of broken lenses.
You can still see the world, but everything you look at is a distorted version of the real thing: a distorted understanding of what life is about, a
distorted picture of who God is, a distorted view of who you are, and a
distorted picture of others.

The Father wants us to know Him. He wants us to find life in Him. He wants us to find complete freedom in Him. But our lives have been filled with so many lies that keep us from seeing Him clearly. We need to expose the lies and lay hold of the truth. We do that by a constant process of recognizing, replacing, releasing, and receiving. We need to:

RECOGNIZE the lies that keep us from understanding the Father's heart, and identify the source of those lies.

REPLACE the lies with the truth.

RELEASE the pain by forgiving those who have hurt us.

RECEIVE the fullness of the love of God as our Father.

You need to know in advance that confronting some of those lies may be very painful for you. But it's worth it, because it leads to life. Where the lies have left a bitter taste in our souls, the truth becomes all the sweeter. Where the pain is at its worst, the healing that comes from the Great Physician of our souls is at its best.

We can't look at every possible obstacle to the Father's heart, but in these next few chapters, let's start together on the road to freedom by looking at three major sources of the lies that so often keep us from Him:

> *the empty promises of the world…*
> *the weight of religious burdens…*
> *and the bondage of family pain.*

If we are going to find the life, healing, and freedom that the Father longs for us to have, we first have to open our hearts to allow Him to speak to us, to reveal the lies that have prevented us from seeing Him for who He is. So before you move on to the next chapter, I want you to pause and say a simple and honest prayer, trusting the Spirit of God to search your heart and to speak to you clearly and powerfully:

> *Lord, help me to see and understand myself*
> *in the way that YOU see me and understand me.*

Chapter 5

Recognizing the Lies:

A World of Empty Promises

Every culture points to certain things and says, 'If you gain those, if you acquire and achieve those, you'll know you are valuable.' Traditional cultures would say you're nobody unless you gain the respectability and legacy of family and children. In individualistic cultures it's different; the culture says you're nobody unless you gain a fulfilling career that brings money, reputation, and status. Regardless of such differences, though, every culture says identity is performance-based, achievement-based. And Jesus says that will never work.[38]

Tim Keller

The World's Oldest Lie

From the beginning, the Father has said, "Find it all in Me."
From the beginning, the devil has said, "God is not enough. You need something more."

From the beginning, the Father has said, "Freely receive."
From the beginning, the devil has said, "You have to earn it."

From the beginning, the Father has said, "You are My beloved."
From the beginning, the devil has said, "Prove it!"

The devil has preached the same sermon since the Garden of Eden, and he has used it skillfully to deceive the hearts of men, women and children in every era and in every culture, leading them away from simple trust in God by convincing them to put their hope in other things outside of Him.

It began with Eve. "Don't think that you have it all in Him," the devil persuaded her. "Do you know why He won't let you eat from this tree? He is holding something back from you. If you really want to find life, you'll have to reach out and grab it for yourself. What could possibly be wrong with this fruit? Just taste it. I guarantee that it would be the best food in the garden. And take a closer look at it. Why should you be so deprived? Surely God wouldn't create something so beautiful if He didn't intend for you to enjoy it! You must have it. If only you had this fruit, you would have everything...you would be like God."

He tried the same temptations with Jesus in the desert (though it didn't work). "Feed Your flesh! Do something spectacular to make a name for Yourself! Accumulate as much wealth and power as You can!" And He has been using the same tactics ever since. Look at how Paul described our life of sin:

> And you were dead in your trespasses and sins, in which you formerly walked according to the *course of this world*, according to the *prince of the power of the air*, of the spirit that is now working in the sons of disobedience. Among them we too all formerly lived in the *lusts of the flesh*, *indulging* the *desires of the flesh and of the mind*.
>
> Ephesians 2:1-3 (italics added)

When we were lost, we lived according to ways of the world around us. The world around us, Paul says, lives according to the ways of the devil ("the prince of the power of the air"). And what kind of life does that lead to? It shouldn't surprise us. It is a life that believes the old lie from the garden, a life that is focused on one thing—indulging myself in whatever looks good to me, living for whatever pleasure my heart desires, living to try to prove to the world and to myself that I am valuable. This so-called wisdom of the world, James writes, is not only empty...it is evil:

This wisdom is not that which comes down from above, but is earthly, natural, *demonic*. For where jealousy and *selfish ambition* exist, there is *disorder* and *every evil thing*.

James 3:15-16 (italics added)

That is serious! Wherever there is selfish ambition, it is *demonic*. And it will lead to disorder and all kinds of evil.

It shouldn't surprise us, then, that the world is in such a mess. Selfish ambition is at the core of our society. Every day, we are assaulted with false promises of life from every direction. Every day, we are exhorted to give our lives wholeheartedly to the pursuit of our personal prosperity. Look at the billboards and the advertisements on TV. Who looks happy? The beautiful. The wealthy. The powerful. The ones who appear to be having the most fun. The winners. The achievers.

And behind the lure of marketing and all of its enticements, I hear the familiar voice of our enemy with his subtle lies: "Obey your thirst." "Wealth is waiting for you." "The Good Life."

Deep in the village, where billboards aren't seen and TV stations don't reach, the lie dresses itself in different clothing, but it is still very much present: "If you get a bigger piece of land...if you add more rooms to your house...if you start a small business in the trading centre...if you become a leader in the community...then you will really be living."

Aren't those things OK, though? Absolutely, unless your sense of identity depends on having those things; unless you are looking to the status that comes with those things to make you feel important or acceptable.

Sometimes it is really hard to recognize our own motives. The temptations are so subtle. And the temptations are relentless. The lust for wealth, status, power, and pleasure is quite able and more than willing to adapt itself to any cultural context. Wherever you find people, it will surely be there.

The apostle John warned us not to be led astray by this lust, because he recognized the voice behind it. John had walked closely with Jesus. He knew the devil's strategy. And he cautioned us, telling us that when the world tries to offer us life, it is nothing more than that old liar making the same empty promises that he has been making since Day One: "Satisfy your physical cravings. If it looks good, go for it. Make a name for yourself." These may seem like harmless distractions, but they are actually dangerous diversions that take us away from the road that leads to the Father's house:

> Do not love this world nor the things it offers you, for *when you love the world, you do not have the love of the Father in you*. For the world offers only a craving for physical pleasure, a craving for everything we see, and pride in our achievements and possessions. These are *not from the Father*, but are from this world.
>
> 1 John 2:15-16 (NLT, italics added)

We haven't heeded John's warning, though. Look around. The majority of the books in the bookshops, even the Christian bookshops, are dealing with topics of riches and success. Corruption is rampant, not because we have a few bad politicians, but because we have all been deceived to believe that every extra shilling we can lay our hands on is like an extra breath of life. And because we have believed the lie, we do whatever we can to get more money and to attain more status, even when it means sacrificing our marriages and our children in order to do it.

My wife met a young lady recently who said that she was getting ready to leave the country for three years in order to get her PhD. She had two small children, a three-year-old and an infant. Knowing that she was planning to leave them behind for three years, my wife pleaded with her, "But your children need a mommy!" Without even a second thought, she said to my wife, "Sometimes you have to make sacrifices for your career." Wow.

And this isn't an isolated incident. Society is teaching this mindset from the very beginning. I saw a signpost for a nursery school not too long ago, and the motto was "We struggle for wealth and success." Are they serious? These are four-year-olds!

It's not that money and possessions are so attractive, in and of themselves. It's the power and status that come with them. In even the smallest of things among the poorest of people, human beings continue to seek ways to improve their position in the eyes of the world.

We long to be accepted, recognized, and admired. The world tells us that if we find this acceptance, recognition, and admiration, we will find life. So we spend our entire lives trying to establish our worth and value, doing whatever we can to earn the approval of others. We have believed the lie.

We have even welcomed the lie into the church. It often comes to us right from our pulpits. This shouldn't surprise us, though, because the apostle Paul told us it would happen, just as it happened in his day. Men who claimed to speak for God were twisting the gospel and drawing people away from the truth. Paul recognized this false teaching as nothing more than the same old lies the devil has been using to distract us from God's purposes since the Garden of Eden:

> But I am afraid that, as the serpent deceived Eve by his craftiness, your minds will be led astray from the simplicity and purity *of devotion* to Christ.
>
> 2 Corinthians 11:3

He warned them that they needed to listen with caution and discernment, because the devil won't clearly identify himself as the one preaching this false gospel. He won't put up a billboard to advertise his lies: COME HEAR FALSE TEACHING FROM THE DEVIL, SUNDAY MORNING, 10 A.M. He is far too clever to do it that way. Instead, Paul says, he will use those who appear to be genuine men and women of God to make his empty promises for him. Paul is telling us to be careful. Someone may call himself a prophet, an apostle, a pastor, or a servant of God. But if he is not preaching the true gospel of Jesus Christ, he is not a servant of God at all:

Such men are *false* apostles, *deceitful* workers, *disguising themselves* as apostles of Christ. No wonder, for even Satan disguises himself as an angel of light. Therefore it is not surprising if his servants also disguise themselves as servants of righteousness.

2 Corinthians 11: 13-15 (italics added)

And many today are doing exactly that. They portray themselves as mighty men of God, but they preach a much different gospel than the one Paul preached. They preach that salvation is a means to getting our problems solved and achieving our goals. They preach a Jesus who exists for our purposes: a sugar daddy who will give us whatever we want, as long as we spend a little intimate time with Him...the Good Witch Doctor who will make sure that we are always healthy and that we will always prosper materially, as long as we perform the right rituals...a fetish who brings good luck on exams...an agent who helps us find the best jobs... a divine ATM where we can draw cash 24 hours a day.

But even if you get all these things, real life may still elude you. Having your circumstances miraculously improved doesn't mean that your heart has been transformed. God might heal you of a terrible disease, but being healed physically doesn't mean you are alive spiritually. God might intervene on your behalf and bring provision in a way that seems as if it dropped out of the sky, but having your school fees paid for doesn't mean that your sins have been paid for. God might set you free from the demons that have been oppressing you, but being freed from the presence of demons doesn't mean that you are filled with the presence of God.

Life comes only through a personal encounter with the love of God, by grace through faith in the death and resurrection of Christ on your behalf. The Father is determined to give you the real thing, and He will not settle for giving you temporary substitutes. He wants to fill you with Himself. He wants to give you a real and living hope, one that lasts forever.

The Deceitfulness of Riches

And people are so desperate for hope. But people are being deceived, and that deceit is spreading like a bush fire in dry season.

"The devil wants to steal your academic dreams! He wants to destroy your finances and kill your future success! But I am here with the Holy Ghost to help you take it all back from the devil," I heard a preacher promise to hundreds of excited students at a neighboring secondary school in our village.

Oh, we definitely have an enemy who is at work in the world, but is that really what the devil is up to? Is that really his goal, to spend his time and energy trying to stop your personal earthly success? There are a couple of major problems with that teaching.

First of all, you won't find it anywhere in the Scriptures that the devil is at all concerned with whether you are rich or poor (unless you twist the story of Job to mean something that it doesn't mean).

Second, it just doesn't make any sense at all, when you read what the Scriptures say quite plainly. This needs a whole book of its own to deal with the issue properly, but for our purposes here it is enough to note that Jesus repeatedly warned His disciples about the desire for riches and the grip that they can have on our souls.

He told them to guard their hearts against the empty promises of wealth, because "life does not consist in an abundance of possessions" (Luke 12:15, NIV). He told them a few chapters later that it is nearly impossible for a rich man to enter the kingdom of God (Luke 18:24-27). He made it clear that you cannot possibly serve two masters, to be devoted to God and to the pursuit of wealth and selfish ambition at the same time (Matthew 6:24). He said that for those who dedicate themselves to the acquisition of wealth and their personal enjoyment of it, their comfort and pleasure will be short-lived, limited to this brief life: "What sorrow awaits you who are rich, for *you have your only happiness now.* What sorrow awaits you who are fat and prosperous now, for a time of awful hunger awaits you" (Luke 6:24-25, NLT, italics added).

Is money evil? Not at all. We can't survive in this world without it. The Scriptures have plenty to say about how money can and should be a tool of immense value in the hands of God's people. We should creatively and prayerfully seek ways to use it to spread the gospel, and to sacrificially meet the needs of people around us. In doing so, we bring lots of glory to God, because in emptying ourselves for the sake of others, we are putting the love of Jesus on display for the world to see. Money is both a great necessity and a great tool.

But the desire for money can be so deceitful, and the lure of it can be so enticing. If Jesus was so persistent to warn His disciples about how the desire for money can easily carry us away from Him (and therefore away from true life), then we need to pay close attention to what He is saying.

The apostle Paul also knew the magnetic attraction of wealth and ambition. He warned his young disciple Timothy about being led astray, not only by people in the world, but by people *in the church* who teach destructive gospels:

> These people always cause trouble. Their minds are *corrupt*, and they have turned their backs on the truth. To them, a show of godliness is just a way to become wealthy. Yet true godliness with contentment is itself great wealth. After all, we brought nothing with us when we came into the world, and we can't take anything with us when we leave it. So if we have enough food and clothing, let us be content. But people who long to be rich fall into temptation and are trapped by many foolish and *harmful desires* that plunge them into *ruin* and *destruction*. For the love of money is the root of *all kinds of evil*. And some people, craving money, have *wandered from the true faith* and pierced themselves with *many sorrows*.
>
> 1 Timothy 6:5-10 (NLT, italics added)

And Paul ends this passage with a word about those who are already rich:

> Teach those who are rich in this world not to be proud and not to trust in their money, which is *so unreliable*. Their trust should be in God, who richly gives us all we *need* for our enjoyment.

1 Timothy 6:17 (NLT, italics added)

It seems to me that the devil would be more than happy to allow you, or even help you to obtain that which Jesus warns you about…that which life does not consist of…that which makes it very difficult to enter the kingdom of God…that which competes with our devotion to God… that which can offer only a short-lived happiness…that which leads people into temptation, into harmful desires, into ruin and destruction, into all kinds of evil…that which causes many to wander away from the faith…that which is so unreliable.

There is much more to be said about this, but the point is this: the devil is not the enemy of your prosperity. He is the enemy of your soul. He is God's enemy, and more often than not, your desire for prosperity is not the devil's enemy, but the devil's ally. His one and only goal for your life is to come against *God's* one and only goal for your life. And he will use whatever means he can to distract you from the real problem, so that you are blinded to the real solution.

Here's the bottom line. The devil doesn't care if your bank account is filled with dollars or shillings…he just doesn't want your heart to be filled with love. He is not terribly interested in putting obstacles in your career path…his focus is on trying to block the path that leads to the Father's heart. He doesn't care if you have financial freedom…he just wants to make certain that your heart is not free. He doesn't care if you experience all the pleasures of this world…he just doesn't want you to experience the joy of Jesus. He wants you to be fatherless, to live your life as a spiritual orphan who feels that the Father has rejected him.

Fatherless Living: My Story

Before I gave my life to Christ, I was the devil's number one customer. I loved the sweet sounds of his promises. I could listen to them all day long. What young man wouldn't sell his eternal soul for the more immediate promise of pleasure, popularity, and power? My dad was a pastor, and he had always preached that life was found only in Jesus, but what did he really know? I was going to find life my own way. I wanted to achieve. I wanted to be loved by everyone. Above all else, I wanted to have fun.

In many ways, I got exactly what I wanted. I was a captain of the best high school basketball team in the district. I was popular. I graduated second in my class, and went to university on an academic scholarship. Once at university, I found new friends who told me that they loved me. I found new people to impress and to use for my own purposes. And I had loads of fun. My life was one party after another. According to the ways of this world, I was doing pretty well. It looked like my dad was wrong about life after all.

Not exactly. I had to learn a hard lesson that millions of young men throughout history have had to learn—young men who thought that they were smarter than everyone else, who thought that they were smarter than their fathers, who even thought that they were smarter than God. Pride really does come before a fall.

On the surface, I was living the good life. But on the inside, I was dying. The emptiness of the devil's promises was gnawing at my soul. I was trapped in a world of alcoholism and I was unable to get out. I had everything I wanted, and everything I wanted had disappointed me completely.

One night in 1985, I was arrested for driving while I was drunk. When I got into the police car, the police officer didn't greet me or start any kind of conversation. He asked one simple question: "What does your dad do for a living?"

"He's a pastor," I said quietly, hoping he wouldn't actually hear my answer.

"He must be really proud of you," he said, sarcastically, and he didn't say another word to me.

If ever I have heard the voice of the devil, it was at that moment: "Did you hear him? You are fatherless!! You are not your father's son, and you are certainly no son of God. You are a complete failure…and you are all alone."

I was devastated, but the enticement of sin is persistent, and for several more years I continued to live according to the plan this world had drawn for me, according to the simple philosophy that says, "Just indulge yourself at all costs." That's exactly what I did, and it continued to leave me empty.

Suddenly, it wasn't fun anymore. My addiction to alcohol consumed me. And bit by bit, everything in my life fell apart. I dropped out of university with only two classes remaining to graduation (I actually did graduate a few years later). I had no money. I had no job, and there was little hope of finding one. I had been engaged to be married, but like everything else in my life, that relationship turned out to be nothing. I was sharing a house with my best friend from high school. He had a great job, a nice car, a house and plenty of cash…a daily reminder to me that I was a failure, that I was as empty as someone could possibly be.

My emptiness wasn't the result of lacking those things (even when I had everything, my heart was empty). But my physical situation was to me a continual picture of the hopelessness that filled my fatherless heart and soul.

Eventually, I just got tired of living (it is exhausting to live for the pursuit of a lie). I had given myself to chase the promises of the world, and the world didn't keep its promises. I decided that I was going to kill myself. I was just going to cut my wrist, go sit in my car, and bleed to death.

I have never felt more alone than I did in that moment as I held that knife in my hand. "Where are all of my friends?" I thought, almost laughing at how ironic it was that this super popular guy could be left to die all alone. You see, the crowds only cheer when you are performing well, and according to the world's standards, even though I was the greatest success only a short time earlier, I was now a miserable failure.

The good news is that I didn't go through with the suicide (obviously), and a few months later, Jesus walked into my life and made me a new man. But I will never forget that feeling of utter hopelessness, of complete rejection and abandonment, of disappointment and disillusionment with a world that doesn't have the ability to deliver on what it promises to give.

Working for Love

And the world can't deliver on its promises because the world doesn't understand real love. Real love, God's love, is where life is found. It's not based on what someone has done to deserve it, but on what is in the heart of the One who gives it. When we have His love, we have everything. We don't need anything else.

But we have swallowed the devil's lie. We have allowed him to define who we are and what makes us valuable. In the world, your acceptance and your identity is based on your performance – marks in school, wealth, popularity, achievement, the clothes you wear, the kind of job you have, the kind of house you live in, whether or not you drive a car, and if you do, what kind of car you drive. Your value is determined by how well you live up to the expectations on the list that the world has made for you.

You've all experienced it to one degree or another. For example, at the end of seven years of primary school—no matter how hard you have worked, no matter what school you attended, no matter what kind of family you come from, no matter what kind of person you are—only one thing matters. A number. If that number is 4, you are the greatest success. If that number is 34, you are one of the greatest failures.

The top students get their names and photos in the newspaper. The ones who fail get caned in front of the whole class. Everyone knows the names of the rich men. Nobody knows the names of the poor. Athletes who win are recognized. Those who lose are forgotten. Don't believe me? Tell me the name of the man who won the gold medal in the 2012 Olympic marathon. For Ugandans, that's easy. Kiprotich! Now can you tell me the name of the man who came in last place? Of course you can't, because we don't value losers. That's how the world works.

So when do we know that we have done enough or achieved enough to be acceptable in the eyes of the world? That's the joke of it all. The world is a brutal judge. It's never enough.

A number of years ago, we had an outreach day at our training centre, inviting orphans in the surrounding villages to come with their caretakers for a day of fun, Bible stories, and receiving clothing that had been donated by some friends. At the end of the day, after all of the children had gone, I found a primary school report that a child had apparently dropped. I was curious, so I decided to check out his results. His percentages were as follows: Math–98; English–100; Science–98; Social Studies–96.

I was impressed. I thought, "This must be the best student in the school. His teacher must really be pleased with his work." Then I read the teacher's comments: "Work harder…aim higher…strive to put in more effort." What?! The kid was almost perfect, and the only encouragement he received was that he wasn't working hard enough?!

I once read a story in the newspaper that was even worse. A secondary school student brought his school report home to his grandmother, who looked at his numbers and immediately flew into a rage: "What kind of results are these? How do you even dare to bring me such numbers? Your brothers bring me good scores, *big* numbers like 7, 8, and 9. But you? You bring me nothing but little ones. Look at these marks: 1…1…1…1!" And she got a stick and began to beat him.

OK, it is a funny story. Grandma didn't understand that on our secondary school reports, the lowest numbers are actually the best scores. But when you really think about it, it's not so funny, because many of you know exactly how it feels to be rejected even when you have done exactly what you were supposed to do, to be treated like the worst even when your performance was the best. "No matter what I did or how hard I tried," I have heard from people so many times, "it was never enough."

Some of you can still hear the words ringing in your ears, and you can still feel the sting of those words in your heart. They may have been spoken by your teacher, your friend, your boss, your neighbor, or someone else. But regardless of who spoke them, the words were powerful, and they have left an open wound: "You are ugly...You're nothing but a villager...You're a failure...You're just not as clever as the other students... You'll never amount to anything."

This world is ruthless and unforgiving. Whether in school, in business, in athletics, or in relationships, the world holds its expectations high, saying, "This is the standard. This is where you are valuable. This is where you are loved. So work harder. Aim higher. Strive to put in more effort."

So we push ourselves to achieve, trying to earn our way into the hearts of the world around us, trying to prove that we are somebody. We pursue education, career success, and wealth, as if our very souls depend on it.

The pressure to perform and achieve is immense. It leads people to make all kinds of compromises in order to gain favor. And those in the position to give favors manipulate those who are desperate for success, taking advantage of the situation and using it to satisfy their own lusts. Girls on campus are repeatedly offered academic success by their professors, if they will offer their bodies in exchange. They are threatened with failure if they refuse. Young ladies going for job interviews are often told that if they expect to get the job, they will need to have a special relationship with the boss. They are reminded that if they don't accept the conditions of employment, there are *many* other qualified applicants who would be more than happy to take their place.

I read a heart-breaking report of the findings from a World Bank study of seventeen districts in Uganda in 2008 which found that more than 40,000 girls from P5 - P7 had been defiled by their teachers.[39] And those numbers only include the girls who had the courage to report it honestly. Those who should be dedicated to teaching them are instead coercing them into sex for a few shillings or some educational favors. Young girls, most of them between ten and fourteen years old, being taken advantage of by the very people whom they should be able to trust the most, being hurt by the very people who should be using their authority to protect them.

The result is a whole generation of young ladies who will grow up with a completely twisted view of life, of themselves, of authority, and of love. Hearts that are so broken and so hurt that it will often lead to a lifetime of unhealthy relationships. Some of them, in order to protect their hearts, will simply harden themselves to the possibility of ever receiving real love, even from God. And why? Because they thought they had to achieve something in order to be someone. They were desperate, and no price was too high to pay.

"Work harder. Aim higher. Strive to put in more effort. Be somebody. Gain. Acquire. Achieve." That's what the world demands from us if we are going to be valued.

And since the world works this way, we make the mistake of thinking that it is also the way that God works. We think that God demands that we perform for Him in order to earn His love, that He accepts us only when we look acceptable. We think He is like the rest of the world, rejecting us whenever we fall and get dirty, and welcoming us only when we have picked ourselves up and made ourselves clean again. We think that He loves us only when we deserve to be loved. We feel safe with Him today when we serve Him well, but what about tomorrow when we fail?

The world's lies are so common and so widespread that we normally aren't even aware that we are living in bondage to them. They are so overwhelming and so relentless that it is hard to imagine that there could be another way of thinking about life.

We need to have a personal encounter with the truth. The world may take notice of what you have done and what you have failed to do. The world might take inventory of what you have and what you don't have.

People might say all kinds of things about you based on their evaluation of your performance in life. But the world cannot really define who you are. That can only be properly done by the One who created you, the One who really knows you, the One who delights in you, the One who calls you His beloved child. He doesn't value you because of anything you have accumulated or achieved. He loves you and accepts you simply because of what is in *His* heart towards you. Nothing more. When you know that, Boan and Yates write, you are free:

> Once God is known as Father all methods to attain security, prosperity and assurance in the world are exposed as useless enslavement. If one knows God as Father then there is security about everything.[40]

The world has held us in bondage to its demands by giving us a distorted picture of the Father. We need to get a fresh glimpse into His heart so that we can be free. And you would think that the best way to get a clear picture of the Father's heart would be to go to church.

Oh, how I wish that were always the case! But the ironic and sad and painful reality is that it is often inside the church and among professing Christians where people find some of their biggest obstacles to understanding who God really is. The community of people which is supposed to be the living body of Jesus in the flesh often makes it so difficult to really see Jesus for who He is.

We should be the ones showing others how to be free. But so many people *in the church* find it nearly impossible to really understand the love of God for themselves, because they have been crushed under the weight of the burdens placed on them by unbiblical forms of religion.

Key Thought:

Once you know God as your loving Father, all methods to attain security, prosperity, and assurance in the world are exposed as useless enslavement. The world cannot really define who you are. That can only be properly done by the One who created you, the One who really knows you. He doesn't value you because of anything you have accumulated or achieved. He loves you and accepts you simply because of what is in *His* heart towards you. Nothing more. When you know that, you are free.

Personal Reflection / Group Discussion:

Through the world, the devil continues to make the same empty promises of satisfaction and life that he has been making since Day One: "satisfy your physical cravings...if it looks good, go for it...make a name for yourself." The world holds its expectations high, saying, "This is the standard. This is where you are valuable. This is where you are loved. So work harder. Aim higher. Strive to put in more effort."

- *Which lies about what makes you valuable are the ones that most easily lead you astray? The desire for riches? Status? Pleasure? Comfort? Popularity?*

- *How do you normally evaluate your life? What do you have to do in order to feel that you are acceptable? Can you think of circumstances which have led to this way of thinking?*

Scriptural Prescription:

For I am convinced that neither death, nor life, nor angels, nor principalities, nor things present, nor things to come, nor powers, nor height, nor depth, nor any other created thing, will be able to separate us from the love of God, which is in Christ Jesus our Lord.

Romans 8:38-39

Further Study:

The world says our value comes from what we have to boast about—our achievements, our possessions, our status. But what does God say?

Read Jeremiah 9:23-24; 1 Corinthians 1:26-31; and Ephesians 2:8-9. Where does our value come from? How does this understanding help us to say no to the empty promises of the world?

Chapter 6

Recognizing the Lies:

The Weight of Religious Burdens

C.S. Lewis observed that what most distinguishes the gospel from legalism is that legalism says God will love us if we are good, while the gospel tells us God will make us good because He loves us. That's a big difference—and getting your heart and mind around it will change your life.[41]

Tullian Tchividjian

"Uncle, He Smokes!"

Not long after we arrived in Uganda in 1997, I was having a conversation with a boy in Kiwoko. He was talking about his cousin, and telling me that we really needed to pray for him. I asked the boy, "Is your cousin a follower of Jesus?"

"Uncle Dave," he said seriously, "my cousin smokes."

OK, so he has a bad habit, I thought to myself. But that didn't answer my question, so I asked him again, "Is your cousin a believer?"

"Uncle," he said with added emphasis, "he *smokes!*"

"Yes, I heard you. But what I really want to know about your cousin is whether or not he is a Christian."

Exasperated, the boy thrust his hands in the air and brought them down forcefully with each word to make sure I didn't miss his point this time: "Uncle…he…*SMOKES!*"

To the boy, it was simple – being a Christian means that you follow the rules. And we all know that smoking is one of the big ones, according to the way we rate sins in the church. So, in his mind, if his cousin was a smoker, then how could he possibly be a Christian? This boy is not alone in his thinking. Millions live with the same distorted understanding of what it really means to follow Jesus.

That distorted way of thinking tells us, "If you are going to be pleasing to God, if you are going to be in right relationship with Him, then it depends on your ability to do all of the right things and avoid all of the wrong things. If you want God's blessing, you have to go to all the church services, you have to say no to the wrong kinds of music, you have to pray a certain way, and you have to be sure that you follow all of the rules perfectly. If you want to be able to enter God's presence with confidence, you first have to make yourself good."

The burdens of religion take on many different forms: believe all of the right doctrines, and you will be right with God...bring your tithes and offerings to the man of God, and you will be blessed...fast twice a week and be sure to come to the overnight prayer meeting every Friday, and you will see the power of God in your life...follow all of the rules carefully, and God will love you and accept you.

Whatever the form, the message is the same: "If you really want to find God, and if you really want to be accepted among God's people, then you have to do things this way."

The burdens that the world has laid on us are already so heavy, telling us from every direction that if we are going to be accepted, then we have to make ourselves acceptable. We have to be beautiful, rich, educated, successful, always laughing, a winner in life. The pressure of trying to live up to those standards is already more than any of us can bear.

So then we come to church, the place where freedom should reign more than anywhere else on earth. We lay our burdens at the foot of the cross. But before we can enjoy our new freedom, we are handed a whole new set of burdens to carry. They look different than the ones the world has laid on us, but underneath the religious disguise, the lying voice of the enemy can be clearly recognized as he whispers to us:

> "If you were a real Christian, you would do this. If you were a real Christian, you would never do that. Real Christians think this way. Real Christians never have those kinds of thoughts. If you really have God's favor, you would have this experience. This is how real Christians dress. This is how real Christians pray. This is how real Christians worship. A real Christian would read his Bible more often. A real Christian would be at all the meetings and fellowships, and he would volunteer to serve every time the pastor needs him. A real Christian would give more money to the church..."

The list goes on and on. And when we carry this list around in our hearts and minds, the burden feels so heavy! If you have been in church for any time at all, you know exactly what I am talking about. You have felt the weight of this burden, to one degree or another. It is absolute bondage. But Jesus didn't come to bring us a new form of bondage. He came to set us free. The apostle Paul had to remind the Christians of his day about this very thing, and they are words that we need to have driven deep into our hearts every day:

> For you have not received a spirit of slavery leading to fear again, but you have received a spirit of adoption as sons by which we cry out, "Abba! Father!"

> Romans 8:15

> It is for freedom that Christ has set us free. Stand firm, then, and do not let yourselves be burdened again by a yoke of slavery.

> Galatians 5:1 (NIV)

Straining Gnats and Swallowing Camels

My friend Peter says that millions of people in Uganda today are being misled by two false gospels: the prosperity gospel and the gospel of legalism. I couldn't agree with him more.

In their book, *The Subtle Power of Spiritual Abuse* (which I highly recommend), David Johnson and Jeff Van Vonderen define legalism in this way:

> It is a form of religious perfectionism that focuses on the careful performance and avoidance of certain behaviors. It teaches people to gain a sense of spiritual acceptance based on their performance, instead of accepting it as a gift based on Christ.[42]

Years ago, at the children's home where we were working, a big discussion arose among the staff concerning certain "worldly haircuts," which led to a ban on the *French cut* and the *Shaolin* styles. I used to give haircuts to some of the boys, and whenever they came, they made certain to remind me multiple times that I needed to be very careful, because they were not allowed to have these sinful cuts.

Well, one day I accidentally set my hair clippers to cut a bit too low, and my customer ended up with what I would call a borderline Shaolin cut. He had mixed emotions. On one hand, he was secretly happy that he had found a way to get the haircut he really wanted. On the other hand, he was afraid that he was going to be disciplined for it. So I walked with him to his family group, and I explained to his family father that his haircut wasn't a sign that the boy was backsliding, but merely evidence that I was much better at being a pastor than I was at cutting hair. He understood, and everything was OK.

But on my way back to my house, I thought, "How ridiculous that we even had to go through this whole process! How easily we can get sidetracked from the heart of ministry!" It was just a haircut (and not so radically different from a normal one, to tell you the truth). Did it really matter that much?

I know what *did* matter. Their hearts mattered. I talked to these kids on a regular basis. I heard their stories. There was so much brokenness. More than anything, they needed to see what love looked like. They needed counseling to help bring healing to their wounded hearts. They needed men and women to walk closely with them, to listen to them, and to pour their hearts into them. Many of them were filled with anger and bitterness towards God. They didn't need stricter hair guidelines. What they really needed was a heavy dose of His love and grace.

The more I thought about it, the more it disturbed me, because it seemed to me that we were becoming more concerned with what was happening on their heads than with what was going on in their hearts. Jesus said that is exactly what religion does. To the Pharisees and scribes, He said:

Woe to you, teachers of the law and Pharisees, you hypocrites! You give a tenth of your spices—mint, dill and cumin. But you have neglected the more important matters of the law—justice, mercy and faithfulness. You should have practiced the latter, without neglecting the former. You blind guides! You strain out a gnat but swallow a camel.

Matthew 23:23-24 (NIV)

The religious leaders knew very well that both gnats and camels were unclean according to the Levitical law, so of course they wouldn't want to swallow either of them. They were very careful when they drank, straining their drinking water through a cloth[43] and sifting their wine through their teeth,[44] to be sure that gnats or other small insects didn't make it into their digestive system, and thus make them unclean before God.

They weren't actually in the habit of swallowing camels, of course. Jesus was using this as a way to tell them that they were completely missing the point, focusing on the strictest interpretation of the tiniest points of the law, but missing the heart of what God wants more than anything—lives filled with love, justice, mercy, and faithfulness.

We do the same when we get too caught up in the "do this" and "don't do that" of religion, but become blind to the heart of God. We try so hard to carefully hold to the externals. For example, we don't drink, we avoid certain kinds of movies, we always dress modestly, we make sure that we tithe faithfully and attend church regularly. And for the right reasons, those are all very good and right standards to have.

Yet even when we are successful at holding to our strict standards, we so often fail to love. We gossip about our sister in Christ (because she doesn't strain gnats as well as we do). In our zeal to teach a struggling brother to obey properly, we completely disregard the pain he is going through. We hold bitterness in our hearts against a coworker. We ignore the needs of those around us, all the while thinking that God must be so pleased because we haven't missed a prayer meeting in two years. Sure, we avoid the gnats...but sometimes in the process, we swallow a whole herd of camels.

Obedience from the Heart

Don't misunderstand me. There are plenty of things we must do as children of God and plenty of things that we should avoid. Jesus isn't saying here that there are no standards of godliness. Far from it! He is saying that what matters is what is in our hearts, because when our hearts are right, we *want* to obey Him. The great missionary to India, E. Stanley Jones, puts it this way:

> Grace binds us with far stronger cords than the cords of duty and obligation can bind us. Grace is free, but once you take it, you are bound forever to the Giver and bound to catch the Spirit of the Giver. Like produces like. Grace makes you gracious, the Giver makes you want to give.[45]

God takes obedience very seriously. He calls us to be holy, just as He is holy. But He isn't interested in a fake, manmade holiness that depends on our ability to make ourselves look good. He wants our holiness to be real, the natural overflow of our love for Him and the result of the work of His Spirit within us. He has never been impressed with the religious efforts of people to clean themselves up on the outside, when there is really not much love on the inside:

> Woe to you, scribes and Pharisees, hypocrites! For you clean the outside of the cup and of the dish, but inside they are full of robbery and self-indulgence. You blind Pharisee, first clean the inside of the cup and of the dish, so that the outside of it may become clean also. Woe to you, scribes and Pharisees, hypocrites! For you are like whitewashed tombs which on the outside appear beautiful, but inside they are full of dead men's bones and all uncleanness. So you, too, outwardly appear righteous to men, but inwardly you are full of hypocrisy and lawlessness.
>
> Matthew 23:25-28

The Gospel of Fear and Shame

The Father is not satisfied with religious observance. He wants our hearts. He wants to love us, and He wants to be loved. That's all. But religion can be so relentless with its demands, so persistent with its attempts to control and to manipulate, so insistent that love and life must be deserved, so adamant that the only way to the Father is to work your way there. And rather than living in the freedom that we are meant to experience as children of God, people instead are so often living in fear and in shame. I see it everywhere. I hear it regularly. And it grieves me.

On a number of occasions over the years, I have asked a room full of Ugandan Christian young people a simple question: "You are all believers, you're saved, you're Christians, right? OK, so let's say that today you have an impure thought, or you tell a lie, or you gossip about someone, and before you get a chance to pray and confess your sin to the Lord, you get hit by a taxi and die. How many of you think that you will go to hell?"

Nearly every hand in the room goes up. It always amazes me. We talk about the power of the cross. We talk about having eternal life. We talk about the love of God. We sing about peace and victory through Christ. We pray with such confidence and authority. Yet religion has told us that we are always on the edge of rejection and judgment, that even if we are OK in God's sight today, it can all be lost when we sin tomorrow.

One of the Scriptures I have heard quoted many times to try to prove this point is from John 5, when Jesus healed the lame man by the pool. After He healed him, Jesus said to the man: "You are well now. Stop sinning, or something worse will happen to you." And I have been told by numerous people, "You see, Jesus is warning us that we need to be very careful, or something bad will happen to us."

Let's think about what was really happening here. Jesus knew that this man didn't have the power to stop sinning on his own. Nobody does. This wasn't a warning to a child of God that Daddy is going to hurt him badly if he does something wrong. Jesus was simply telling a man *who wasn't saved* (very important to understand here) that being physically healed was great, but having a new set of legs wasn't his primary need. What he really needed was the healing of his soul, and unless his soul finds forgiveness and healing, the consequences of being lost are much worse than any physical sickness. Jesus wasn't threatening the man. He was pointing him to real salvation. Not salvation through perfect obedience, but salvation through faith in Christ. This is clear by what He says a few verses later:

> Truly, truly, I say to you, he who *hears My word, and believes* Him who sent Me, has eternal life, and does not come into judgment, but has passed out of death into life.
>
> John 5:24 (italics added)

What Jesus is saying is obvious. But those who live in the bondage of religious performance misinterpret it, seeing it as a confirmation of their beliefs. They think that Jesus was saying, "You think that being lame for thirty-eight years was bad? Wait and see the bad things God will do to you if you sin! So you'd better watch out, you'd better be on your best behavior, or God is going to get you!" They twist this story, and many other Scriptures, using them to put fear into the hearts of God's people, thinking that the threats will somehow scare them into holy living.

That kind of thinking doesn't come from the hearts of sons who know the love of their father. It comes from the hearts of slaves who are terrified of their master. But if we are children of God through Jesus Christ, the Bible says that we don't need to live in fear: "There is no fear in love; but perfect love casts out fear" (1 John 4:18). We don't sleep in the servant's quarters. We have a safe and permanent room in the Father's house. Because we are not slaves...we are His *sons*!

But the burdens of religion often weigh us down so much that we aren't even able to look up long enough to see the truth. As a result, so many people in the church continue to live with no sense of peace, with no assurance of His love, and with no certainty of their place in God's family. And without that assurance, they will never find life. They will never be free. That grieves me.

Then there are those people who are pretty sure they are going to heaven, but they still live with a constant feeling that God is displeased with them. Why? Because every time they fail, their pastor shows that he is displeased with them...because every time they sin, the gossip in the church begins to flow...because every time they fall, their brothers and sisters push them away.

The result? People have a hard time believing that they can run to the Father with confidence, unless they are sure that they have a clean record to present to Him. But if something has gone wrong, if there is any blemish on their record at all, legalistic religion has led them to believe that they are not welcome in God's presence. That grieves me.

I was once involved in a ministry situation where a fellow staff member had fallen into serious sin. As his pastor and friend, I went to see him, along with another man. When we confronted him about what had happened, he immediately repented, and was assured of God's forgiveness. As we prayed and counseled together over the next couple of weeks, the Holy Spirit worked powerfully in his heart, restoring his relationship with God and beginning to bring healing to his marriage.

But then a few church leaders stepped in and decided to put him to shame by forcing him to publicly confess a sin that nobody needed to know anything about. It had nothing to do with his process of restoration. The sin had been dealt with–forgiven and cleansed by the blood of Christ, cast "into the depths of the sea," as Micah 7:19 puts it. For some reason, though, religious people often feel the need to go fishing for what God has cast away, so that they can bring it all up to the surface again.

I know that public confession of sin is not at all a new thing in Uganda, dating back to the time of the East African Revival. But during the early years of the revival, it was much different than it is today. The confessions weren't used to put someone's guilt on display, nor were they demanded by the leaders. People were encouraged to testify, but it was all rooted in the freedom that was being experienced when people came into a deep understanding of the power of God's love through the cross of Christ. Because of this tremendous freedom, it was common for people to *voluntarily* confess their sins publicly, and the whole fellowship of believers would then rejoice together in the Lord's love and forgiveness. It was a time of joyful testimony, not a time of public shame. In his book, *Revolutionary Love*, Bishop Festo Kivengere describes the beauty of those times of confession in the early revival days:

> It was in this atmosphere that we were transparent with each other, knowing that we were loved and instantly forgiven by the brethren when we were forgiven by God. It was reassuring to me, after telling them what God had dealt with in me, to have them celebrate the forgiveness by lifting a praise chorus. With them, as with God, the past was forgiven and forgotten. No one ever brought it up again. We came to know each other as well, as sinners together at the foot of the cross. Down there we felt free to share anything.[46]

Unfortunately, what began years ago as a beautiful expression of freedom and joy in the grace of God, has too often become a tool of fear and manipulation. Public confession is forced on people as a consequence for sin, or threatened as a way to try to scare people into being holy (or at least to get them to be obedient to the pastor). It isn't much like the revival days at all. It's a lot more like when the Pharisees caught a woman in adultery and dragged her before Jesus. That makes it really hard for people to see the heart of the Father. That grieves me.

It grieves me when during a time of Holy Communion, I see many of my brothers and sisters in Christ refusing to take the bread and the cup, because they have been told to "examine themselves," being warned that if they take it in an unworthy manner, they will bring judgment on themselves. I am not talking about unsaved people who happen to be in the church when we take communion. I am talking about adopted sons and daughters of the Father through faith in Jesus Christ.

Based on a wrong interpretation of Paul's discussion of communion in 1 Corinthians 11, they have been led to live in fear that maybe their heart is not right, that maybe there is a sin they forgot to confess. So, just to be safe, rather than risking taking it in an unworthy manner, they let the bread and the cup pass them by.

But if you read the passage, it is clear that Paul is talking about a specific situation where the Corinthian believers were not taking communion seriously. It was becoming a time to feast and drink, rather than a time to focus on Christ. Paul certainly wasn't telling us that if we have had sinful actions or sinful thoughts that we couldn't participate in the Lord's Supper, that we had to be "worthy" to take part in it. If that were the case, the Lord's table would always be empty…because *none* of us can make ourselves worthy. And we don't need to try to make ourselves worthy, because *He* has already made us worthy!

Communion is meant to be a celebration of the freedom and assurance that we have because of the finished work of Christ on the cross, not a test of how well we have performed in the previous week. The only people at the cross are people who don't deserve to be there. It's not about what we have failed to do for Him…it is about what *He* has done for us. That's the whole point of the celebration. That's the heart of the gospel.

If you are a child of God through Christ and you choose not to take communion because you feel you are unworthy, that grieves me. More importantly, it grieves the heart of the Father who Paul says poured out

His love for you and me at the cross...and He did it *while we were still sinners*:

> For while we were still helpless, at the right time Christ died for the ungodly. For one will hardly die for a righteous man; though perhaps for the good man someone would dare even to die. But God demonstrates His own love toward us, in that while we were yet sinners, Christ died for us.
>
> Romans 5:6-8

When you understand that love, you don't run away from the cross because of your sin. You run *to* the cross because of your sin. And there is no probationary period. You simply confess your sin to Him, and then receive His promise...immediately:

> If we confess our sins, He is faithful and just and will forgive us our sins and purify us from all unrighteousness.
>
> 1 John 1:9 (NIV)

Knowing that every sin has been paid for by Jesus, you can go boldly and confidently into the presence of your loving Father (Hebrews 4:14-16). When the Holy Spirit convicts you of sin, it isn't to fill you with guilt that keeps you away from God. It is to remind you of who you are and to draw you close to God. He is simply calling you to live in your identity as a son or a daughter of God: "Run away from sin, because you are no longer its slave. And run *to* the Father, because you are forever His child."

That is a beautiful truth, but it is so hard to hear because the voice of the enemy is so loud in the midst of our religious activity. He wants to push us away from the Father so that we feel alone and abandoned in our condemnation. The same kinds of lies he tells us in the world are repeated over and over in the church: "If you want to be accepted by God, then you need to make yourself acceptable. If you succeed in being faithful, God will love you. But if you fail, He will reject you. It all depends on your performance. If you want eternal life, you've got to earn it. And the standards are strict. So work harder. Aim higher. Strive to put in more effort."

An Exhausting Pursuit: The Gospel of "Not Enough"

But no matter how much we strive, it could never be enough. Trying to make ourselves like God would be like trying to clean Kampala with a dirty toothbrush. We can't do it!

Here's the good news—we don't have to. When Jesus forgives us, He plants His heart and His Spirit in us, leading to the beautiful freedom of knowing that the Father has blessed us with "every spiritual blessing in Christ" (Ephesians 1:3, NIV), that by His power He has already given us "everything we need for a godly life through our knowledge of Him" (2 Peter 1:3, NIV).

Yet religion refuses to give up, and it keeps pounding our hearts with the message that it all depends on our efforts. So we try and try and try, and we work and work and work, hoping to make ourselves presentable before God. I think we all know deep down that it isn't working, but we keep trying because we've believed the lie that our position before God depends on our performance before God. It's what my good friend Jim Robbins calls the "not enough" gospel. So what happens when it becomes obvious that our efforts aren't enough? In his book, *Recover Your Good Heart*, Jim writes:

> Any "gospel" that *pressures* people to be good inevitably brings shame; because 'good enough' is never good enough. How do we recognize the gospel of duty and pressure, and therefore, shame? This false gospel comes with the following message: "You're not doing enough, you're not spiritual enough, committed enough, selfless enough."[47]

Like the Pharisees who piled hundreds of their own rules and regulations on top of God's law, the "not enough" gospel says, "If you want to find life, then do this and this and this, and don't do that or that or that. And even if you get 99% of it right, we will totally condemn you for the 1% that you got wrong."

So as we go through our day, we are constantly reviewing this check-list in our minds: *Did I do this right? Did I give enough last Sunday? Did I pray enough this week? Why don't I have those special experiences like other Christians... do I not have enough faith? Should I be listening to this song? Can I wear this dress? Should I be having these kinds of thoughts? Probably not. I guess I need to give my life to Christ...again.*

As we live with the constant pressure that we must do everything on the list, we also live with the constant awareness that we are *not* doing everything on the list. The inevitable result? Shame. "I'm a failure. How could God love me?"

Some people just decide to give up, and they walk away from God. Others aren't willing to give up, but they also aren't willing to admit that they have failed. So they put on heavy layers of spiritual make-up, in order to *appear* as if they are succeeding at being good and holy by their own efforts. They learn to say "Praise the Lord" at the beginning of every sentence and "Hallelujah" at the end of every sentence. They are at every church event and every outreach, smiling and quoting Scripture the whole time. They have the longest prayers, complete with shouts and tears. They let everyone know that they tithe and that they read their Bible at work. They are always quick to help, and even quicker to tell you what joy it brings them to be able to lay down their lives in service to you.

If they can't actually succeed at being holy, then at least they are going to do their best to appear holy. What happens after some time is that they actually begin to believe that they are the super holy person that they have been pretending to be. And then shame turns to self-right-eousness. They become proud of their tireless efforts and their devo-tion to God, and they look down in judgment on those who are "not as committed."

But no matter how hard you try or how much you pretend, it will never bring peace. It will never bring joy. It will never bring freedom. Whether you are trying to get rid of your shame by working to make yourself acceptable, or trying to cover your shame under the mask of self-righteousness, it is absolutely exhausting to live under the weight of the burdens that religion has laid on us. We go to church. We sing. We dance. We pray. But so many people are just weary from a lifetime of trying so hard to be and do everything they have been told they are supposed to be and do.

Some of you, if you could be totally honest with God, would say, "Lord, I am tired. I'm tired of trying to fit into the system. I'm tired of trying to live up to all of the expectations. I'm tired of pretending. I'm tired of trying to please everyone. I'm even tired of trying to please You."

An Offer of Freedom: The Gospel of "More Than Enough"

If that is you…if you are exhausted from trying to be everything that religion demands you must be, then Jesus has an offer for you:

Come to Me, all who are weary and heavy-laden, and I will give you rest. Take My yoke upon you and learn from Me, for I am gentle and humble in heart, and YOU WILL FIND REST FOR YOUR SOULS. For My yoke is easy and My burden is light.

Matthew 11:28-30

He's not saying that life in Him will be easy. And He is not saying that the standards of holiness have all been dropped, and therefore we can live however we want to live. He is inviting us to find fullness of life *in Him*. Not by trying hard to make ourselves what He wants us to be, but by surrendering to Him and allowing *Him* to make us what He wants us to be.

He's saying, "I don't want disciples who think they are strong enough, who think they are wise enough, who think they have something impressive to offer to Me. I am inviting those who are tired of trying, who understand very well that they aren't strong enough or wise enough, who know that they can't do it on their own. Religious leaders place heavy burdens on you, burdens that no one was ever meant to carry, and then they reject you and condemn you for not being able to carry them. But that's not My way. My heart is turned towards you. You can come to Me. I am gentle. I won't use My strength against you, to add on more burdens. I will use My strength for you, to lift your burdens and to carry them as we walk together. Come to Me. I will give you every bit of My heart and every bit of My strength. In Me, you will find the freedom and the power to be everything that you were created to be."

Wherever the lies bring bondage, the truth can bring freedom. The *world* deceives us with empty promises of life. Jesus offers Himself as the fulfillment of the deepest desires of our hearts. *Religion* weighs us down with heavy burdens, telling us that keeping the rules and making ourselves good is the way to work ourselves into God's heart. Jesus says, "*I* am the Way," the One who has already purchased our place in God's heart. And He offers Himself as the source of all of our strength and goodness.

There is one more environment where the enemy tells his lies, to try to keep us from finding life and freedom in the heart of the Father. And quite often, the lies that come from this source present us with the biggest and most difficult obstacles. I am talking about the pain that people have experienced at *home*.

As we confront the lies of the enemy in this area, know that he will do his best to drive those lies even deeper into your heart. He will tell you what he thinks about everything you have done or failed to do. But we're not interested in his opinions. We want to see the Father's heart. We want to know what *He* thinks. So, before you go on, I want you to just pause and repeat that simple prayer again, expecting the Father to flood your heart with His love as you face some things which might be painful to face:

> *Lord, help me to see and understand myself*
> *in the way that YOU see me and understand me.*

Key Thought:

When you understand His love, you don't run away from God because of your sin. You run boldly and confidently into the arms of a loving Father, knowing that every sin has already been paid for!

Personal Reflection / Group Discussion:

The Father is not satisfied with religious observance. He wants our hearts. He wants to be loved. But religion can be so relentless with its demands, so persistent with its attempts to control and to manipulate, so insistent that love and life must be deserved, so adamant that the only way to the Father is to work your way there. And instead of living in the freedom we are meant to experience as children of God, we are so often living in fear and in shame.

- *How would you evaluate your relationship with God? Is your evaluation based on what you have done for Him or on what He has done for you?*

- *What is your usual motivation for obeying God? Be honest. Is He a Master whom you serve out of fear? Or is He a Father whom you serve out of love?*

- *You have felt the weight of religious burdens, the gospel of "not enough." Think of some examples in your life.*

Scriptural Prescription:

Come to Me, all who are weary and heavy-laden, and I will give you rest. Take My yoke upon you and learn from Me, for I am gentle and humble in heart, and YOU WILL FIND REST FOR YOUR SOULS. For My yoke is easy and My burden is light.

Matthew 11:28-30

Further Study:

The believers in Galatia were being told that the cross of Christ was not enough, that if they wanted to be made right with God, they had to be circumcised as well (in our context today, there are many different things that people say are requirements in order to really be "Christian").

Read Galatians 3:1-3 and 5:1-6. What does Paul say to us about trying to fulfill all of the obligations that religion tries to place on us?

Read Galatians 2:20 and Philippians 2:13. Think about how walking in these truths frees us from the weight of religious burdens.

Chapter 7

Recognizing the Lies:

The Bondage of Family Pain

This is the enemy's one central purpose—to separate us from the Father. He uses neglect to whisper, "You see—no one cares. You're not worth caring about." He uses a sudden loss of innocence to whisper, "This is a dangerous world, and you are alone. You've been abandoned"...And in this way he makes it nearly impossible for us to know what Jesus knew, makes it so very, very hard to come to the Father's heart towards us.[48]

John Eldredge

Memories of Dad

Since we came to Uganda in 1997, I have counseled with so many people who just cannot understand the love of God, because of a lifetime of being rejected. They think that every time they sin, He rejects them and pushes them away...just like their father did...just like their mother did....or their grandmother...or their uncle...or their auntie. They wonder how God could possibly care about the details of their lives, because their own father had abandoned them. They can't believe that God's desire for them is to have life, because all they ever received at home was pain. The people are different. But their stories all sound so similar:

> "On the day I was born, my father held me, handed me back to my mother and said, 'I don't want him.' And he walked out of my life."

"Every time I brush my teeth, my gums bleed, and I remember the way he used to hit me."

"He told me, 'You are a burden to this family. Why should we waste our money feeding you? You are just taking food away from those who really deserve to be eating it.'"

"The only thing I could do to survive was to obey everything my father told me to do. If I disobeyed even the smallest command, he could beat me badly, or even send me out of the house and make me sleep in the bush."

"From the time I was eight years old, my father beat me every day, telling me that it was my fault that my little brother had died. Eventually, in order to comfort himself, he would come to me in my room…and that's when the regular rapes began."

"My dad never did anything bad to me. He just never did anything good. It's as if he wasn't even there."

"My father paid my school fees. He bought me the things I needed. But he never hugged me. He never told me that he loved me. Even when I performed so well, he never once told me that he was proud of me (which is what I wanted more than anything)."

"I didn't experience any love from my parents. Every time I heard about the Father, Father God, I almost burst into tears, because it didn't make sense to me."

"If God loves me and wants me to know Him, then why didn't He give me a different father?"

Many of you are nodding your heads in understanding as you read this. You know the feeling. It's all around us, so common that many people have told me that they have just accepted that this is how families are. So it's very difficult for many people to receive or even imagine the love of God. They can easily trust that He is able to do powerful things, but it is hard for them to trust that He loves them. In his book, *The Central Event*, Ed Piorek says:

> As children we had a physical and psychological need to feel the love of our natural father and mother. Our ability to feel love as adults has been greatly affected by our parental relationships. The need for a father's love runs deep into the created core of our being.[49]

When that need is not met, the result is that there is never a place in our hearts where we can rest, a place of love and acceptance, a place that we can call home. We wonder if there is anyone who will really love us, if there is anyone we can really trust. We feel alone, left like spiritual orphans. So we close our hearts to others in order to protect ourselves from being hurt again, or we try really hard to be good enough to earn everyone's love (including God's).

The Hunger for a Father's Love

I find in counseling that the biggest and most painful obstacle that keeps people from experiencing the love of God is the relationship they had with their fathers (or people who functioned like fathers). Fathers are meant to point us towards the heart of God, to be living examples of what God the Father is like. They are meant to bring a sense of safety, identity, purpose, and value. Our family life, says Floyd McClung, was meant to be a doorway through which we experience our true home in the family of God:

> You were briefly loaned to human parents who, for a few years, were supposed to have showered you with love like His love. The love and security of a good home and family were intended by God to prepare you for His love.[50]

When our earthly fathers have failed to do that in one way or another, it gives us a distorted picture of who God is, and it gives us a distorted picture of who we are. It makes it so hard to understand His heart towards us.

Many of us respond to the pain by lowering our expectations. We harden our hearts to the idea of love, because it hurts too much when we long for it but don't receive it. So we try to guard our hearts, thinking that if we don't expect too much, then we can't be too disappointed. One young man said to me, "I know that my dad will never really love me, so I decided that if I can at least get him to pay my school fees, I can get an education and find a good career. Then I can go out into the world and figure out life on my own someday."

I have counseled with people who begin the conversation by saying, "My father was a good father. He always paid my school fees, and made sure I had food and clothing." But within an hour, they are weeping, because deep in their hearts they know that they needed much more than school fees. They needed their father to be there...to talk to them...to laugh with them...to guide them...to love them. No amount of money can take away the pain or fill the emptiness that fatherlessness leaves in our hearts. Children need fathers, not sponsors.

These are not isolated examples. As our Ugandan son Paul says, "The world is full of fatherless people." Wherever you go in the world, the effects of fatherlessness can be felt. Here in Uganda we feel it acutely, but to deal with it we have lowered our expectations, reducing the role of a father (and even of God) to someone who exists simply to provide and protect. That is definitely an important part of being a father, but it isn't enough to give children what their hearts are hungry for. We can lower our expectations to try to block out the pain, but the hunger remains. Physical provision and prosperity can satisfy the hunger of our bodies, but it can't even begin to satisfy the hunger of our hearts and souls.

Robert McGee, author and president of an internationally known mental health ministry, says, "We don't just want our fathers to love us; we *need* them to love us." We can't just ignore it. We were created with a hunger for love. And McGee says that this hunger of the heart acts very much like physical hunger, in the sense that if it is not satisfied, we will seek some kind of substitutes, even very unhealthy ones[51] (a person who is starving can become pretty desperate). We see it happening all around us.

Men work so hard to try to create an appearance of self-assurance, power, and authority. They hide behind their positions and titles in order to cover up the insecurity and weakness that they really feel inside… because their fathers never gave them the confidence to really lead like men, to use their influence to serve others rather than to get others to serve them.

They try to prove their manhood by showing how tough they are, doing whatever they can do to try to make us believe that they are strong. They control, manipulate, and often even abuse their wives, their children, their students, and their employees in so many ways…because their fathers never showed them that real strength is found in love, or that a real man uses his strength on behalf of those in his care, not against them.

And many men dedicate their entire lives to the pursuit of wealth, power, and status…because they are still trying to prove their value to fathers who never told them they were valuable.

Women feel the effects of fatherlessness, too. Girls are meant to find love and security from their fathers, but when they don't get it, they will seek it elsewhere. Some women will give themselves to any man who will offer to take care of them. Others will become independent, and seek wealth and success on their own…because they are trying to somehow find the safety and security that their fathers were supposed to make them feel, but didn't.

Girls need to know they are beautiful. That confidence should come first from their father. But when it doesn't, they'll go looking for another man who will make them feel beautiful. No wonder so many girls are getting pregnant at an early age. No wonder so many young ladies find themselves in painful and abusive marriages. They just want to feel safe. They just want to feel beautiful. They just want to feel loved. Lectures, sermons, and abstinence programs won't solve the problem. The solution begins at home, in the heart of a father who treasures his daughters in the same way that God does.

We see the effects of fatherlessness in the church, too. When we aren't secure in the love of Father God, we seek spiritual substitutes.

We seek power and anointing. We look for exciting spiritual experiences. We work hard to be successful in ministry. We become so religious in order to show everyone how happy, holy, and spirit-filled we are. We do all of this to try to cover up the pain and emptiness that is deep inside, and eventually we even begin to believe that we are as spiritual as we are pretending to be.

But underneath all of the smiles, the shouts of "Hallelujah," the preaching, and the busy church activity, there is a lot of pain in our hearts that has never been healed, a lot of emptiness that has never been filled. As the Congolese proverb says, *"The teeth are smiling, but is the heart?"*[52]

"That's not me," I hear some of you saying. "My father was fine. I don't see any negative effects in my life." I hope that is true. But if the pain is there, you can't cover it for a lifetime or hope that it will just go away. It *will* come out. McGee writes:

> If children fail to receive enough love from their fathers, they carry the painful effects for a long time to come—usually for the rest of their lives. Our natural tendency is to block out the painful past. But the wound is too severe. While the hurt may be suppressed for a time, it will eventually emerge, frequently in unexpected and undesired ways. As we form relationships with a spouse or offspring or anyone else, the unresolved pain from the past will cause emotional havoc in the present.[53]

Going to the Heart Doctor

Here's the good news. We don't have to try to cover the pain or pretend it isn't there. There is another option...*healing*. What we have experienced in our families has a huge impact on our lives. And it can be so painful. But it doesn't have to stay that way. As my dad always says, "We are products of our past, but we don't have to be prisoners of our past."

We can be free. And the first step towards healing and freedom is to recognize the lies, to see how our family lives have affected our view of God, our view of ourselves, and our view of others.

As I have walked through this process with people in the past, some have struggled with the idea of identifying the sins and weaknesses of their parents. It feels to them as if they are dishonoring their parents, as if they are accusing them. But the goal of this process is not to blame your parents or to make an assessment of whether they are good or bad people. They are people just like you: people who have experienced their own share of pain...people who are also struggling, because they have been deceived by the lies that life has told them...people who also need to come home to the Father. The goal of this process is not to put together evidence to make a case against your family. The goal of this process is *healing*.

When you go to the doctor, he asks you questions to help figure out what is wrong in your body. You tell him what you have been experiencing and feeling: fever, joint pain, and headache. He doesn't just treat those symptoms, though, because he recognizes that the root cause of them is malaria. He doesn't accuse and condemn the mosquitoes for biting you and giving you the disease. He doesn't curse the hole in your mosquito net which allowed this to happen. That is not his purpose. His purpose is to identify the sickness so that your body can be made healthy.

That is what we are doing here, simply allowing the Great Physician to identify the source of the pain in our hearts so that the healing process can begin. As we do this, I want to encourage you to open your heart to Him, to allow the perfect Father to take your hand as you walk through some things which might be difficult, and to trust all along that the desire of His heart for you is life and freedom.

I want to look at some different types of fathers and the effect that they often have on our hearts and lives, particularly in our relationship with God and with others (and remember, Jesus said our relationship with God and with others is everything that life is all about). These are not perfect descriptions of every father who exists, but they are useful tools to help us evaluate the experiences we have had at home, tools which can help us to identify some of the lies we have believed about God and about ourselves.[54]

As you read through this next section, you might look at a certain type of father and say, "That is my dad exactly!" But if that is not your immediate reaction, don't feel pressured that you have to force him into one of the categories. Some of you will see bits of your dad in two or three of the father types. Some of you won't see much of your dad at all. Your dad might have generally been a good dad, but there are still some things you will recognize that have in some ways made it hard for you to see God clearly (sometimes even small flaws can become big obstacles in our hearts).

It may be that you have more than one father figure who has influenced you in a big way. As you recognize some things about your father, you might also recognize some things about your mother, your auntie, or some other person who was involved in raising you.

Read these next pages prayerfully, and please remember that the goal is not to place blame on anyone, but simply to identify the source of the lies so that the Spirit of God can lead you to healing.

The Performance-Oriented Father

This is the father who expects you to do everything right. There is no room for you to make a mistake. He expects you to be one of the top performers on exams. He expects you to have a successful career, because your success makes *him* look good. At home, you have to cook everything just right, your clothes have to be ironed perfectly, you have to look smart and speak well when visitors come…so that you won't embarrass your father.

I believe that many of these fathers actually do love their children, but their own background and the lies they have believed about life make them think that pushing their children to achieve and perform is the best thing for them.

"Of course," Mark Stibbe writes in his book, *I Am Your Father*, "it is not wrong as a father to want your children to do well." The problem comes "when a father causes his children to believe that they have to earn his love through performance."[55]

This type of father often criticizes everything you do, and even when you do well, it's still not enough to please him (you get 98 on your exam, and he wonders why you didn't get 100). It's like living with a building inspector. He is always looking for something wrong that needs to be repaired or corrected, down to the smallest detail. It is bondage, and you live in a constant state of fear and insecurity, knowing that if you make even the slightest mistake, you will be rejected.

Sometimes, it may actually be the case that he doesn't make very many demands with his words at all. But his own life is so dedicated to achievement, success, and perfection, and his example communicates very clearly to you what makes a person valuable in his eyes. Without a word, you just know that you have to live up to those standards, if you want to be pleasing to him. He doesn't actually say, "If you want my love, you have to earn it." But he doesn't have to say it. It is obvious just by watching him.

So you begin to believe that God is like your father, demanding your good performance before He is willing to give His love. There is no freedom in that kind of life…no joy…no peace. You live in bondage to the pressure to perform, or at least to appear as if you are performing.

Many times, the children of these fathers grow up to be the people who seem to have everything. They are the successful ones, the beautiful ones, the intelligent ones. They become skilled at pretending that they are doing very well. In the church, they are the ones who always have a testimony to share (one which makes them look good, of course). They are the ones who always seem to have the right answer, the ones who always have a smile on their face. They try to always appear strong, to never show any weakness or allow tears in their eyes (unless the tears are necessary to give the appearance of godly humility).

They look great on the outside, but on the inside they're not happy. They have believed the lie that they are lovable only when they do things right. They are driven by their fear of failure, and by their concern about what others think of them. They typically become very critical of other people, holding everyone else to the same unrealistic standards that they are trying to live by. And they normally end up treating their own children the same way that their father treated them, expecting them to perform perfectly if they want to be accepted.

After years of trying to achieve enough to be worthy of love, many of them get so tired that they decide to just give up. "I always fall short. Whatever I do, it is not good enough. So why should I even try?" They retreat and live a very safe life, attempting to achieve little so that there is little risk of failure. They are unmotivated, just existing day by day for no apparent reason. "If I don't try," one person told me, "I can't fail. And then no one can criticize me and tell me I am a failure."

This affects believers as well as unbelievers. Committed church members and even pastors fall away from God, because they have been led to believe that they have to perform in order to earn His love. They try so hard, but they realize that they just can't achieve the kind of life that He requires. And since they don't understand His love and grace, they just give up, saying that the Christian life is unattainable.

The Authoritarian Father

In some ways, the effects of this type of father are similar to those of the performance-oriented father, but the goals are different. This harsh, controlling father doesn't necessarily care about good performance in school or success in the world. As the name "authoritarian" suggests, what this father cares about more than anything, and demands at all costs, is absolute obedience to him, complete submission to his authority.

This father is normally extremely impatient, he criticizes everything, and he is overly harsh with his words and his punishments when his children disobey. He doesn't have the ability to express compassion or grace (or he is afraid to, because he thinks that too much grace might cause his children to lose respect for him).

He appears to be very strong, but the truth is, this kind of father is usually a very weak and insecure man. He attempts to cover his weakness and insecurity with an outward display of strength, like the headmaster walking around the primary school compound with a cane in his hand. Stibbe writes:

> He exercises authority in order to manipulate, control, dominate and coerce his children, and in the process creates a culture of fear. Children in the home of an authoritarian father are constantly intimidated into being compliant to the father's rules... Authoritarian fathers tend to be very judgmental, injuring their children by devastating judgments and the unjustly tough use of punitive discipline.[56]

What matters to this father is that he is completely in control, not questioned by anyone, and definitely not defied in any way. He may communicate a lot with his children yet not make any real efforts to have a relationship with them. His communication focuses mostly on making sure that they follow all of the rules. He is not normally very interested in his children's dreams, their goals, or what is going on in their hearts. What he is most interested in is that they do what he wants them to do.

He is paranoid, always on the lookout for anything that might undermine his authority, and he will do whatever he needs to do to keep his children perfectly under his rule. These are the men who become politicians who rule like dictators, bosses who treat their employees like slaves, or pastors and Christian leaders who lead as if they own their people, using threats and shame to make it nearly impossible for the people to ever think of going to another church or working for another ministry.

The children of these fathers learn how to survive. They fear failure, because it has always led to harsh punishment. So they learn how to appear to be obedient and compliant with what their parents want, even when their hearts are far from them. They will do and say whatever they need to do to avoid another beating. They learn when to deny that they did anything wrong and when to just give in so that the punishment doesn't get any worse. They learn how to please people, whether it is actually in their heart to please them or not.

Don't misunderstand me. These fathers are right to expect their children to obey them. That is God's desire as well: "Children, be obedient to your parents in all things, for this is well-pleasing to the Lord." (Colossians 3:20). But the obedience God desires is not an obedience that comes from fear or manipulation, but from *love*. Jesus says, "If you love Me, you will keep My commandments" (John 14:15).

There was a young lady who came to stay with us for a while, who had grown up under this kind of fatherhood. Over the years, she had learned how to play the right games in order to survive. When we would rebuke her or correct her, she would often say something like, "Just tell me what you want me to say, and I'll say it." And we would tell her, "We aren't interested in forcing you to say anything. Our goal is not to control you. What we want is your *heart*."

But it was hard for her to understand, because children of harsh, controlling fathers often have a very difficult time relating to any kind of authority. They have a difficult time believing that anyone in that kind of position could possibly love them and have their best interests in mind. They assume that all kinds of leaders just want to use them for their own purposes, that they just want to control them like their fathers did. This young lady finally realized that whenever she was talking to anyone in authority–a pastor, a school teacher, or even me–she had a hard time trusting them or receiving correction in the way it was intended. To her, it always sounded harsh because, as she told me, "Whenever I talk to someone in authority, I see *him*."

Because of their desire to avoid authority, many of these children grow up to be very independent, self-reliant people (or they at least try to be). They have always been required to do what someone else wants them to do, but now they want to be their own boss. They want to take control of their own lives. This sometimes leads to a life of total rebellion against all authority and rules, sometimes even leading to addictions, crime, and unhealthy sexual relationships. They are unhappy, but they think they have freedom. As one woman said to her counselor, "My life is a mess, but at least I am in charge of the mess."

As parents, these children will unfortunately often grow up to treat their children in the same way that they were treated. I have known men who love the Lord and who are so kind, but when they get into a position of authority, what is deep in their hearts is revealed. They are gentle with other people, but with those under their leadership, including their own children, they are harsh and controlling. Why? It's the only way they know how to lead. It's what was modeled for them. They have believed the lie that acceptance comes only through proper obedience and submission.

When it comes to their view of God, people who had these kinds of fathers typically base their relationship with Him on discipline and duty. They can only see the Scriptures that talk about the fear of God, the law, obedience, and judgment. But the Scriptures about love, grace, and mercy don't make any sense to them. So they do what they have always done—they try hard to do and say whatever they believe He expects them to do and say. Not because they love Him, but because they are afraid of Him. They live with what Paul referred to in Romans 8:15 as "the spirit of slavery." They're never free in the Father's love, always knowing that they are just one mistake away from big judgment.

Sometimes, when these children grow up, they decide that they don't want to have anything to do with God at all. If He is going to demand every bit of their life like their fathers did, then they want to get as far away from Him as possible, because they really can't trust Him. They might decide to go to church and be involved in some activities, but they will serve Him on their own terms. One young lady once told me, "I am afraid to surrender my whole life to God, because I don't know what He will do with it." She'll let God partially into her life, but she won't yield control to Him, because her childhood taught her that she can't trust anyone else to be in charge.

The Abusive Father

The most painful wounds come from this kind of father. I don't need to describe it too much, because if you have had this kind of father, it is obvious. You know it. An abusive father inflicts pain on his children in a variety of ways. Sometimes it is through kicks, slaps, or punches. Sometimes he uses his words like weapons, tearing up the heart of a child: "You're useless." "I wish you had never been born." "You are a burden to me." Sometimes the abuse is emotional: locking the child alone in a dark room...telling them that the dog is going to come and get them if they don't obey...neglecting them when they really needed comfort or help. And sometimes the abuse is sexual, which is the deepest and most difficult wound to heal.

The worst thing about any kind of abuse, McGee says, is that it is usually continuous:

> Abuse is almost always repeated over and over. You aren't likely to meet many people who were abused once, and then their parents somehow decided to stop. Once it begins, it usually continues.[57]

Children of abusive fathers live in a very lonely, confusing, and frightening world. The ones who should be protecting them are the ones who hurt them. The ones who should make them feel safe more than anyone else are the ones they fear more than anyone else. Children long for the love of their fathers. They need the security of their fathers. And when they receive abuse instead, it is devastating.

These kids often grow up with a lot of anger in their hearts. Sometimes the anger is obvious, and sometimes it is hidden deep within (but it will eventually come out).

Sometimes a child is so angry that he wishes his father was dead. But even if the father was gone, it wouldn't take away the pain. It is such a strange mix of emotions. The child hates his father, but the longing for his father's love is still there. McGee says:

> While they may wish their domineering, unreasonable fathers were dead, at the same time they wish that some miracle would suddenly make the abusive fathers recognize the worth of their children and begin to express love.[58]

Sometimes, the anger is directed at God. They wonder, "If God loves me, why didn't He give me a different father? And since He had to give me this one, why couldn't He have at least protected me from him?"

Angry at their fathers. Angry at God. Maybe angry at both. And the sad reality is that some of these children even become angry with themselves. They believe the lie that they were somehow responsible for what was done to them, that they are just bad people who must have done something to deserve it. Often they are filled with all kinds of guilt, shame, and self-hatred, and they can't imagine that God has any good intentions towards them. In a counseling session, a Bible college student once said to me, "I know that God loves *you*, but for me, His plan is pain...because I am just dirty."

After enduring years of abuse, understanding the love of God can become so difficult. They know that God is supposed to love them, protect them, and take care of them. But their father was supposed to do that, too. So it is hard to get close to God and to trust Him, because they are afraid that it will just bring more disappointment and more pain. They often struggle with any male authority image, and reject any kind of mentor or father figure, even when that Father is God Himself. Years ago, a university student gave me this response to the idea of God being his Father: "I already had one father, and it was so painful. Why would I want another one?"

The Absent Father

The last type of father is a father who didn't necessarily do anything bad to his children...he just wasn't there. Though it isn't always as obvious as with some of the other father types, the impact of absent fathers is massive. And it is growing on a nationwide level.

Children long for and need the input of a loving father. When that father isn't there, it leaves a huge gap that cannot easily be filled. There are a lot of different reasons for the father's absence. It could be death, divorce, abandonment, or frequent traveling for work. It could be that the father is always at home, but he just doesn't care. He just sits in the corner of the sitting room, reading the New Vision or watching TV. You exist in the same space with him, but practically, it's as if he isn't there at all. Whatever the reason for his absence, the effects on his children are generally the same.

There are a couple of other big contributors to the absence of fathers in Uganda: the growing number of fathers who live and work in different districts or different nations, and the separation from fathers due to the increasing number of children who are in boarding school (and these days, they are being sent there when they are so young). With boarding school, it is the child who has gone away, but the impact is still the same. The child needs a father, and the father is not there.

The current trend is leading us towards an entire generation of children who will grow up without any concept of what a father is supposed to be...simply because they haven't been with him. It is a serious issue that the church needs to pay attention to, to provide leadership in helping a nation understand that the biggest need in a child's life is not to be sent to the best school, but to be *loved* and *actively parented*.

A 17th-century Anglican priest named George Herbert once wrote, "One father is worth more than a hundred schoolmasters."[59] It's great to get a quality education, but an institution can never be what a father is meant to be: someone who is there when his children need him, someone who teaches them about life and talks with them about things that matter, someone who tangibly shows them love, who makes them feel safe and secure, who encourages them, and makes them know that they have identity, value, and purpose.

When a father is not actively involved in the lives of his children, whether by choice or by circumstance, it leaves a big hole in the heart of a child. And though they are not often as painful as the wounds of abuse, the wounds are still there...and they are very real.

Children of absent fathers often grow up unable to enter into intimate relationships and friendships with others, because they fear that they, too, will disappear from their lives, just like their dad did. They have difficulty trusting others, because they don't want to get hurt again. This is especially true of children who get passed around from one relative to another, and moved from one school to another. How can they believe that anyone, including God, will ever love them *permanently*? At the children's home where we used to work, the most common question we were asked by the kids in our first few months was, "How long are you staying?" In other words, "I want to know whether or not I should even begin to get to know you. Because if you aren't planning to stay for a long time, the last thing I need is to be abandoned by someone else that I love."

Children of absent fathers often struggle to believe that God cares about them, that He is really concerned about their needs, that He listens to them, and that He wants to speak to them. Why? Because their father, who was supposed to give them a clear picture of what God the Father is like, was never around. They might believe that God will provide for them from a distance, just like their dad did. But they doubt that He really cares enough to get close to them. They doubt that He really loves them.

As with the children of abusive fathers, there is often a lot of hidden guilt in children of absent fathers. They somehow blame themselves, thinking that he must have left or not been interested in them because of something that was wrong with them. I have counseled with young adults who still blame themselves for the fact that their father *died* when they were very young. It's not rational to think that it could possibly be true that it was their fault. But that's not the issue. The issue is that it *feels* true.

Because they feel a sense of guilt for his absence, and because they never received the "well done" that they so desperately needed specifically from their father, children of absent fathers often feel a compelling need to prove themselves. There was no father to give them value, so they work tirelessly to try to earn their value in the eyes of the world, in their own eyes, and even in the eyes of God. But no amount of work can help them find what their hearts are hungering for. And no amount of gifting, education, or career success can do it, either.

A few years ago, one young man asked me to disciple him. He is very bright, lots of fun to be around, hard-working, and extremely gifted in ministry. It didn't seem like there could be much that he really needed at all. In our first meeting, I asked him what it was that he was looking for from me. I expected him to say, "I want you to help me learn to teach and preach more effectively," or something involving ministry skills. But without hesitation, he said, "I need a *daddy*." You can have so many things going for you, but the presence of a father is irreplaceable.

I know and have worked with many pastors and Christian ministry leaders who so clearly exhibit the effects of absent fathers. They are so busy, the hardest working pastors I know. They are so good at mobilizing people for ministry (but often don't have any idea how to build real relationships with them). They preach with passion. They work and work and work. They build big successful ministries. But underneath it all, I can see the insecurity of boys who are trying so earnestly to earn the approval of fathers who are nowhere to be found, boys who more than anything want to hear their fathers say, "You are a good man. I am so proud of you."

Finally, children whose fathers are absent because they died (especially when the child was young) are often angry at the father for leaving them, and angry at God for allowing him to leave. I will never forget the first time I was confronted with this anger, when Justine, a girl at the orphanage where we were working, told me very bluntly, with almost no emotion at all, "Uncle Dave, I am so angry at God for taking my father. If He loved me, He would have never done that." The pain was so intense and so real that you could almost feel it in the air. Thankfully, Justine's story has a beautiful and happy ending, which I will share with you in the last chapter.

An Orphaned Nation

One of the most common statements I have heard in our fifteen years in Uganda is this: "I don't trust other Ugandans." People have so little trust for one another. They are so suspicious of the hearts and motives of those around them. It isn't because Ugandan people are more untrustworthy than others. It isn't because they have worse hearts than people in other nations. It isn't that at all. It is because we are a nation of people who have never really learned how to trust *anyone*.

I believe we can attribute it to what we call the "orphan heart," meaning that people are living fatherless lives. By "fatherless," I don't mean only those who have physically lost their parents, but those who, for some of the reasons we have discussed, are fatherless in many other ways—emotionally, psychologically, and spiritually. There are many characteristics of the orphan heart, but I want to just mention this issue of trust specifically, as I believe it has huge implications for the life of the entire nation.

Someone with an orphan heart is someone who has not really understood the love and security of having God as their Father.   Trust was supposed to be created at home, when a child from the very beginning finds safety and love. But for countless people, that safety and love hasn't been found. Those who were supposed to make us feel secure made us scared. Those who were supposed to provide for us neglected us. Those who were supposed to give us a sense of identity made us feel like we were nobody. Those who were supposed to fill our hearts with love broke our hearts instead.

When fathers have been absent, abusive, neglecting, or harsh and demanding, that early sense of trust is not developed in the child. And the eventual result is a man or a woman who doesn't have the ability to trust anyone at all, including God.

As with physical orphans, those with orphan hearts learn very early in life that since they can't trust anyone else, they have to look out for themselves. They wanted love and they needed love, but instead they were hurt, they were neglected, and they were abandoned. It is up to them now to make sure it never happens again.

They learn to do whatever they need to do to survive. They learn to mistrust everyone around them. They only get close enough to people to get what they can from them. But they never really give anyone their heart, keeping a safe distance from everyone in order to avoid being hurt or disappointed again. As one young lady once told me in our sitting room, "I have decided that I will just never trust anyone again. It's much safer that way." Thankfully, the Lord brought tremendous healing to her heart, and she is now free to really love and be loved. But her words reflect the mindset of millions of other people in our churches who are still in bondage to fear and pain, and as a result they are unable to really trust anyone. They desperately need the love of the Father to set them free.

The effects of the orphan heart on an individual life can be devastating. And when fatherlessness of any kind becomes common among an entire group of people, the resulting mistrust can spread like an infectious disease, harming not only individual lives, but destroying the lives of entire families and communities as well. It can even destroy a nation. Mark Stibbe says this about the multiplying effect of mistrust in the orphan heart:

> The trouble with all of this is that the person with the orphan heart not only becomes mistrustful of others, they also become mistrusted by others. Mistrust breeds mistrust. The person wounded by his or her father finds himself or herself not only the subject of mistrust but the object of it, too.[60]

Eventually, Stibbe says, it becomes a mentality that says, "I don't trust others because others don't trust me."[61] When this mentality spreads throughout a nation (as it has done in Uganda), it has a very harmful effect on the way that we do everything–business, politics, education, marriage, family, and yes, even church.

There Is ALWAYS Hope

But pain was never meant to be the end of the story. I don't talk about all of these things just so that you will feel pain in your heart. I talk about these things because I know the power of the truth. I don't know exactly where you came from, and I don't know exactly what kind of father you had, but I do know this–Psalm 103:4 says that He is the God "who redeems your life from the pit, who crowns you with love and compassion."

You are never alone. You are never without hope. "There is only one place where there is no hope," my dad always says, "and that place is called hell. You are *not* in hell…therefore, you have hope." As long as you are alive and breathing, the good news is that there is always hope…no matter what kind of person you have become…no matter what anyone else has done to you or told you about yourself…no matter how painful the wounds are…no matter how much you've been deceived by all the lies. No matter how deep the pit is, the love of the Father is always deeper.[62] And He will pursue you to the bottom of that pit, take you in His strong and loving arms, and bring you out with Him to the place where He is.

His plan for you is not striving, or pretending, or pain, or loneliness, or despair. His plan for you is love. Jesus wants to take you outside of Jerusalem to a hill called Calvary, where He took *all* the lies of your past and *all* of the pain in your heart onto Himself, and He nailed them to the cross and buried them there forever. He wants to raise you to a new understanding of what life is all about. He wants you to be fully at home in the heart of the Father who loves you perfectly. I'm not talking about getting saved again. I'm talking about complete healing. I'm talking about being free. I'm talking about fullness of life, the way that God designed it to be.

He's not required to offer us life. We haven't done anything to deserve it. He does it because He is love. He does it because He *wants* to.

It's His delight. It's your destiny.

Key Thought:

As long as you are alive and breathing, the good news is that there is always hope…no matter what kind of person you have become…no matter what anyone else has done to you or told you about yourself…no matter how painful the wounds are…no matter how much you've been deceived by all the lies. No matter how deep the pit is, the love of the Father is always deeper. And He will pursue you to the bottom of that pit, take you in His strong and loving arms, and bring you out with Him to the place where He is.

Personal Reflection / Group Discussion:

We don't just want our fathers to love us; we *need* them to love us. We can't just ignore it. We were created with a hunger for love. And this hunger of the heart acts very much like physical hunger in the sense that if it is not satisfied, we will have to seek some kind of substitutes, even very unhealthy ones.

- *As you read through the various father types, which one(s) described your father (or parental figure)?*

- *What substitutes have you sought in order to fill the unsatisfied hunger for a father's love?*

- *What evidence do you see of the "orphan heart" in your life, your family, your community, our nation?*

Scriptural Prescription:

For my father and my mother have forsaken me, but the LORD will take me in.

Psalm 27:10 (ESV)

I will not leave you as orphans; I will come to you.

John 14:18

Further Study:

Read Psalm 139:13-18. Your father may not have showed much concern for your life, but see the heart of your Father in heaven who has had wonderful plans for your life since before you were born, and who continues to work out those plans today!

Read John 8:32. Look ahead with confidence, believing that Jesus will keep His promise to bring you freedom in the truth about who He is.

Chapter 8

Replacing the Lies
with the Truth

Sociologists have a theory: you become what the most important person in your life (wife, father, boss, etc.) thinks you are. How would my life change if I truly believed the Bible's astounding words about God's love for me, if I looked in the mirror and saw what God sees?[63]

Philip Yancey

"I Want My Daddy"

A couple of years ago, my daughter Sarah was climbing a tree with her brother, Joshua. Even though she was only about four years old at the time, she was actually able to move up pretty quickly, without much problem. But as many people can testify, moving up the tree is one thing.... but getting down from it is a different story altogether.

So there she was, three feet tall and ten feet above the ground, not at all confident that the same hands and feet that got her safely up could possibly navigate the same branches to get her safely down.

So what do you do when you're in a situation like that? Well, Sarah did exactly what she had learned to do when life proved to be bigger than she could handle: she called God, and she called Daddy.

Joshua said that the first thing she did was to pray. But what do you pray when you're four years old and stuck in a tree? I suppose she could have tried to impress God with one of those big, long prayers that we say in church, thinking that if we say the right words, if we are loud, and if we sound confident and full of faith, then God will respond by doing something for us:

> Lord, You are the One who created all the trees, which Your word says clap their hands in praise to You. And right now, I commit this particular tree into Your hands, so that You might do a miracle for me. Fill every bit of this tree with Your mighty presence, from the highest leaf to the deepest root. May Your power rest on every bird that nests in its branches and every caterpillar that moves on its trunk. Lord, Your word says that cursed is he who hangs on a tree, but by the blood of Jesus I declare that I am not cursed, I am blessed. I claim that every branch on which I set my foot belongs to me. I come against any spirit of wind that would seek to cause me to fall. You promise that whatever I loose on earth has already been loosed in heaven, so in the name of Jesus, I loose myself from this tree. I speak to these branches, and I command them to lower themselves, so that when I open my eyes, I will be on solid ground.

That may sound very spiritual in an overnight prayer meeting, but this was definitely not the time for one of those prayers. And the truth is, God is never really impressed with our many words. He's not impressed with shouting. He's not impressed with great claims. He is impressed with a *heart* that trusts in His heart. Not just in a church service, but in the midst of the circumstances of real life.

Real life calls for a real God. Sarah needed the God who she could talk to when it's not Sunday, the God who speaks Sarah's language. She wasn't calling on a faraway God who created all the trees, hoping that maybe she could convince Him to come down from on high and do a miracle for her. She was calling on the loving and merciful God who knows her intimately, the One who is near, the One whom she knew was already with her in this particular tree.

Her prayer was simple and brief: "God, my brother knows how to get down from this tree, but I can't get down."

Do you know why her little prayer was so beautiful? Because she did the most basic thing that the Lord asks of us: she *trusted* His heart. This four-year-old little girl, who was stuck in a random tree in the middle of a small town in Ohio, believed with all her heart that the God of this universe loved her like a Father, and that He was right there in that tree with her. How could she be so confident in that? Because she knew that His heart was turned towards her.

And why was she so confident in the heavenly Father's love for her? Because she was so confident in her earthly father's love for her. As soon as she had prayed, she said, "I want my Daddy. "

When I went out to her, she didn't remind me of how well she had behaved that week, thinking she needed to convince me that she deserved to be helped. And she wasn't afraid at all. She just looked down and smiled....because Daddy was there. When I told her to step down on the next branch, she did it with confidence. And when I told her to let go, that I could take her the rest of the way, she gladly took her hands off of the branch, and just let herself fall into my arms. She did it because she knew for certain not only that I *could* catch her, but that I *would* catch her.

That certainty brings freedom, even freedom to take risks, because do you know what she did later that same day? She climbed it again.... and she got stuck again. But she did it with the security of knowing that Daddy would come, and since she knew that Daddy would be there, she knew without a doubt that God would be there as well.

Sarah knew the truth, and the truth made her free. Not a freedom that came because she was delivered from her circumstances, but a freedom that filled her heart *in the midst of* her circumstances. She knew the truth about God, and so she knew the truth about herself. And when you really know the truth, there is no room for lies.

The Test of Freedom

So how do you know whether or not you are free in the Father's love? Ask yourself these questions:

How do I respond when things go wrong in my life? How do I respond when I have failed?

How do I respond when people don't love me as they should? How do I respond when people ignore me, abandon me, falsely accuse me, disagree with me, or reject me? How do I respond when I have done something wrong, when I am corrected or rebuked?

How do I respond when I do something good and nobody gives me credit or appreciates me for it? How do I respond when someone else receives all of the praise?

How do I respond when I am not able to control a situation? How do I respond when people don't do what I want them to do?

Do I worry? Do I seek to earn the love of others by trying harder to make myself lovable? Do I try to prove that I am right? Do I work to try to gain control of the situation? Do I get discouraged and depressed? Do I get jealous? Angry? Bitter?

Or do I fall into the arms of a loving Father? Henri Nouwen says it is all a matter of whose opinions you are really living for:

> The main issue is this: 'To whom do I belong? To God or to the world?' Many of my daily thoughts suggest that I belong to the world rather than to God. A little bit of criticism makes me angry, and a little bit of rejection makes me depressed. A little bit of praise raises my spirits, and a little bit of success makes me excited. It takes very little to either raise me up or throw me down.[64]

Lies and Accusations

How we respond to situations in our lives reveals a lot about what is going on in our hearts. It reveals if we're believing the truth about God and about ourselves, or if we're believing lies. And we have plenty of opportunities to test ourselves on this, because no matter what life brings, we can be sure that in every situation, the enemy of our souls will be there. He is the one that Jesus refers to in John 8:44 as "the father of lies," the one that John refers to in Revelation 12:10 as "the accuser of our brothers and sisters" (NIV). He will do whatever he can to deceive us, to make certain that we are unable to believe the almost unbelievable truth that God delights in us. And the lies he will use are the same ones he has used so many times before…yet they are still so effective:

> "You failed again."
> "If only you were more…"
> "You are worthless."
> "You didn't do enough."
> "God will never forgive you now."
> "Just give up."

He will pound us relentlessly with his lies and accusations, in order to give us a distorted picture of ourselves, in order to keep us from really understanding who God is and what He really thinks about us. My friend Jim says that what we really need is to know that God delights in us as His children. But after we have heard the lies so many times, it is difficult to imagine:

> "What do you really think of me, God?" I suspect I've always been a bit afraid of what He'll say. Don't we believe that God's response would be disappointment? "You're not doing enough to please me." Or the indictment: "I really wish you were more… (faithful, loving, obedient)." Isn't this the kind of painful assessment we think we'll hear if God lets us know what He really thinks of us?[65]

That is what we have been led to assume, that He is always disappointed in us, that He is never really pleased with us. But that assumption is so far from the truth. Our Father is not a "work harder, aim higher, strive to put in more effort" kind of Father. His one desire is to give us life. His life. Not because of anything we have done for Him, but because of what He has already done for us…and because He delights in us.

The devil wants to accuse, to lead us into fear, guilt, and shame. But that's not at all the heart of the Father. His desire is not to accuse your heart, but to *heal* it.[66] He won't just sit around and wish that your heart was OK. He will pursue you relentlessly. He will fight for your heart. In fact, He is fighting for you right now. And He will win the battle. He won't rest until He has completed His work in you.

The Battle for Your Heart

We need to understand that the enemy has only one objective—to keep God from accomplishing His purposes in this world. And what are God's purposes? He is building a family, a family of sons and daughters who will live together in the freedom of His love, and who will put that love on display throughout the world. Revelation 12:12 says that the devil knows he is running out of time, that he is fighting a losing battle. Because of that, he is filled with anger, and in his anger he will do whatever he can do to destroy God's family, to try to keep the sons and daughters of God from walking in the power and truth of His love. The devil doesn't have the power to just take your heart from you, though. He only has one method. He's a liar.

And fighting his lies is of the utmost importance, because what you believe to be true will rule your life. What you believe to be reality in this world will determine everything about how you live—your character, your goals and motivations, how you use your time and resources, how you relate with God, and how you relate with others. What you really believe to be true will impact your life greatly, both now and for all eternity.

So how do you fight an enemy whose only real weapons are lies and deceit? You fight him with the *TRUTH*. Truth is our only defense, and truth is our only weapon. Not truth that comes from a textbook, but truth that comes from the Father's heart.

In Ephesians 6:11, Paul tells us to "put on the full armor of God, so that you will be able to stand firm against the schemes of the devil." The armor of God is not what many have claimed it to be, something magical that we speak onto ourselves in order to prevent the devil from touching our finances, our health, and our families. Remember, three chapters earlier, Paul said that if we really know the love of God, then we will be "filled to the measure of all the fullness of God." If it is true that we find everything in His love, then we can be certain that the devil's schemes are aimed at trying to prevent us from understanding that love. The battle is about truth–the truth about who God is, the truth about who we are, and the truth about His heart towards us as His children.

All of the armor has its strength in the truth. The devil assaults us with his lies to try to distract us, to cause us to fear, and to keep us from walking in God's purposes. But we have shoes that protect us, that enable us to stand firm, that give us confidence to move forward. Paul calls these the shoes of the *gospel*–the good news, the truth of what God has done for us through Jesus Christ. The enemy tries to convince us that we are guilty, condemned, and rejected. But his lies will fail, because we are covered by the breastplate of *righteousness* and the helmet of *salvation*–the truth about our right relationship with God, and the truth about the security of our position in His family.

The devil tries to make us doubt God's heart. He tries to make us think that we have been abandoned, that things are hopeless, and that we are alone in this world. But the Bible assures us that his arrows of deceit will not find their mark, when we defend ourselves with the shield of *faith*–our trust in the heart of God, our confidence in the certainty of His victory at the cross, and our assurance that all of His promises will one day be fulfilled. And all of the armor is held together by one thing–it shouldn't surprise us–the belt of *truth*.

When I am rooted in the truth, the devil's weapons become absolutely useless, because the armor of God cannot be penetrated. The truth of God's love is our perfect defense.

But it isn't only to be used for defending ourselves. The truth is also a powerful weapon, a weapon against which the devil has no defense. Paul tells us to take up "the sword of the Spirit." Again, this isn't some kind of magical tool that you wave around to get whatever you want, nor is it a real sword that you actually attack the devil with. I recently heard a preacher claiming that he had just used it to "slice the devil into pieces" (I wish it were that easy!).

The weapons we fight with, Paul says in 2 Corinthians 10:3-5, are weapons of *truth*, given for the purpose of fighting against anything that would keep us from the real knowledge of God. And our weapon for this battle is the sword of the Spirit, which Paul says is "the word of God."

Right at the beginning of the public ministry of Jesus, the devil met Him in the wilderness and tempted Him. He tried to distract Jesus from the Father's purposes, to try to get Him to either doubt His position as God's Son or to use His position as God's Son for selfish reasons. And Jesus fought back. He didn't argue with the devil. He didn't sing "lower, Satan, lower." He didn't shout at him, or curse him, or use any kind of special prayer methods. Every time the devil brought His temptations and lies, Jesus used the one weapon that the devil absolutely cannot resist—the truth. Jesus fought back with the word of the Father: "It is written…"

After the third time, not only did Jesus defend Himself by resisting the temptation, but He took the offensive and told the devil to leave Him. And he left. Jesus was standing firm against the devil's schemes. He was saying, "I won't be enticed by you. I won't be deceived by you. I won't be intimidated by you. And I certainly won't worship you. Now go away from Me. I don't have time for you. I belong to the Father. I only do His will."

Jesus was confident in the truth, not only because He knew the Scriptures, but because He knew the heart of the Father from whom the Scriptures came.

Our enemy is crafty. He is good at what he does (he's been at it for quite some time). But when we know the truth of the Father's heart, there is no room for the devil's lies. Even the best of his tactics will fail, because the truth of God's word is a powerful defense…and an even more powerful weapon. That power is rooted in the understanding and the ongoing experience of two life-changing realities: the certainty of our forgiveness and redemption, and the assurance of our identity as His adopted children.

It Is Finished

"I felt so much pressure from everyone in the church, especially the pastor," Grace told me. Listen to her story:

> I was expected to do whatever he said to do, no matter what else I had planned for a particular day, or for my whole life, for that matter. I was told by him that he knew what was best for me, because he was my pastor and my spiritual father. If I made any decisions that didn't agree with him, I felt so guilty and condemned, as if I had offended God Himself. It made me think maybe I wasn't committed enough, that others were better or more spiritual than me. There was so much competition for the pastor's approval (which was seen as the same as having God's approval). Everyone wanted to appear to be the most dedicated church member, to look the most righteous. There was so much pressure to conform to what everyone else expected, and if you fell and did something wrong, you just felt so terrible and dirty. Coupled with the effects of growing up with a demanding mother, it made me feel like I could never be acceptable. I didn't serve God out of a sense of love, but out of a sense of duty, out of a sense of fear.

Her story is not at all uncommon. Maybe as you read it, you thought of a friend who is going through this. Or maybe you thought, "I know exactly how that feels," because you yourself have been in that kind of situation. It is bondage! Thankfully, at least for Grace, that is not the end of the story:

> It was so hard to see the truth. I knew that the way my pastor tried to control people in order to promote himself and his ministry wasn't right, but I felt so guilty for thinking that. I mean, he was a pastor, so he must be right. And that means I had to be wrong! But I thank God that someone walked closely with me, loving me for who I am, and constantly pointing me to the truth about who God is. I began to realize that God doesn't want us to be bound. The Bible says, "It is for freedom that Christ set us free." So if I am bound, something is wrong. I realized that God doesn't expect me to do things for His love, but that He just loves me because of who He is. When I fall, I know He won't reject me, but He will come to pick me up. If God is love, then there is no reason to fear, because perfect love casts out fear. I thank God that I am free to live as His daughter, free to be who He created me to be.

That freedom was purchased for us at the cross. God never intended for us to be bound by duty or fear. He never intended for us to strive to try to become something for Him, but rather to rely on what He became for us—our perfect sacrifice, our Redeemer, our Savior. He set us free so that we could really be FREE! The apostle Paul tells us that we should stand firm in the knowledge of that freedom, that we should never let ourselves "be burdened again by a yoke of slavery" (Galatians 5:1, NIV).

The liar tells us that we are still condemned. The truth tells us that at the cross, Jesus has already taken our guilt, our shame, our failures, and our sins—all of them—onto Himself. And because of that, the apostle Paul assures us in Romans 8:1 that "there is now no condemnation for those who are in Christ Jesus." How complete was His work?

> He made you alive together with Him, having forgiven us all our transgressions, having *canceled* out the certificate of debt consisting of decrees against us, which was hostile to us; and He has

taken it out of the way, having nailed it to the cross. When He had *disarmed* the rulers and authorities, He made a public display of them, having *triumphed* over them through Him.

Colossians 2:13-15 (italics added)

But He, having offered one sacrifice for sins *for all time*, SAT DOWN AT THE RIGHT HAND OF GOD.

Hebrews 10:12 (italics added)

"It is finished!"

John 19:30

At the cross, *all* of our sins were forgiven. The record of charges and accusations against us was *canceled.* That word literally means that it was "wiped out."[67] You can no longer go to the files and find any record of a case against you. Whatever case was there before, Jesus took it and *nailed it to the cross.* The old record has been canceled, removed, taken away! The only records remaining in your file are *His* perfect records that He submitted on your behalf!

Paul tells us that when Jesus did this, He *disarmed* the devil and his angels. When the devil comes to accuse, there is no longer any evidence for him to work with, no record of sins to consult. Jesus has already dealt with it all, and by doing so, He has taken the weapons out of the enemy's hands! This disarming was so complete that Paul says the devil and his army were publicly put to shame.

In those days, when the Roman military would win a great victory, they would have a big parade in the city to celebrate. The commanders from the conquered army would be stripped of all their armor and forced to march through the city. Their weapons were taken from them and put on display for everyone to see, making it clear to everyone that this was an enemy who had been totally defeated.[68]

That is exactly what Christ has done through the cross. By taking our sin onto Himself and canceling all charges of sin against us (even those which have not yet been committed), Jesus has stripped the devil of his power. When we know the truth of the gospel, the enemy has nothing left to accuse. He is defeated!

Martin Luther, the great German theologian whose teachings inspired the Reformation in the 1500s, talked of numerous encounters with the devil, in which he tried to discourage Luther by accusing him and naming all of his sins. Luther responded by telling him it was true that he had committed all those sins, and he informed the devil that there were actually some other sins he had forgotten to name. But it didn't matter anymore, because Christ had taken all of his sin onto Himself at the cross. And because of that truth, this is what Luther advises us to do with the devil's lies and accusations:

> When the devil throws our sins up to us and declares that we deserve death and hell, we ought to speak thus: "I admit that I deserve death and hell. What of it? Does this mean that I shall be sentenced to eternal damnation? By no means. For I know One who suffered and made a satisfaction in my behalf. His name is Jesus Christ, the Son of God. And where He is, there I shall be also."[69]

We have to understand how perfect and complete the work of Christ on the cross really was! One sacrifice. For all sins. For all time. And when He had done it, the writer of Hebrews says that He "sat down." Why do you sit down when you've been working? Because the work is *finished*. And that is exactly what Jesus said, just before He bowed His head and died: "It is *finished*."

The fulfillment of the Law—His perfect, sinless life offered to the Father in place of our broken, sinful lives. Finished! The one sacrifice for all sins. The payment for our redemption, making our adoption possible. Finished! Fear of judgment. Finished! The need to strive and to try to earn our way into God's presence. Finished! The power of the devil's lies. Finished!

When you know that, you are free! Andrew Murray, a great pastor and writer in South Africa in the late 1800s and early 1900s, says that if we ever have any doubts at all about whether or not the Father loves us, all we need to do is look to the cross, where Jesus "washed us from our sins in His own blood":

> Is that not proof enough that He will never reject me; that I am precious in His sight, and through the power of His blood I am well-pleasing to God?[70]

The lies say, "You haven't yet done enough to be acceptable to God." The truth says, "It is finished!" And we know without a doubt that it is finished, because when He buried our sins, Jesus Himself didn't stay buried with them. He rose again to new life, ushering us into what Peter calls a "*living* hope." The Father's plan for you is life, and this is His promise to you:

> I will not leave you as orphans; I will come to you...because I live, you will live also.
>
> John 14:18-19

And for each one of His children, not only a promise of life, but a promise of *home*:

> My Father will love him, and We will come to him and make Our abode with him.
>
> John 14:23

Jesus didn't just purchase our forgiveness, so that we don't have to go to hell. He made a way for us to come home to a completely new life as sons and daughters of God.

A New Identity

We need to understand just how "new" this completely new life really is! Many people teach that we are still just as bad, just as sinful, just as hopeless as before, but somehow the cross has blinded the Father, so that He can't see our sins. Nothing could be further from the truth. Floyd McClung says this:

He sees *you*! He sees you as the unique special person He has created you to be, and He sees you as the new creation you have become. He sees your sins when you commit them. He sees your weaknesses and failures, but most important of all, He sees you as His child. He sees you through eyes of love.[71]

But many people don't really understand the transforming power of the cross and the empty grave. They know that they are forgiven, but in their hearts they still carry the same old identity card—the one that says I am a failure...the one that says I always fall short...the one that says I am hopelessly selfish and full of sin...the one that says I am not pleasing to God.

But when the Bible says that we are new creations, it really means "new!" God didn't just forgive us. He has *changed* us. We are new people. McClung continues:

A Christian is a person who has become someone he or she was not before. Becoming a Christian is not just getting something from God, no matter how great those things are, but becoming a brand new person. This is not just a position we have been given, nor is it something we receive because of making right choices. When we receive Christ by faith into our hearts, we are no longer sinners, but children of God. We are loved, destined for heaven, adopted into God's family because we have been born again.[72]

As His child through faith in Christ, the Father has given me a new identity card! The new ID card says that I am...

- a new creation (2 Corinthians 5:17)
- a child of God (Romans 8:16; 1 John 3:1)
- not in the flesh, but in the Spirit (Romans 8:9)
- delivered from the powers of darkness (Colossians 1:13)
- a partaker of His divine nature (2 Peter 1:4)
- led by the Spirit of God (Romans 8:14)
- an heir of God and joint heir with Jesus (Romans 8:17)

- blessed with every spiritual blessing (Ephesians 1:3)
- being transformed into His image (2 Corinthians 3:18)[73]

He didn't just forgive us for being dead in our sins. He has made us *alive* in Christ (Ephesians 2:1-4). He didn't just forgive us for being incomplete. He has made us *complete* in Him (Colossians 2:10). He didn't just forgive us for being far from Him. He pursued us and brought us *near* (Ephesians 2:13). He didn't just forgive us for not doing His will. He Himself is at work in us, leading us to *desire* His will, and giving us the *ability* actually *to do* His will (Philippians 2:13).

"But without Jesus, I am just a hopeless sinner," some people have reminded me. That is true, but here is the good news – I am NOT without Jesus!! Jesus said that when the Holy Spirit comes and takes residence in our hearts, He not only reveals the truth about Christ to us, but He actually unites us with Christ. This is our new reality as children of God: "In that day, you will know that I am in My Father, and you in Me, and I in you" (John 14:20).

The devil still wants me to live in my old identity. My old identity said that I was dirty, unacceptable, a spiritual orphan, with no hope of ever finding my way home. But Jesus has given me a new identity. My new identity says that the Father has brought me home, He has made me clean and acceptable to Him, and He has given me His name. I am a full and permanent son in His household. I am inseparably His!!

New Creations

I could fill chapter after chapter with stories about the powerful transforming work of Jesus in my life and in the lives of people I know. But space doesn't permit, so let me just introduce you to a couple of them.

I met Francis Mugwanya in 1998, when we were working at a ministry near his home. I still remember sitting and talking with him in a little grass-thatched shelter in our compound one day, and seeing his eyes light up as the Lord revealed to him a new understanding of the heart of the gospel. But there is much more to the story than that. His life is yet another beautiful example of the Father's artwork! Here is a bit of his story, in his own words:

> When I was 3 years old, I got polio and have been unable to walk since that time. I was forced to crawl on my hands and knees to get around. I hated always being dirty. In Uganda people with disabilities are mocked and considered to be second class or cursed. Some people did not think I was even worth educating, since "cripples don't amount to anything." I hated the names they called me, and I stayed close to home where I was safe. I started to believe what everyone said about me. I believed I was useless and crippled.
>
> We tried for years to find a wheelchair, but there didn't seem to be any in Uganda. One day, when I was eleven years old, an organization that helps kids with disabilities gave me a wheelchair! My life dramatically changed that day. I began to go to church, and I accepted Jesus as my personal Saviour when I was twelve years old…and God gave me my smile. Throughout the next several years, the Lord blessed me with discipleship from a godly man who taught me what the Bible has to say about my true identity. God knit all the parts of my body together and created me wonderfully (Psalm 139); He made me in His image (Genesis 1:27); and best of all He has planned for me to be His very own son. I am a child of God! He is my Father.

Francis didn't just go off and enjoy his new position as God's child, relaxing and living a blessed life. When the Father gave Francis a new identity, He also gave him a new heart…His heart. This new heart led Francis to establish The Father's Heart Mobility Ministry, which has enabled him in the past several years to give wheelchairs to thousands of disabled people throughout Uganda. And not only have they received new wheelchairs, but many of them have also received new life as sons and daughters of God, through faith in Jesus Christ (the ultimate goal of his ministry). Francis explains:

Today I am compelled to share the love of the Father with those who do not know Him yet. God alone can change their lives! And I am compelled to give mobility to those who are right now still crawling in the dirt. I cannot sit idly by, I must use whatever the Lord has given me to be a blessing to someone. There are over 2.5 million people with disabilities in Uganda, still living in the mud, still thinking they are cursed, still hopeless. We have been given the wonderful opportunity of making a difference in their lives!

The lies of the world said, "Francis, you are cursed. You can't even walk. How will you ever achieve anything that will make you acceptable in our eyes? You are useless."

The Father says, "Francis, you are blessed. You can walk *with Me*. Not only are you acceptable to Me through My Son Jesus Christ, but you are also the object of my deepest delight. And you are not useless at all. In Me, you are absolutely complete, and I will do things through your life that are beyond anything you could have ever imagined. You are My beloved Son. And I am your Father. Forever."

My friend, Pastor David Zijjan, understands the power of that truth, too. Listen to his story:

I was raised without a father. I never saw my dad until the age of seventeen. So, as I was getting into adulthood, I wanted to know my father. And so I asked my mom to take me to my dad. So my mom took me to this place. This guy had thirteen other children, nine other boys. And I get there, and all his children looked like him. I was the only boy who didn't resemble him. And by African standards, that was like failing a DNA test. I was told point blank, "You do not belong to this family. Because look at these boys, they look like their dad. The appearance is as their father. You don't originate from here."

And so I was rejected. I was sent away from this family. I had longed to meet my dad for the first time in seventeen years, and here I appear, and I failed to pass the test. I was very devastated. My dreams were crushed. The world had crumbled upon me. After waiting for seventeen years to meet my father, I meet him for the first time, and he's not my dad, because I couldn't prove beyond appearance that he was my father.

I didn't know who I was or where I was going. But in my wanderings, in my identity confusion as a teenage boy, a seminary student shared Christ with me, and I believed. I went on by the grace of God to join a ministry called Youth With A Mission, and I did their discipleship training school. There was a subject in the school called "The Father Heart of God." That was a turning point in my life. I realized that God was a Father, a Father before whom we did not have to bring any more evidence to prove that we were His sons. Christ had given me the right to become a child of God.

I realized that you can fail a DNA test before biological parents....but you will never fail a DNA test with God. Realizing my sonship to the Lord and His Fatherhood to me, grasping His Father heart, changed my life.

I got confidence in me, and I wanted every African child who had not experienced the love of a father to get the experience that I had received—the Father heart of God. I want them to know that He will never reject them, that He is their Father who loves them tenderly, who created them for a purpose.

That purpose David is talking about is not only to receive the Father's love, but to invest it into the lives of others who desperately need it. David is not only a son, but now he is also a father, many times over. He is the founder of Father's Divine Love Ministries, and through David, the Lord is giving a home to many fatherless children, sharing the good news of the Father's love through Jesus Christ, and impacting lives all over the world with his testimony of the power of the truth.

The lies said, "David, you are nobody. You belong nowhere. Nobody wants you. Just give up on life. It is hopeless."

The Father says, "David, before the world ever began, you were in My heart. You are My son, and I love you. Nothing can ever change that. You will never fail to show yourself acceptable to Me, because Jesus has already made you acceptable. And as My Spirit works in you, as you pour My love into the lives of these children, it is clear that you are My son. You resemble Me more and more each day."

The Truth Will Set You Free

The world tells you that you aren't acceptable unless you accomplish, achieve, and accumulate according to its standards. Legalistic religion tells you that you can't be acceptable until you clean yourself up, obey all of the rules, and follow the traditions properly. Painful family experiences tell you that you are worthless, that you are alone, and that you are without hope of ever being of any value to anybody. But when you really know the truth of the gospel, it changes everything.

When my heart is filled with the love of Jesus, there just isn't room for the devil and all of his accusations. When I am walking in the confidence of God's love, I just can't seem to find time in my schedule to sit down and listen to lies. I am too busy fixing my mind on the truth that pours from the heart of the Father.

"Meditate on this day and night," Andrew Murray says, "until you have the assurance: *He loves me unspeakably.*"[74]

When you really know it, when you have that assurance, then as a true son or daughter of the Father, you are free. Free from accusation. Free from condemnation. Free from the power of sin. No need for striving, because at the cross, He has done it all on your behalf. It is finished. You are acceptable. Your value doesn't depend on what anyone thinks about you. Your value comes from who you are. You are no longer the same person you used to be. You are a new creation, with a new identity and a new heart. You have *His* name. You are His child. You don't have to perform for it. You don't have to earn it. It all comes from His heart. And it all belongs to you.

It's His delight. It's your destiny.

Key Thought:

The truth is this—you can trust His heart. You don't have to listen to the lies any more. If you put your trust in Jesus Christ, you are completely free. Free from accusation. Free from condemnation. Free from the power of sin. You are acceptable. No need for striving, because at the cross, He has done it all on your behalf. It is finished. He has raised you to new life. You are no longer the same person you used to be. You are a new creation, with a new identity and with a new heart. You have *His* name. You are His child.

Personal Reflection / Group Discussion:

At the beginning of the chapter, we took "The Test of Freedom," to get us thinking about how we respond when things in life don't work out the way we would like them to, when people don't treat us as they should, when we have failed. It helps us to see whether or not we are free in the Father's love or still in bondage to human opinion and the lies of the devil.

- *How did you answer? Do you work to try to do better, or to try prove that you are right? Do you become angry, discouraged or bitter? Why do you think your response is normally that way?*

- *How would your response change if you really understood what Christ did on the cross, that "it is finished"? How would your response change if you really understood your new identity in Christ as a child of the Father?*

Scriptural Prescription:

Therefore there is now no condemnation for those who are in Christ Jesus.

Romans 8:1

Therefore, if anyone is in Christ, he is a new creation. The old has passed away; behold, the new has come.

2 Corinthians 5:17 (ESV)

Further Study:

God didn't just forgive us. He really changed us! So how do changed people live?

Read Colossians 3:1-17 and Ephesians 4:17-5:10. Paul makes it clear that those who have put on the "new self" ought to be "imitators of God," since we are His "beloved children." What are the marks of this new life in the family of God? How should the Father's children live, not only as individuals but together?

Chapter 9

Releasing the Fathers
Who Failed Us

To be a Christian means to forgive the inexcusable, because God has forgiven the inexcusable in you.[75]

C.S. Lewis

As we pour out our bitterness, God pours in His peace.[76]

F.B. Meyer

The Bondage of Bitterness

"If forgiving my father is my way to avoid going to hell, then I am ready to go to hell," Dulton had vowed to other family members when they suggested that he should forgive his father.

Wow. So bitter that, if given the choice, he would have chosen to suffer for all eternity rather than to release the anger he felt towards his father. That is a classic case of bitterness. You think you are punishing someone by withholding forgiveness from the person who has hurt you. But the truth is, the one you are hurting is yourself. Anne Lamott says that "not forgiving is like drinking rat poison and then waiting for the rat to die."[77]

Bitterness is so common in our world that many people don't even recognize that it is there. It's like an unseen cancer, eating away at our souls. It becomes such a familiar companion that we begin to embrace our bitterness and think of it as our friend. We see it as an acceptable way of trying to take control of the pain we feel in our hearts. And bitterness is especially deep when the one who hurt you is someone whom you so desperately wanted to love you. That was Dulton's story:

> I had never seen what it means to be loved by a father. All I ever received from my father was rejection, neglect, and abuse. He didn't take care of me. He had plenty of money, yet I still had to strive to find food for myself. He used to tell me that I was useless, that I did everything wrong, and he would punish me by beating me without mercy. He would always make it clear that he didn't want me around, saying things like, "I have a lot of children, so if you go away, what is that to me? And when you leave, don't ever come back here." But even though he told me not to come back, he said he knew that I *would* come back, because I was hopeless and unable to live on my own, unable to survive without him. He would say, "When you go away, you will come back one day. And when you do, you will be rotting with jiggers all over your feet. You will come back begging for my help."
>
> He would embarrass me so much by abusing me physically and verbally in front of other people, and he would do the same to my mom, which made me so angry. I couldn't bark back at him or do anything in response, though, because in our culture we have a belief that if you hurt your father, he may pronounce a curse on you, and then you will surely suffer. If he curses you, then your children will do the same to you, as you have done to him.
>
> So I didn't respond in anger, because I wanted to avoid giving him any reason to curse me. I tried so hard to please him all the time, because I thought that then he might stop beating me and mistreating me. But even when I did what he told me to do, even when I did what was right, he would beat me anyway. No matter what I did, it was just more of the same. He seemed to be always against me, and I thought to myself, "I don't have a father. I have an enemy." I thought of poisoning him, so that I could just be rid of him, but I didn't have the courage to go through with it.

In my heart I would say, "I wish God could just punish him." But that never happened. So I tried to ignore that he even existed. I wanted to try to just move on with my life and leave it behind. But I couldn't forget. Every headache reminded me of when he hit me with a brick. Every time I brushed my teeth, my gums would bleed, and I would feel pain in my mouth…and I would remember him on top of me, punching me over and over. Whenever I got dressed, I would see the scar on my side from being pierced by a knife that he threw at me when I was trying to get away from him. I could never forget. Everything I did reminded me that this is how it was. I wanted to break my mirror, because I didn't want to see the blood. I didn't want to see the scars. I didn't want to face myself and the pain I felt in my heart. It made me so angry at him, and I just wanted to forget it all.

But pain won't just go away. If it is not dealt with and healed, it will become bitterness. And bitterness is deadly to your heart and soul. Lee Strobel says it this way:

> Bitterness inevitably seeps into the lives of people who harbor grudges and suppress anger, and bitterness is always a poison. It keeps your pain alive instead of letting you deal with it and get beyond it. Bitterness sentences you to relive the hurt over and over.[78]

Grieving the Past

It doesn't have to be that way. You can find healing and freedom. Forgiveness really is possible. But how do we do it? The first step in forgiving is to *grieve*.

Hope told me in a counseling session, "I remember happier times, before all of the beatings and the rapes, when my father used to buy me gifts, and we would have fun together as a family. I just want those times to return." Here is the sad reality: Hope's father had been dead for years. And there are many people like her who are still waiting for their fathers to come and make things right for all of the pain they have caused, to finally give them the love and happy childhood that they should have had. But for most people, the reality is that it's never going to happen. Those days are past, and they can never be recaptured. The beginning of forgiveness is to recognize that reality, to let go of what you wish could happen…to grieve. Anne Lamott writes, "Forgiveness is giving up all hope of having had a different past."[79]

When you lose someone you love, the beginning of healing is to be able to grieve. When you accept that the person has died, when you allow yourself to feel the pain of their absence in your life, it opens your heart to make it possible for healing to begin.

Finding healing from the pain your father (or others) caused you is no different. Your family life was meant to be happy. But maybe it wasn't. You were supposed to receive love. But maybe you didn't. You lost something. But it is gone. You can never make yourself young again. You can never return to those years to try to live them differently. Whatever has happened has happened. It is too late to change it. The beginning of healing is to face that truth, to look the painful reality right in the face, and then take it to the Lord.

I want to encourage you to pause for some time right now to do this. Take as much time as you need. The point is not to get through the chapter as quickly as possible. The point is to let God do His work in you.

Ask the Holy Spirit to reveal to you pain that needs to be released. Ask Him to show you those things that you have been holding onto, things about your father (or other parent) that you want to be different, even though deep in your heart you know that you can never go back and change them.

Spend some time in prayer. Open your heart to God, the perfect Father. Tell Him everything that you are feeling: "It hurts, Father!" "I am angry!" "I needed my father's love, but I didn't get it." "I don't understand why my childhood couldn't have been different." Be honest with Him…and then let the Great Physician begin treatment. This is the first step on the road to forgiveness.

Beginning to Heal

It is not at all easy to forgive, especially when the pain is severe. But for someone who has been hurt badly, it is a big and necessary step on the path to true freedom. That is what Dulton had to learn. He recalled with me the beginning of his healing, which came last year when He gave His life to Christ:

> When I accepted Christ, it was the turning point of my life, from just working to be good in the eyes of people to really accepting the work of God in me. Walking through Ephesians in evening devotions with your family was the foundation of knowing that I am forgiven, that I am a dwelling place of God. I could now look back and see that I had been living in a lie, thinking that I could somehow live as a good person, and then everything would be OK. But I realized that no matter how much I had been hurt, and no matter how much I tried to be good, I myself was in such great need of forgiveness. Before, I had always been covered by pain and anger. Now, I knew that I was covered by His love and forgiveness.
>
> The only drawback at first was my lack of forgiveness for my father. Though God had changed me, it was still hard to trust in the love of others. It was still hard to open up my heart to others. Would someone else turn and hurt me? Could I give my heart to anyone else?

I knew that Dulton needed to forgive his father if he was going to really be free. So I began to talk with him about his past, asking him questions that would dig into his heart, to try to open him to the possibility of forgiving his father. He said it was so difficult when I would ask those questions, because they were hard memories to think about. It just seemed like it was painful for no reason. He said, "I never knew that healing was possible, that God could really reach the depths of my heart."

One day I was teaching at a nearby missions training centre, doing an all morning session on the Father heart of God. I asked Dulton to go with me, praying that God would use it to bring some real healing. I taught through many of the concepts that you have read about in the previous chapters of this book: God's desire to give life; how we were created for love; the lies that have become obstacles to understanding the heart of the Father.

"When you talked about the different types of fathers," Dulton said, "I thought to myself, 'My father was *ALL* of those types.'"

It was hard for Dulton. But as I said earlier, where the pain is at its worst, the healing that comes from the Great Physician of our souls is at its best. That is Dulton's testimony. And this is what he shared with me about that day:

> It almost killed me. I have never had God dig deep into my heart like that. I didn't know that healing was so painful. I kept praying during the teaching, "God I wanted You to give me relief... but You are killing my heart." But that was the painful moment I really needed. I learned that day that forgiveness is not accomplished by running away, because pain will always come and find you. I knew that I needed to face it and confront it. Later that evening you told me, "This story is going to end in a good way." That gave me a lot of confidence to move forward.

It's Time to Let Go

It is absolutely necessary to face the pain, and to grieve what has been lost. But grieving is only the beginning of the process. We need to *release* the bitterness. We need to forgive. Before we go into what forgiveness is, I want to mention a few important items about what forgiveness is *NOT*.

First of all, forgiveness does not mean that you are excusing what has been done, that you are saying it is OK. In our years in Uganda, that has been the most common way that I have heard people respond to someone who asks for forgiveness, whether for something big or something small. The answer is almost always the same: "It's OK."

But it is *not* OK!! It is sin, and we must recognize it as sin. If it's "OK," then there is nothing to be forgiven. Maybe it seems like it is just a matter of words, but this is really important. So often, we want to deal with sin by brushing it aside and trying to forget about it. We don't want there to be any more conflict, so we try to ignore what happened, hoping it will go away.

But as Dulton learned, the pain in our hearts won't just go away. It is like cancer. It will spread. It will grow. It will consume our hearts, and eventually, it will destroy us. If we are going to find real healing, we have to honestly assess the injury. We have to acknowledge that our fathers (and others) have sinned against us. Not because we want to prosecute them, but because we really want to forgive them.

That is what God does. When God looks at our sin, He doesn't say, "It's OK." He hates sin. It is terrible. It is rebellion. In the Old Testament, sin is likened to spiritual adultery. It is not OK! God doesn't brush sin aside as if it didn't happen. He deals with sin completely. At the cross, Jesus didn't say, "It's OK." He looked our sins directly in the eye and recognized them for how terribly sinful they really are.

And then He took all of our sins, even the worst of them, onto Himself. Paul says in 2 Corinthians 5:21 that Jesus actually became sin on our behalf. He literally felt the unbearable weight of our guilt, the disgraceful depths of our shame, and the hopeless sense of abandonment and separation from the Father. He saw our sins for what they are. They are sinful. They are not at all OK. But they are paid for. He has set us free. That freedom gives us the ability to forgive.

Second, when you forgive, you are not seeking to place blame on the other person. Did their actions have a big impact on your life? Of course they did! But you cannot use this person's sin against you as an excuse for every bad thing that has happened to you since then, nor can you blame them for the sinful ways that you have responded to the pain. Your actions are your own responsibility.

Many people want to continue to see themselves as the victims of everyone else's actions. But if you have put your trust in Christ, you are not a victim who has had everything taken from him. You are a child of God who has had everything given to him! If you have everything in Him, then you don't need to hold on to anything else, including your pain. You are free to forgive, to release your fathers from blame. By the power of your Heavenly Father's love, you no longer have to live under the power of your earthly father's pain.

Third, forgiveness is not an option. Jesus says that we must forgive others, if we are going to receive and walk in the forgiveness of God. A heart that is bitter and unwilling to forgive closes itself to the ability to receive love and forgiveness, even from God. If you are struggling to forgive, then you are the one who is responsible to seek God for healing and for the power to forgive. It is not an option. It is absolutely necessary.

But many people don't really want to forgive. Why not? Well, the biggest reason I normally hear is that they don't want the other person to get away with what he has done to them. They want him to be punished. But here is the reality. You aren't really punishing that person by not forgiving him. He is probably not even thinking about what he has done to you.

Years ago, I struggled for a long time to really forgive someone who had sinned against me. He had spread all kinds of lies about me. He had schemed to try to bring trouble for me and my ministry. It was especially difficult because I knew that he would never humble himself to repent, and because I knew that he would never be brought to justice for what he had done to me. So in my heart, I didn't really want to release him. One day as I was praying, the Lord said, "Do you know that he is not even concerned with what he has done to you? He slept peacefully last night, without a thought as to whether or not you have forgiven him. The person you are really killing is yourself." That is so true. Lewis Smedes says, "To forgive is to set a prisoner free and to discover that the prisoner was *you*."[80]

Is it easy to forgive? Not at all! It can be a difficult and painful struggle. But it is absolutely necessary, both because Jesus requires it and because your freedom depends on it. Recognize that what they did to you is not OK. Don't live like a victim, but take responsibility to seek God for healing. And realize that your father may never repent, but *you* will be free. It was for freedom that Christ set you free. It's time to release.

So what does that look like?

Forgiving Like God Forgives

People who have been hurt are often bitter, angry, and filled with a desire to take revenge. That's how things work in this world. But in Ephesians 4, Paul says that children of God must be different than the rest of the world:

> Let all bitterness and wrath and anger and clamor and slander be put away from you, along with all malice. Be kind to one another, tender-hearted, forgiving each other, *just as God in Christ also has forgiven you."*
>
> Ephesians 4:31-32 (italics added)

Our forgiveness must be like His forgiveness. So the question we need to answer is, "What does His forgiveness look like? How did God forgive us through Christ?" This also needs a whole book of its own to really explain, but let me just look briefly here at some of the important aspects of God's forgiveness, so that we begin to get a good idea of the kind of forgiveness that He calls us to offer as well.

First and foremost, it is *based on the cross.* It has to begin here. The cross is the ultimate expression of love, and it is the means by which God has forgiven us. When we realize the depths of what Christ has done for us at the cross, we will freely offer forgiveness to others. That person who hurt you is someone for whom Christ died. Your father is someone for whom Christ died. Jesus took all of your sin onto Himself, offering you complete forgiveness and life as a son or daughter of God. But God wants your father to be His son, too. And He also took every one of your father's sins upon Himself, including those that caused pain to you.

Many have said to me, "I want to forgive, but I just don't feel forgiveness in my heart towards him." Or they say, "But you don't understand what he has done to me!" I understand that the pain that people inflict upon others in this world is terrible, that fathers do things that no child should ever have to endure. But you don't forgive because you feel good about what happened to you. You forgive because of what happened at the cross. You don't forgive based on your assessment of what they have done to you. You forgive because of what was done to Christ…for you, and for the one who has hurt you. At the cross, you find freedom in Christ's forgiveness. And at the cross, you can find the freedom and power to forgive. Ken Sande writes:

> Christians are the most forgiven people in the world. Therefore, we should be the most forgiving people in the world.[81]

It is *immediate*. Sometimes we don't want to forgive right away. We want to first see if they change, and then maybe we will be willing to forgive them. Or we say that we have forgiven them, but we don't really give it. In our hearts we say, "Let me wait and see how he behaves from now on. Let's see if his repentance is really genuine." Many people are like that. We are willing to forgive as long as the person who offended us proves to us that they have changed, that they aren't going to hurt us anymore.

But that is not God's way. He doesn't say "I forgive you," and then wait to see if you have changed enough to deserve it. His forgiveness is immediate, and it is without conditions.

When the rebellious son returned home in Jesus' story in Luke 15, the father (who is a picture of God the Father) threw his arms around him and restored him to full sonship, without hesitation. The reason that the father loved his son wasn't because he saw how genuine his repentance was. The son's repentance was genuine because he saw how much his father loved him. The father forgave his son, but not because he saw how much he had changed. The son was changed because he saw how much his father had forgiven him.

God's heart is already turned towards your father (or whoever has hurt you), whether he ever turns his heart towards God or not. Your father may never receive the benefits of God's forgiveness, but it has already been offered to him nonetheless. The price for all sins for all time, including those committed against you, has already been paid at the cross. God doesn't delay to offer forgiveness. So who are we to withhold forgiveness from those to whom He freely offers it…even those who have hurt us the most?

It is *complete*. We forget so many things. We forget an important meeting that we were supposed to attend. We forget someone's name. We forget facts that we learned in school. But when it comes to sin, our memories are amazing. Most people don't forget anything that someone has done to them. We often keep long lists in our hearts of wrongs committed against us. I have counseled with people who can talk about it for hours, reliving the details of one sin after another, remembering vividly how it had hurt them.

So many times, people have said to me, "Pastor Dave, I want to forgive him, but how can I forget what he has done to me?" Forgiveness doesn't mean that the sin has been taken from your memory. It means that you no longer hold it against those who have hurt you. Certainly God is still aware of the many times I have sinned against Him. It is not as if He mentally is unable to recall what happened. But He "forgets" my sins in the sense that He has released me fully from the guilt and shame of my sin. My record is as clean as if the sin never happened, and through the cross my relationship to the Father has been fully restored.

Psalm 103:12 says, "As far as the east is from the west, so far has He removed our transgressions from us." If you begin traveling east and continue all the way around the world, you will eventually come back to the point where you began. But as long as you continue moving in the same direction, you are still going east. And if you continue moving east, there is never a time when you will suddenly find yourself traveling west.

East and west never meet! That's what God is saying. No matter how long you live on this earth, His forgiveness is so complete that it is not possible that you will ever again come face to face with the guilt of your sins. It is finished!

Love, the apostle Paul writes, "keeps no record of wrongs" (1 Corinthians 13:5, NIV). That means when someone sins against us, we forgive them in such a way that we never bring the guilt of that sin before them again. We don't pull it out of the file when conflict comes, saying, "That is just like the other time when you…"

And if we are to forgive completely, it means there is no room for us to take revenge. Paul says in Romans 12 that we should not condemn, but instead we should love others and let God decide how to deal with their sins: "Never pay back evil for evil to anyone…Never take your own revenge…Do not be overcome by evil, but overcome evil with good."

God's forgiveness means that the record of our sins is gone. It is paid for. Deleted from the file. Thrown away and never to be found again! Our forgiveness must be the same, even for those whose record of sins against us is so long.

It is *offered even before we ask.* A lot of people wonder, "But what if they never ask for forgiveness? Do I still have to forgive?" In Romans 5, Paul says that Christ died for us "while we were *still* sinners," when were we still His "enemies." Ephesians 2 says that life was offered when we were still "dead in our transgressions." The father of the proud, rebellious son in Luke 15 felt compassion for his son and ran to him *before* the boy had even said a word to him. Christ offered forgiveness to you, for even the worst of your sins, nearly two thousand years before you were born! He knew that many people would never repent. But He died for them anyway.

Christ didn't wait to be asked for forgiveness. He just offered it. We shouldn't wait, either. We can't withhold forgiveness until they repent… because that may never happen. They might never ask for forgiveness. The person you need to forgive might even be dead. But the need for you to forgive them is still just as real.

If we don't feel like forgiving, or if it seems too difficult, we can ask the Father to help us. Hebrews 4:16 says that we can approach Him boldly, expecting to find the grace to help us in time of need. That includes the grace to forgive everything from the past, and it includes the grace to determine in advance that we are already offering forgiveness to whoever will hurt us in the future. He will give us that grace, because the heart of forgiveness is at the heart of who He is.

It is *offered repeatedly.* "Love," Jean Vanier writes, "is an act of endless forgiveness."[82] In Matthew chapter 18, Peter asked Jesus, "How many times must I forgive my brother when he sins against me? Should I forgive him even as many as seven times?"

Jesus said, "Not only seven, but seventy times seven." If you do the math, that equals 490 times. But Jesus isn't saying that you are allowed to withhold forgiveness for sin #491 and beyond. He was just using a big number to make a point, and the point He was making is that we should never stop forgiving. The cross was enough to cover all sins. It really is finished. His well of love and grace never runs dry, and we can draw from that well continually, for ourselves and for those we need to forgive.

That means that our forgiveness is not based on whether or not the person stops hurting us. Many of you will have to face an ongoing battle. You forgive today, and then the same person hurts you tomorrow. You forgive again, and they hurt you again. You continue to forgive, and they continue to hurt you. It seems crazy to keep forgiving, but that is exactly what God does for you. Hebrews 7:25 says that, as our living High Priest, Christ continues to make intercession for our sins. What He did two thousand years ago is still enough to cover your sins of today, and it is more than enough to cover those that will come tomorrow.

There will never be a time when He says, "OK, you have reached your limit of grace. That is one sin too many. There is no more forgiveness for you." Jesus says, "The one who comes to Me, I will certainly not cast out" (John 6:37). You will never stop needing His forgiveness, and He will never stop giving it. We are called to do no less for those who have wronged us and for those who continue to wrong us.

There may be a time when you have to physically remove yourself from a situation where you are being hurt repeatedly, in order to protect yourself. Forgiving repeatedly doesn't mean continually subjecting yourself to pain. But as far as your heart is concerned, no matter how many times someone has hurt you, you cannot hold on to the bitterness. The call of Jesus, based on what He has done for you and for them at the cross, is always to forgive. It's not at all easy, but it's the only way for your heart to really be free.

Finally, it is *compassionate*. When Jesus hung on the cross, He said something very interesting: "Father, forgive them, for they don't know what they are doing." That is a powerful statement. The men were sinful, yes. And what they were doing was the most wicked act in all of human history, the execution of the Son of God. But Jesus said they didn't really understand their actions. They were blinded by their lust for power, by their jealousy, by their misunderstanding of who Jesus was, and by their misguided religious zeal. Because of that, they didn't really understand that the man they were putting to death was the Messiah. Jesus wasn't excusing their sin. He wasn't saying, "It's OK." He was looking into their hearts. He knew their weaknesses. He understood what was going on inside of them. And He loved them.

His one desire for them was that they would have life, but they weren't finding it. They were deceived. That filled Jesus with compassion, and His compassion moved Him to action on their behalf. These were the very men who plotted to have Him killed, and as Jesus was in the act of making their forgiveness possible, He prayed for them from the depths of His love: "Father, forgive them, for they don't really know what they are doing." That is the heart of God:

> The Lord is like a father to His children, tender and compassionate to those who fear Him. For He knows how weak we are; He remembers we are only dust.
>
> Psalm 103:13-14 (NLT)

A good father understands the limitations of his children. He doesn't expect a four-year-old to know how to cook, how to drive a car, or how to manage his accounts. He doesn't rebuke him or punish him for his failure to do these things, because he understands that a young child simply doesn't have the ability to do them yet. He is patient with him, showing compassion because he understands that he is still growing. That is the heart of God towards us. He doesn't excuse our sin. He hates our sin. But He has patience and compassion, because He understands our weaknesses.

We need to understand that our fathers also have limitations. They are products of their pasts. Many of them never learned how to love. Many of them were hurt badly by their fathers. They don't know how to be fathers, because they never really experienced being sons in a healthy way. Your father may have never even stopped to think about what he was going to do to you. Quite often, the way he treated you is not at all what really he wanted to do. It was a sign that he was hurting, too. And he responded to his pain by hurting others, including you.

I am not suggesting that we should excuse their sin. Not at all. Remember, it is *not* OK! But we need to seek to understand their weaknesses. We need to seek God's grace to have compassion on them, because it is the heart of God to forgive, and because forgiveness is your path to freedom.

I counseled with a young lady who was struggling to forgive her mom. Her mom was so critical, so demanding, always complaining about every little thing her daughter did, even if she did it right. Years and years of that treatment had been painful, and now that pain was turning into bitterness. One day I asked her a question: "Do you know your grandmother?"

She said that she did, so I went a bit further: "How does your grandmother treat your mother?"

She quickly replied, "She is so critical of my mom. No matter what my mom does, my grandmother criticizes it. It has always been that way."

I said, "That sounds familiar, doesn't it? Do you ever want anyone else, even your mother, to go through the pain that you have gone through?"

She looked down and said, "No, because it is terrible."

I said to her, "Your mom has gone through it for her entire lifetime, not only in her childhood but even throughout her adulthood, up until this very day. Can you imagine how much your mom must be hurting?"

She began to be able to see her mom a bit differently, not just as someone who hurts her children for no reason, but as someone who has also been hurt and continues to be hurt. She realized that her mom didn't know any other way to parent. And even though the way her mom had treated her was completely wrong, and though it had been very damaging to her, she began to feel compassion for her mom. She was able to say, "Father, forgive my mom, because she doesn't know what she is doing." That compassionate understanding was the beginning of healing.

Freedom!

We don't excuse the sins of those who have hurt us, but we seek to understand their weaknesses and the pain that has bound them for so long. For many, this is the beginning of great freedom. That is exactly what Dulton found to be true:

> I prayed a lot that God would protect my heart, so that my pain didn't lead to anger. I really wanted to find healing. I had been forgiven so much. I wanted to be able to forgive. I also realized that I wasn't holding my father by not forgiving him...I was actually holding myself.

> When we talked about my father's childhood, I was relieved a lot to think about the fact that my father was also treated in the way he treated me. Not because I enjoyed knowing that he was hurt, too, but because it helped me to understand what had happened a bit more. I thought that maybe he didn't really want to mistreat me like that, but he was just acting that way because it is what he knew. Before then, it was always pointing to ME. Am I the wrong person? Am I not good enough? But now I realized that there were other factors, that there were things going on in my dad that had nothing to do with me. It made me revisit those

times. Why did he do it? Maybe there was another reason besides me. That understanding set me free.

Finally, I was able to decide to forgive him in my heart. And when I released him, I felt like I was so tall, but with no weight at all, because the relief in me was so great. Just from a night to another day, and suddenly you feel like you are the opposite of what you were last evening. It's amazing.

"But if I forgive my father today, how do I know that it is real? How do I know that the bitterness won't come back and consume my heart again?" That's a common question. Here is where the story gets even better. This forgiveness, this new freedom that Dulton had in his heart, was soon tested.

Dulton had been managing the daily details of our training site for about five months, but until that day I had never sent him to Kampala for anything. That morning, I suddenly decided that I should send him to take care of a couple of things for me. Looking back, they were minor details, not at all worth a trip to the city. But this was God's arrangement, not mine! Listen to the rest of the story, as he told it to me:

I was walking along Jinja Road, near the Ministry of Internal Affairs, and a car pulled over in front of me and stopped. A man got out of the car. I couldn't believe it. It was my dad! Before, I had vowed to myself that I would never face him or talk to him again. I was afraid I would only want to kill him if I saw him. But I didn't want to kill him. I felt something I had never felt before. I saw my father walking towards me, and even though I had no idea why he was coming, to see him made me feel joy.

When he reached me, we just stood there for about 15 seconds, looking at each other. Then my father did two things that he had never done in my life, as far as I can remember. First, he hugged me. Right there on Jinja Road, for about a minute! And then he said, "I am sorry for everything. Do you have some time that we can sit and talk?"

We went and talked for about 45 minutes. The first thing he said was, "You've changed." I told him that I had given my life to Christ. I told him that I understood God's forgiveness towards me, and that I had forgiven everyone, including him (even before we met). And I told him that I had been praying for him, that he would never do again to anyone else what he had done to me.

I have forgiven my father. Through the love of God, and specifically through your family, I have finally begun to experience the love of a father. Before, I wanted to destroy my mirror. Now, every night, I want to look. I want to see my scars. I want to let them remind me of who I was, so that I really realize who I am. I am free!

Getting Ready to Release

But this isn't just Dulton's story. This is God's story, a story that He is continuing to write in millions of lives all over the world. Does He want to write a new chapter in *your* life? Is it time for *you* to be free from the pain? There's only one way. You need to destroy that file called "bitterness," to erase every single item on that record of wrongs you have been keeping in your heart for so long. It's time to forgive. It's time to be free.

First of all, set aside plenty of time to prayerfully walk through this process. It is worth it! Find a quiet place where you can be alone with the Lord and not disturbed by others. If you want to walk through this with a friend or with a church leader, that's OK. But please be certain that he or she really understands the heart of the Father (even many pastors do not really know His heart, so be careful!). Otherwise, they will not be useful to you, because you are asking them to help you find a freedom that they themselves do not understand.

Second, you're going to need some help from the Lord. If forgiving seems too difficult, then you can ask the Father to give you strength. Remember, He promises that you can approach Him boldly, expecting to find the grace to help you in time of need. That includes the grace to forgive your father for each area of his life where he failed to represent the Father's love to you. God will give you that grace, because the heart of forgiveness is at the heart of who He is.

As you begin this process, ask God to help you understand your father (or your mother or other parental figure). I would encourage you to use a prayer that is just like the one you prayed earlier, when you asked the Father to help you to really see yourself as He sees you. Only now it is someone else you are seeking to understand:

> *Father, help me to see my father*
> *in the way that You see him.*
> *Help me to understand my father*
> *in the way that You understand him.*

Finally, expect to receive healing and freedom. Know that even in the most painful, lonely times of your life, the Father has always been there, loving you and desiring nothing but life for you. I don't know why He allowed certain things to happen. I don't know why He didn't stop it from happening. But I do know this—whatever has happened in the past, He is here with you now. And He is offering you deep healing and complete freedom. He is offering you His heart.

Jesus says in Luke 11:13 that we can be certain that our heavenly Father will give the Holy Spirit to all who ask Him. Reading a book is good. Listening to powerful teaching is good. But if healing and freedom are going to come, you need more than an explanation of the love of the Father. You need to *experience* the loving presence of the Father. In Romans 8:16, the Bible promises that the Holy Spirit will continually remind you that you are a child of God. Ask Him and expect Him to keep His promise right now. Ask Him to fill you afresh with His Spirit. Ask Him to remind you of the Father's love for you.

As you walk through this with Him, He might lead you into one of those life-transforming encounters that you will talk about for the rest of your life, or He might just plant a seed in your heart that begins a beautiful process of healing. Either way, if you ask Him, He *will* work in you. Meditate on that assurance, and let it open your heart to be ready to forgive.

And as you move forward, know that I and many others are praying for you: that the Father would take you into the safety of His strong and loving arms…that He would touch you and bring healing to the most painful places in your soul…and that He would overwhelm you with a love that no earthly father – not even the best of them – could ever give.

Breaking the Chains

You have already asked God to give you the grace to forgive your father, for every way that he has hurt you and for every way that he has failed to show the Father's love to you. As you read the previous chapters, a lot of things had probably already come into your mind. Now, as you begin to release your father, trust the Holy Spirit to reveal to you any other negative words, attitudes, or actions of your father that you need to release to the Lord.

Remember the nature of God's forgiveness. It is *based on the cross…*it is *immediate…*it is *complete…*it is *offered before we ask…*it is *offered repeatedly…* it is *compassionate.*

Now it is time to go to the cross, where every sin committed by you and against you was placed on Jesus. See Him bearing every bit of your guilt, every sin, every bit of your pain, and every bit of your shame. And hear Him say triumphantly, "It is finished!"

In his teaching on the Father's heart, Jack Frost says that when you go to the cross, imagine taking your father there with you. Imagine your father asking you to forgive him. Of course, he may never have the ability to actually do this, but it can be very helpful in enabling you to really feel as if you are releasing him. Remember, it is *you* who is really being set free. Frost says to imagine your father saying these words to you, and as he does, begin to release him in your heart as if he were really there:

As a father, I committed the worst sin against you. I misrepresented the Father's love. I failed to create a special place in your heart. God gave me the gift of your life, and I was not faithful to nurture the gift of God within you. And I ask you to forgive me. You were not the problem. There was not something wrong with you that caused me to treat you this way. I couldn't be a father to you, because I was never a son in my own father's house. Forgive me, for I knew not what I was doing. I was doing the deeds of my father. Forgive me for never taking you into my arms in a healthy way. Forgive me for not being safe enough for you to risk crawling into my arms. Forgive me for not being able to say the words, "I love you." Forgive me for disciplining you in anger. Forgive me for all the times I devalued you with words and actions. Forgive me for hurting you with words of criticism, rather than encouraging you with words of affirmation. Forgive me for not laughing with you, for being too busy for you. You weren't broken. You were created for love, created to be nurtured by me and my love. It was *me* who was broken, and I failed to represent God to you. Forgive me.[83]

And now it is time to take a huge step on the road to freedom. It is time to release him. Frost continues:

Place the cross between you and the fear and disappointment of your earthly father's house. And say, "I forgive you, Dad. You couldn't be a father, because you had never experienced the love and joy of being a son. You have hurt me, and I have been angry with you. But I forgive you, because you didn't know what you were doing."[84] Lay your father at the foot of the cross and release him. Lay at the cross the pain, the anger, the bitterness, and the disappointments. Now, turn and walk away. Turn to Father God: "I have nowhere to go for love. I know the door to Your house is always open. You said that You would not leave me like an orphan. I ask You, Father, to come to me now and reveal Your love and Fatherhood to me. I choose to receive You as a Father to me. I choose to be Your child."[85]

This is not about getting saved (though some of you may actually be understanding the gospel for the first time). This is about finding freedom from years of pain and bitterness that have kept your heart in bondage. This is about entering into the fullness and beauty of life as a beloved son or daughter of Almighty God.

He has never stopped fighting for your freedom. Through every painful moment, through every heartache, through every disappointment, He has always been there as Father—loving you, holding you, and inviting you to come home and be free in His love. It's all that He's ever wanted. It's all that you've ever needed.

It's His delight. It's your destiny.

Key Thought:

It is time to go to the cross, where every sin committed by you and every sin committed against you was placed on Jesus. See Him bearing every bit of guilt, every sin, every bit of pain, and every bit of shame, both for you and for those who have hurt you. And hear Him say triumphantly, "It is finished!"

Personal Reflection / Group Discussion:

It is not at all easy to forgive, especially when the pain is severe. But it is a big and necessary step on the path to true freedom. Pain won't just go away. If it is not dealt with and healed, it will become bitterness. And bitterness is deadly to your heart and soul. It doesn't have to be that way. Healing and freedom are possible. Forgiveness really is possible.

- *What is the biggest obstacle that hinders you from being able to forgive your father (or others who hurt you)?*

- *Have you opened your heart to allow God to help you see your father through His compassionate eyes?*

- *Has God given you a breakthrough and a new sense of freedom as you forgave your father? If so, tell somebody about it! Testify to the power of God's grace.*

Scriptural Prescription:

Be kind to one another, tender-hearted, forgiving each other, just as God in Christ also has forgiven you.

Ephesians 4:32

Further Study:

Our ability to forgive depends on our understanding of how much we have been forgiven ourselves.

Read Luke 7:36-50 and Matthew 18:21-35 and see how this understanding is the key factor in our love for God and in our love for others.

Chapter 10

Receiving from the Father Who Never Fails

God loves you. He always has—He always will.[86]

Dr. David Jeremiah

Daddy Will Always Be Here

I will never forget the day my daughter Hannah was born, the day I became a father for the very first time. This was a completely new experience for me, and even though God had given me nine months to prepare for it, it seemed like it all came upon me so suddenly.

Before she came along, I was just a guy with a wife. Then suddenly this little head popped into the world, and in one moment, my life was changed forever. I had held lots of babies before, but this was not just any baby. This beautiful little girl was *my* daughter. When I held her for the first time, I felt such joy, like a man who had been given the greatest gift anyone could ever be given. And at the same time, I felt a heavy weight on my shoulders, like a man who had just been given the most important responsibility that anyone could ever be given. For years to come, this little creature would be dependent on me for everything she needed. But what was really weighing on my mind was the understanding that most of her early opinions about who God is would be based on what she saw in me.

On that first night in the hospital room, Hannah woke up crying. I wanted to let my wife rest, so I went over to Hannah, picked her up and held her in my arms. Now I had never practiced for this moment. I hadn't read about it in a book. Nobody had counseled me so that I would know what to say. But something very real happened in my heart at that moment. I already knew very well how much God loved me, but when I held my newborn child He did something in me that made me understand His love in a whole new way. The heart of the Father came alive in me…and I knew exactly what to say.

I just said, "It's OK, Daddy's here." And then I made her a promise: "Daddy will *ALWAYS* be here." She is a young lady now, and she has never doubted that promise…not even for a minute.

How was I able to make that promise to her? I could do it because the love of the Father had taken root in my heart. I could do it because I knew without a doubt that He would always be here for me and that He would always love me. I could do it because He had proved it to me through my dad.

Remember the story I told you in chapter 5, about the time I was arrested for drinking and driving? The policeman made it clear to me that my father, the pastor, must be so disgusted with me. And the lies of the enemy were so convincing: "Did you hear him? You are father-less!! You are not your father's son, and you are certainly no son of God. You are a complete failure…and you are all alone. You will *always* be alone."

But that wasn't the end of the story, because the heart of the Father doesn't give up. His love is relentless.

Several years after that incident, I was at my parents' home, and I was telling my dad some stories about different things that had happened, things that I was certain he didn't know anything about. And then he said, "Oh, I know about a lot of things, much more than you think I know. I even know about the time you were arrested for drinking and driving."

Oh no. I thought I had hidden it from him. I didn't think it was possible that he could have known. But he *did* know. I felt so guilty. I was filled with shame. And I knew that what the policeman had communicated to me, that my father was disgusted with me, was about to be made very clear.

But what happened was the complete opposite of what I expected. And though nearly a year passed before the power of my dad's words really took root in my heart, what he said to me on that day changed my life forever. He said, "You know, there are many things that you think you can't talk to me about. But you are wrong. I don't at all approve of the way that you are living your life. It grieves me. But no matter what you decide to do, there is one thing that will never change. I will always be your father, and you will always be my son." That was all he said.

I was speechless. It was amazing enough to know that he still loved me. But what made it so powerful was the assurance that he would never stop loving me, no matter what.

"Always," he said. That's what kept me from committing suicide a few months later. *Always.* That's what opened my heart to believe that if my parents still loved me, then maybe God still loved me, too. *Always.* When I gave my life to Christ, that's what made me certain that what He had done on the cross wasn't only for others, but that He had really done it for me. *Always.* That's why I know without a doubt that I am now and forever a full son of my Father in heaven.

Always. That's how God loves. And if we are going to walk in the freedom that the Father desires us to have, then we have to be assured that He is not just a God who has love sometimes, but that He *is* love… all the time. We have to know that His heart never changes. He is not unpredictable, depending on what kind of mood He is in. He doesn't hug you today and slap you tomorrow. He is always the same. The good news you have read about in the earlier chapters is always good news. The love that offered you a place in His family is the same love that secures your place in His family forever.

Unfailing Love

In the Old Testament, there is a Hebrew word that is used over and over to describe the unchangeable nature of the love of God. It is often translated in the English Bible as "lovingkindness," "mercy," or "kindness." But this word, *hesed*, means so much more than that. It is so full of meaning that my theology professor in seminary took two full weeks of classes to try to explain it to us. He said that if we don't understand the meaning of this word, then it is impossible to really understand the relationship between Father God and His children.

It describes a love that can't be moved by circumstances…a love that doesn't change with moods…a love that is based on pure commitment.…a love that is expressed, not primarily in feeling, but in action…a love that is rooted in the perfect faithfulness of God towards His people. In each of the following Scriptures, I have inserted *hesed* after its English counterpart so that you can see how it is translated:

Though the mountains be shaken and the hills be removed, yet My unfailing love *(hesed)* for you will not be shaken.

Isaiah 54:10 (NIV)

The steadfast love *(hesed)* of the Lord never ceases.

Lamentations 3:22 (ESV)

Surely goodness and mercy *(hesed)* shall follow me all the days of my life.

Psalm 23:6 (ESV)

Give thanks to the Lord, for He is good. His faithful love *(hesed)* endures forever.

Psalm 136:1 (NLT)

Unshakeable. Never ceases. Follows me all the days of my life. Endures forever. Even if the mountains could somehow be unsettled. Even if the immovable could be moved. Even if the unshakeable could be shaken.

Even if everything we thought we could rely on were taken away, His love could never be moved in the least bit. That is *hesed*. That's the love of God.

A Father Forever

The apostle Paul describes this love in 1 Corinthians 13:7-8. He says it is a love that *bears all things*. God is not a Judge who is seeking to condemn us and put us to shame. He is a Father who covers all of our sins by bearing our pain and taking our shame onto Himself. It is a love that *believes all things*. He doesn't look at us with disappointment and doubt, but He believes the best for us, looking past what we are and looking ahead to what He knows we will be. It is a love that *hopes all things*. He is certain about the power of His love to transform, and so He is unwilling to accept failure as the final word. And it is a love that *endures all things*. He will fight for us to the end with a love that cannot die, refusing to give up even when all hope appears to be gone.

In case we still had any doubts, Paul adds one final statement: *Love never fails*. Never. When He decides to be our Father, He intends to remain our Father...forever.

In chapter 4, we looked at the beautiful truth of what it means that you are an adopted son or daughter of God through faith in Jesus Christ.

It was planned by the Father. Your adoption is not based on anything that you have done. He chose you! He knew everything about you, and just like me, you didn't qualify to be His child. You didn't deserve to be part of His family. But He chose you anyway. Why? Because He loved you. No other reason. He saw you, He knew you completely, and He loved you. It is all based on His choice, on His heart. And His heart doesn't change.

It was purchased by the Son. Not only did He choose to adopt us and bring us home, but He did so at a tremendous cost—the life of Jesus, the One the Father loves more than any other.

It was promised by the Spirit. His Spirit continually reminds us and assures us that we are, without a doubt, beloved children of God, and that one day we will enter fully into the joy of life in the Father's house forever (we will talk about that more in the final chapter).

But how secure is our adoption? Is it possible that He would ever decide to give us to another father? Would He really pay such an extravagant price for something He didn't intend to keep? Would the Holy Spirit waste so much time reminding us and assuring us of a position that is only temporary? Is it at all possible that He would reject or abandon His child after He had gone to such great lengths to bring that child home? Could the Father ever grow tired of loving us?

To help us answer those questions, let's look briefly at the custom of adoption in the Roman Empire at the time when Paul was writing to the churches about our adoption into the family of God. When someone (usually a young adult) was adopted into a family, there were two steps to the adoption. The first step was a symbolic "sale," which was done three times. The first two times, the biological father would sell his son, and then he would buy him back. But when they acted out the sale for a third time, he did not buy him back, signifying that the son had fully passed from the authority of one father to another. That may sound more like slavery, but it wasn't. It was a symbol that a very real change had taken place, that the boy no longer belonged to his biological father. It was as if he had never known him, and he was now a son of his new father, a full member of his household.

The second step was to present a legal case before the magistrate. Once he approved it, the adoption was final. The one who was adopted was now completely disconnected from his past life in every way–all debts were canceled, he received a new name, and he became a full son of his new father.[87]

He became an heir to his new father's estate. There was no difference between his position and that of his father's biological children. He was a co-heir with them in every way. In order to dispel any doubt, the adopting ceremony was carried out in the presence of seven witnesses. So, if the adopting father died, and someone tried to challenge the young man's right to his inheritance, the witnesses would then come forward and testify that they were there when he was adopted. They would verify that this was, in fact, a genuine adoption. Based on their testimony, he was confirmed as a full son of his father.[88]

And once the adoption was complete, the son's place in his new family was final. According to the Roman-Syrian law book of that time, a man was able to send away his biological son, if he had good reason for doing so. But the law stated clearly that an adopted son could never be sent away...not for any reason.[89] The adopted son's position in his family was actually more secure than that of the biological son!

If the law of sinful men could offer such security, how much more we can be certain that our adoption in Christ is secure! How much more certain we can be that He will never abandon us...that He will never grow tired of loving us...that this relationship is much more than a temporary arrangement. As we begin to understand what adoption meant to Paul and to his readers, the truth of God's word regarding our adoption comes alive in our hearts with powerful assurance:

> For you have not received a spirit of slavery leading to fear again, but you have received a spirit of adoption as sons by which we cry out, "Abba! Father!" The Spirit Himself testifies with our spirit that we are children of God, and if children, heirs also, heirs of God and fellow heirs with Christ.
>
> Romans 8:15-17

Preaching or teaching can't make you certain of that love. Words on the pages of a book can't do it, either. The certainty of the Father's love has to be revealed to you. You need the Holy Spirit to testify to you deep in your soul, confirming that you are a full son or daughter of God, that you are loved with a love that never fails. You need the Holy Spirit to fill your heart with His love so that you can cry out, "Abba! Father!", with the complete confidence of a child who knows that he is perfectly and permanently loved.

Howell Harris, a great evangelist in Wales in the 1700s, describes an experience he had just three weeks after he was saved, a revelation of the Father's heart that changed his life forever. This new understanding made him a powerful tool in the hands of God, and he was used greatly to help bring about revival in his country:

> Suddenly I felt my heart melting within me like wax before a fire, and love to God for my Saviour. I felt also not only love and peace, but a longing to die and to be with Christ. Then there came a cry into my soul within that I had never known before—Abba, Father! I could do nothing but call God my Father. I knew that I was His child, and He loved me and was listening to me.[90]

A little over a year ago, I witnessed the tangible power of this revelation at a missions conference in Apac. I was teaching a large group of pastors, evangelists, and local believers, leading them through several sessions on understanding the heart of the Father. In those two days, the Lord moved in a big and wonderful way in the lives of many people. But it was the visible transformation in the lives of two particular ladies that really grabbed my heart.

They were simple women from the village. I noticed them at the beginning of the first session. They were right in front of me, in the center of the room near the platform. They looked so broken and beaten down. When I looked at them, I just prayed in my heart, "Oh Lord, those ladies have so much pain. I don't know their stories, but I can see the results of their stories so clearly. They are hurting. Bring healing to their hearts. Show Your love to them today. Let them know that You are their Father."

When we walked through a time of forgiving our earthly fathers, it sounded like a labor room. Groans came from deep within people's souls as they released years of pain and bitterness into the hands of the Lord. I watched these two ladies as they wept and repeatedly lifted their hands to the Lord, as if they were handing Him one load of pain after another. After about forty-five minutes, it was over. The pain was gone. You could see it on their faces. But there was still something missing. They needed to encounter His love. They needed to come home.

As we talked in the next session about our adoption through Christ, they giggled with delight at the idea that Almighty God rejoices over them with singing. They put their hands over their mouths in amazement when they heard that He had chosen them for Himself. Their eyes sparkled with joy when they heard that there was nothing that could change His heart towards them. With each new statement of certainty, they leaned forward as if they couldn't wait for the words to reach their hearts. The Father was revealing Himself to them. It was so obvious… and it was so beautiful.

Just a few hours earlier, they were as beaten down as anyone I have ever seen. But now their faces were beaming with love. There was peace. There was freedom. The message was clear. You could see it in their eyes, a declaration of confidence that said, "He is _MY_ Father!!"

When the Spirit of God reveals the heart of the Father to us, it fills us with a wonderful certainty about who we are. Because of His love, we know that He chose us. We are not slaves who have to worry about earning the master's favor. We are sons and daughters who already have the Father's favor. Because of His love, we are certain of our inheritance in Him (the Holy Spirit is our witness that the adoption was genuine). And because of His love, we know that His heart towards us will not change, or as Paul says at the end of Romans chapter 8, that "nothing can separate us from the love of God, which is in Christ Jesus our Lord."

When He decides to be our Father, He intends to be our Father forever. You might be willing to stop being His child, but as long as you still have breath in your lungs, He is not willing to stop being your Father. His heart is immovable. His love is relentless.

In Hosea chapter 11, though the people of Israel had continually rejected Him and chased after other gods, God showed that His heart towards them was steadfast. An earthly father might have been willing to give up. But not this Father. He says, "I know My son has been rebellious. But I chose him. I have loved him from the very beginning. I am the One who taught him how to walk! How could I ever give up on him?"

In Isaiah 49:15-16, God asked if a mother could possibly forget the child she is nursing, or if a woman could possibly feel no love for the child that she herself bore. The tone of the question suggests that this is one of the most unlikely things that could ever happen. But even if such a thing were possible, He says, it is absolutely impossible that Father God could ever forget His children. He has engraved His children on the palms of His hands. His love for us is permanent!

How permanent? Song of Solomon 8:6-7 says it's a love that is as permanent as a seal engraved on His heart. It's a love that is unwilling to let us go, just as the grave is unwilling to give up its dead. It's a love that is as durable as a blazing fire, unable to be put out by the waters of any difficulty. And it's a love that is more valuable than all of the riches a man could possess.

Always really does mean always. You can't do anything good that will make Him love you more, and you can't do anything bad that will make Him love you less. You don't have to do anything to earn His love, and you don't have to do anything to make yourself worthy of keeping it. It is a gift from a loving Father. Unfailing love is what He rejoices to give. Unfailing love is what you were created to receive.

It's His delight…it's your destiny.

Key Thought:

Always really does mean always. You can't do anything good that will make Him love you more, and you can't do anything bad that will make Him love you less. You don't have to do anything to earn it, and you don't have to do anything to make yourself worthy of keeping it. It is a gift from a loving Father. Unfailing love is what He rejoices to give. Unfailing love is what you were created to receive.

Personal Reflection / Group Discussion:

In the Roman practice of adoption, once the adoption was complete, it was final. But sometimes an accuser would come forward and say that the child was not really the son of his adopted father, and so they would call forward the witnesses who were there when the adoption took place, to testify and confirm that he was in fact the rightful son of his father.

- *What realities in your life and in the world around you sometimes make it difficult to really believe that your place in the Father's heart and home is secure?*

- *Do you need the Holy Spirit to step forward as a witness, to remind you that you are an adopted child of God through the death and resurrection of Jesus Christ, and that your sonship is secure forever? Ask a friend to pray for you, or pray alone. Ask the Holy Spirit to speak to you, clearly and powerfully. He will be faithful to answer.*

Scriptural Prescription:

For you have not received a spirit of slavery leading to fear again, but you have received a spirit of adoption as sons by which we cry out, "Abba! Father!" The Spirit Himself testifies with our spirit that we are children of God.

Romans 8:15-16

Can a mother forget the baby at her breast and have no compassion on the child she has borne? Though she may forget, I will not forget you! See, I have engraved you on the palms of My hands.

Isaiah 49:15-16 (NIV)

Further Study:

Read Luke 15:1-32. How do the father's actions towards both of his sons who had brought him shame demonstrate the unfailing love of God that we have been talking about (first, the younger son in vv. 11-24 and then the older son in vv. 25-32)?

Read Jeremiah 31:20. Israel (Ephraim) had continually rebelled against God, their Father. How does the Father's response show the depths of His unfailing love?

Part III:

Walking in the Freedom
of the Father's Heart

See what great love the Father has lavished on us, that we should be called children of God! And that is what we are!

1 John 3:1 (NIV)

Chapter 11

The Father's Voice:

the Assurance of Freedom

I have been led to an inner place where I had not been before. It is the place within me where God has chosen to dwell. It is the place where I am held safe in the embrace of an all-loving Father who calls me by name and says, "You are My beloved son, on you My favor rests." It is the place where I can taste the joy and the peace that are not of this world.[91]

Henri Nouwen

The Most Powerful Voice in the World

Several years ago, I was doing quite a bit of preaching at a church in Kampala. And every Sunday morning, as I was praying and finishing up my message, and as my family finished getting themselves ready for church, the parade would begin. One girl after another would walk into the room and stop in front of me with a big smile of anticipation, just waiting for me to notice the results of her preparation.

During the whole process of getting ready, the girls are always asking one another for feedback about how they look: "What do you think about this dress?" "Does my hair look OK?" And they make adjustments based on that feedback.

But when my daughter is standing there in front of me, my opinion becomes the most important opinion on earth, the only opinion that really matters to her. Not because I have a unique sense of fashion, but because I am her father. You see, she isn't coming only to find out if

I think that she *looks* beautiful. She does want to hear that, but what she is looking for is much deeper than that. What she really needs to know from me is that she *is* beautiful, in every way. She needs to know that I delight in her. She needs to know that I treasure her and cherish her.

She is looking for safety, for security, for acceptance. She just wants to know that she is mine, no matter what. She wants to be assured that she is of infinite value to me, that whenever she needs me, I will be there. She just wants to be fully confident of my love for her. She already knows that all of those things are true…but sometimes she just needs to be reminded.

"You look so pretty," I say enthusiastically. Those were the words she came to hear. She dances away with a smile, maybe even adding a twirl of delight. She goes out of the room with compete confidence and freedom, because she doesn't just think she is beautiful. She *knows* she is beautiful….because Daddy said so. The voice of the father is powerful.

It is true for boys as well. A boy doesn't really need to know that his dad thinks he looks nice (in fact, it is usually the furthest thing from his mind). His needs are different. He knows that he is destined for manhood. He knows that the qualities of a man have been planted in his heart. But that's not enough. He needs to know that *Dad* thinks that he has what it takes to be a great man someday. He needs to know that when Dad looks at him he sees strength, wisdom, leadership ability, problem-solving skills, and courage.

A few years ago, when we were back in the U.S., my son Joshua was playing on a basketball team, and I was his coach. He didn't really know much about basketball, but basketball was the game that I had excelled at when I was young, so Josh wanted to do his best to be good at the game Daddy loved. He practiced and practiced, and he became quite good at dribbling the ball.

But he had never played in a real game before, so he wasn't very confident that he could do it. For several games, whenever he had the ball, he would look over to me to be sure that he was doing it the way that

Daddy wanted him to do it. But I just wanted him to stop looking at me and get moving. Over and over I would tell him, "Josh, just go!" But he kept doing the same thing.

Finally, before the last game, I decided to have a talk with him. I said, "Joshua, you are so good at handling the basketball. There is not a single kid in this league who can stop you when you have the ball."

That was what he had been waiting to hear from me all along. He just needed to hear me say, "You can do it!" The opposing players spent the entire game watching Joshua fly past them with the ball. They couldn't stop him. He played like the best, because Daddy said he was the best. The voice of the father is the most powerful voice on earth.

But when Jesus says, "Follow Me," He is inviting you to hear something much more powerful than the voice of even the best earthly father. He is inviting you to come and hear the voice of your Father in heaven speaking to you. He is inviting you to come and find the same love, the same security, and the same perfect confidence that He Himself found in the heart of Father God.

Sometimes even free people need to be assured of their freedom. We know the truth, but life brings so many challenges and distractions, and we need to be reminded of what is true. We all hunger for that assurance...daily. Maybe we were confident in His love yesterday, but now it is today, and the lies of the enemy are ringing in our ears. It can leave us so confused, and the doubts come rushing in:

"I have been struggling. I thought I forgave my father, but now the pain seems to be coming back. Maybe I am not really free after all."

"I was feeling great about my life and about my new understanding of my position as God's child. But I have fallen into sin, and I feel so guilty. Can He still really accept me?"

"I know that Jesus said, 'It is finished.' I know that He said, 'If the Son has set you free, you are free indeed.' I know that the apostle Paul wrote that nothing can separate us from His love.

But how 'finished' is it really? How free is 'free indeed'? And what if Paul left something off of the list in Romans 8? What if there really is something that could separate me from His love? I believe the truth…but how can I be sure?"

If you feel this way, it doesn't mean that you are losing your faith. It doesn't mean that something is terribly wrong with you. It simply means that you are human, that you are living in the midst of the uncertainties of real life. Even though you know the truth, the lies will keep coming at you. The world will still judge you according to its standards of performance. Religion will continue its effort to weigh you down with its many burdens. And people will still hurt you and disappoint you. That's life.

Just because you are now free in the Father's love doesn't mean that the enemy will give up and leave you alone. Actually, your newfound freedom increases his hatred for Jesus and for you, and it makes him even more determined to do whatever he can to put obstacles between you and the full understanding of the Father and His love for you. As we said before, the devil's only method of attack is to come at us with his arsenal of lies and deceit. His lies are loud. His lies are relentless. And his lies can sometimes be quite convincing.

But there is a voice that is much more powerful than the devil's lies – the voice of the Father. When He whispers our name, there is peace. When we hear His voice clearly, we have confidence. When He speaks words of love over our lives, there is hope and freedom. The voice of the Father is the most powerful voice in the world.

Let's look at the power of the Father's voice in a couple of very key moments in the life of Jesus.

"This Is My Beloved Son"

The first of those two events happened in Matthew chapter 3, at the edge of the River Jordan, where large crowds of people were coming to John to repent and to be baptized. But then Jesus came, and He told John that *He* would like to be baptized, too. John was a bit confused by this. This was the One that John had declared to be "the Lamb of God, who takes away the sin of the world." He didn't have any sins of His own that needed to be taken away, yet here He was, asking to be baptized.

John said, "Jesus, if the two of us are going to be here in the water for a baptism, it should be You who is baptizing me, not the other way around."

Jesus didn't offer John a detailed explanation. He simply said, "It needs to be this way, if we are going to fulfill what I have been sent to do."

So John agreed, and he baptized Him. As Jesus came up out of the water, it says that the heavens were opened, and the Spirit of God descended on Jesus in the form of a dove. And then came the voice of the Father, speaking from the heavens for everyone to hear…but especially for Jesus to hear: "This is My beloved Son, in whom I am well-pleased."

Think about what Jesus was about to face. He was just about to launch into His public ministry. For the next three years, He was going to be poor, homeless, and often hungry and physically exhausted. He was going to be misunderstood, hated, rejected, plotted against, falsely accused, betrayed, and ultimately killed. He needed strength. He needed assurance. He needed to hear the Father's voice.

So the Father spoke. What He said to Jesus was so simple, yet it is the most powerful truth on earth. It was exactly what Jesus needed to hear at the beginning of His ministry, and it was the truth that carried Him throughout His ministry. Everything about who Jesus was and everything that Jesus did arose out of His intimate knowledge and sheer delight of who He was in the Father: "This is My beloved Son, in whom I am well-pleased."

The voice of the Father is powerful!! It communicated three important things to Jesus: His *identity* as the Son of the Father, the *delight* that He brings to the heart of the Father, and His *security* in the hands of the Father.

First, it affirmed His *identity*. The Father was making sure that Jesus' entire life and ministry was rooted in the assurance of His place in the Father's heart: "You are Mine. No matter what happens, no matter what anyone says about You or does to You, You are My Son. That is a fact that can never be changed."

After the baptism, when Jesus went to the wilderness to be tempted by the devil, it was His identity that the devil attacked immediately. The devil knew that if he could win that battle, then he could win the whole war. So the first words he spoke to Jesus were, "If You really are the Son of God...." He was trying to build strongholds in the mind of Jesus, those big walls of lies that stand between us and the true knowledge of God. He knew that if he could just get Jesus to doubt His identity or misuse His identity, then he could keep Jesus from accomplishing what He was sent to do. So he tried to distract Jesus by turning His mind away from the Father's business and focusing His mind on the emptiness of His own stomach.

"You are hungry, Jesus. You have been fasting for 40 days. If You really are the Son of God, then why don't You use Your power to turn these stones into some bread so that You can eat?" Jesus responded to the devil by quoting from Deuteronomy 8:3, saying, "It is written, 'MAN SHALL NOT LIVE BY BREAD ALONE, BUT ON EVERY WORD THAT PROCEEDS FROM THE MOUTH OF GOD.'"

And what was the most recent word that had proceeded from the mouth of God? "You are My beloved Son." Jesus is saying, "Yes, I am hungry. But My greatest need is not bread. What I need is to know that I am the Father's Son!" Wherever Jesus went, whatever Jesus did for the next three years, He did it with the full knowledge of who He was.

That knowledge wasn't just something official, like holding a birth certificate that legally stated that Jesus was the Father's Son. What the Father was communicating was something that came from deep within His heart. Jesus was not just His Son...He was His Son in whom He *delighted*: "This is My beloved Son, in whom I am well-pleased."

This was a statement of pure love. It wasn't a matter of the Father saying, "Jesus has performed well, so therefore I am very happy with Him." Yes, Jesus was perfect, and He always did the Father's will, but that was not the basis of the Father's delight. The word that we translate "well-pleased" appears 21 times in the New Testament, and in nearly every instance it involves a choice. Not a reaction to something someone has done, but something that begins within the heart of the one who is pleased.[92]

The Father is saying to Jesus, "You are My beloved Son because it pleases Me for You to be My Son. So no matter what happens, know that Your place in My heart can never be changed. You are Mine, and I delight in You...simply because You are Mine." Jesus knew that the Father had loved Him with an endless delight since before the foundation of the world (John 17:24). The Father is reminding Him of that love: "It is still that way. It will always be that way."

That knowledge gave Him *security*. And Jesus definitely needed to know that He was secure! He was always being criticized, always being rejected, always being threatened. He was misunderstood, even by His closest disciples. It would have often been tempting to think that the whole thing was a failure.

But Jesus was secure in the knowledge that He was the Son who was infinitely loved by His Father. He knew that He wasn't here to be popular or successful in the eyes of the world, but only to do what the Father had sent Him to do. And no matter what anyone said or did to Him, He was secure in the Father's hands.

When He was misunderstood, He rested in His identity. He said, "I know where I came from and where I am going" (John 8:14), and "the Father who sent Me testifies about Me" (John 8:18). When He was threatened, He didn't fear, because He knew that the Father would never forsake Him. He said, "I do nothing on My own initiative, but I speak these things as the Father taught Me. And He who sent Me is with Me; *He has not left Me alone*" (John 8:28-29, italics added).

When He faced failure and opposition–when people didn't seem to understand what He was trying to do, or they weren't interested in following Him–He didn't worry. He knew that the Father's plan would not fail:

> All those the Father gives Me will come to Me, and whoever comes to Me I will never drive away. For I have come down from heaven not to do My will but to do the will of Him who sent Me. And this is the will of Him who sent Me, that I shall lose none of all those He has given Me, but raise them up at the last day.
>
> John 6:37- 39 (NIV)

How was He so certain that He would accomplish what He was sent to do? Speaking of Himself, Jesus said, "On Him God the Father has placed His seal of approval" (John 6:27, NIV).

And when the crowds started going away from Him, when it looked like everyone might desert Him, He didn't despair. He simply turned to His disciples and said, "Do you want to go away as well?" (John 6:67, ESV). Even if those who were closest to Him decided to leave, He had no fear, because He was fully confident that He was the Son of the Father…fully confident that He was doing the will of the Father who never fails…and fully confident that He was completely secure in the Father's hands.

How was He so confident? When did the Father place His seal of approval on Jesus? How did He know the Father was with Him? When did the Father testify about Him? How was Jesus so certain about who He was? It all happened right there at the edge of the River Jordan, when the heavens opened and the Father spoke: "This is My beloved Son, in whom I am well-pleased."

But that day at the Jordan wasn't the only time it happened. There was another time, late in the life of Jesus, when the Father knew that He desperately needed to hear it again.

Clinging to Abba

It happened in Matthew 17. Jesus had just told His disciples (again) that He must go to Jerusalem, that He would suffer many things at the hands of the religious leaders, and that He would be killed. A few days later, He took Peter, James, and John up on a mountain to pray. While He was praying, His face began to shine like the sun, and His clothing became white like lightning. Moses and Elijah appeared and were talking to Jesus (in Luke 9, it says that they were talking about His coming death, most likely encouraging and strengthening Him).

Peter thought it would be a good idea to make three tabernacles, one each for Jesus, Moses, and Elijah. But while he was still talking, a bright cloud enveloped them, and the voice of the Father spoke again: "This is My beloved Son, with whom I am well-pleased."

Peter, James, and John needed to hear this. They needed to be reminded that Jesus was not just another prophet like Moses or Elijah. He was the Son of God. And in 2 Peter 1:16-18, Peter writes that it was the voice of the Father on this occasion that confirmed to them that Jesus was the Son of God, making them certain of what had been revealed to them. But Peter and his friends were not the only ones who needed to be reminded.

This was for Jesus, too. Things were about to become very difficult. It was going to be more painful than anything He could have ever imagined. The Father wanted to be sure that Jesus understood that nothing had changed: "You are still My beloved Son, in whom I am well-pleased." Jesus would need the strength of this knowledge to carry Him through the dark days that lay ahead. When He was praying in the Garden of Gethsemane, right before His arrest and crucifixion, it was that knowledge to which Jesus clung with all of His heart. It was that knowledge that enabled Him to surrender Himself to the Father's will:

And He was saying, "Abba! Father! All things are possible for You; remove this cup from Me; yet not what I will, but what You will."

Mark 14:36

Who did Jesus pray to at the most important and difficult moment of His life? Not to a distant God who is somewhere faraway in heaven. At the moment of His greatest need, Jesus prayed to "Abba," the Father who was right there with Him in the garden...the Father who loved Him with an everlasting love...the Father who would never leave Him. Jesus willingly placed His life into the Father's hands because He had complete assurance of what was in the Father's heart.

That assurance came at the beginning of Jesus' ministry, when He heard the Father's voice at the edge of the River Jordan. It came towards the end of His ministry, when He heard it on the mountain. We only know about the Father's voice speaking on those two occasions, because the disciples were there to witness it. But I am certain that Jesus must have heard the Father's voice speaking His love over Him many other times in the three years between those events.

We know from the gospels that Jesus made a regular habit of meeting the Father in prayer. We know that life continues to bring all kinds of challenges, and with those challenges comes the need for assurance. And we know the heart of the Father. Because of that, I think we can be very sure that in each of those many times of prayer, the Father reminded Jesus of who He was: "You are My beloved Son, in whom I am well-pleased." And that knowledge set Him free.

The voice of the Father is powerful.

That Assurance Is For YOU

And the beauty of it is that Jesus doesn't just soak up all of the love and delight of the Father for Himself, and then invite us to something less. He prayed that we would experience the same love that He Himself has experienced since before the beginning of time:

> "Father, I want those You have given Me to be with Me where I am, and to see My glory, the glory You have given Me because You loved Me before the creation of the world. Righteous Father, though the world does not know You, I know You, and

they know that You have sent Me. I have made You known to them, and will continue to make You known *in order that the love You have for Me may be in them* and that I Myself may be in them."

John 17:24-26 (NIV, italics added)

Life will continue to bring pain. It will bring confusion, frustration, disappointment, and doubt. The devil will continue to come at you with his collection of accusations and lies. But if you have put your trust in Christ and what He has accomplished for you through His death and resurrection, if you have committed your life to Him, then the same assurance that Jesus had is for you, too...because you have a Father. You have a wonderful identity. You are a child of Almighty God. You are the delight of His heart, and His heart never changes. And you are secure. Your life is safely in His hands...forever.

You know that it's true, because Father God says that it's true. The voice of the Father is the most powerful voice in the world. He invites you to continually live in the life-changing reality that you are deeply loved by God. When you know that, you are free.

And as often as you need Him to remind you, He will speak the same powerful words of assurance and love over you that He spoke over Jesus: *"You are My beloved child, in who I am well-pleased."*

Every day, He wants to speak those words to you. And every day, He wants to speak those words to others through you.

It's His delight...it's your destiny.

Key Thought:

If you have put your trust in Him, then the same assurance that Jesus had is for you, too. You have a wonderful identity. You are a child of Almighty God. You are the delight of His heart, and His heart never changes. And you are secure. Your life is safely in His hands... forever.

Personal Reflection / Group Discussion:

We tend to see our circumstances as the obstacles that keep us from having life, joy, peace, and freedom. Most of our prayers focus on asking God to fix our circumstances so that we can be free. But everything about who Jesus was, and everything that Jesus did arose out of His intimate knowledge and sheer delight of who He was in the Father. His freedom came from what He knew in His heart. It didn't depend on His circumstances at all.

- *If that is true, then how should that change the way that we pray? What should we be seeking from the Father more than anything else?*

Sometimes even free people need to be assured of their freedom. We know the truth, but life brings so many challenges and distractions, and we need to be reminded of what is true. We all hunger for that assurance.

- *Do you need to hear the Father's voice right now? Listen to Him speaking the assurance of His love over you: "This is My beloved child, in whom I am well-pleased."*

Scriptural Prescription:

See what great love the Father has lavished on us, that we should be called children of God! And that is what we are!

1 John 3:1 (NIV)

Further Study:

Read John 8:12-55. In the midst of opposition and accusations, look at how, time after time, Jesus doesn't defend Himself, but He simply points to His identity as the Son of the Father and trusts Himself into His hands. How can the understanding of your identity and your security as His beloved child give you the strength to obey Him and to do His will, even when it is not popular, or even when it causes you to be hated?

Chapter 12

The Father's Business:

the Fruit of Freedom

True love is a revolutionary experience. And far above any love is the love of Christ, causing the most radical revolutionary experience in human life.[93]

Festo Kivengere

If we have got the true love of God shed abroad in our hearts, we will show it in our lives. We will not have to go up and down the earth proclaiming it. We will show it in everything we say or do.[94]

D.L. Moody

The One Jesus Loves

Last year, I spoke at a missions conference in Kampala, and as they were making the final preparations I got a text message from the pastor, saying, "Dave, you know in Uganda we love our titles, so I need to know what title we should put next to your photo on the poster. We can't just write 'Dave.'"

He said it that way because he knows that I am a bit like my father. Dad was a pastor for 50 years, and he didn't really like being called Reverend, or anything else that sounded too official. He always told people, "I don't need a title. Just call me John." I feel the same way. But we had to put something on the conference poster, so I told the pastor, "I guess we can just write *Pastor Dave Carroll.*"

A few days later, when they gave me a copy of the finished poster, I looked at my picture and just chuckled to myself...and I thought about my dad. And as I thought about my dad, I thought about another guy named John–the apostle John, the disciple of Jesus. John didn't make a big deal about his titles and positions, either. He certainly could have. If anyone had the right to an impressive title, it was John.

He was an important leader in the early church. He wrote five books of the New Testament. He had walked closely with Jesus for three years as one of His specially chosen twelve disciples. Among the twelve, John was part of the inner circle, the three who were closest to Jesus (along with Peter and James). And among those three, John was the one who was always right by Jesus' side. So he could have rightfully claimed a huge title to put next to his name, maybe something like "The Most Excellent Right Arch-apostle John." Yet when he referred to himself, he never did it in a way that drew attention to John. He did it in a way that drew attention to Jesus. He simply called himself *"the one Jesus loved."*

He wasn't saying this because he believed that he was the only one who was loved by Jesus. And He wasn't saying it because he believed that Jesus loved him more than anyone else. This wasn't a statement of pride at all. It was a statement of humility, because John was so amazed that someone like Jesus could love someone like him. You see, John's life wasn't defined by what he accomplished. It wasn't defined by his position in the church or in the community. John's life was defined by only one thing–the simple reality that he was loved by Jesus, the Son of God.

I like that. And so I was thinking that if they ask me to speak at the conference next year, maybe I will request that on the poster next to my photo they write *"Dave, the one Jesus loves."* Because that is who I am!

My title only tells you what I do, but it doesn't tell you what's in my heart. My wife doesn't call me "Pastor." My children don't call me "Pastor." Jesus doesn't call me "Pastor." That's just a title. If you want to know who I am, you have to go to the cross. At the cross, my life is defined by one reality, that through the death and resurrection of His Son Jesus Christ, God has paid for my sins, He has transformed me, and

He has filled my life with His love. At the cross, all of the pretense and all of the striving for position and popularity is stripped away, and I am simply Dave, the one Jesus loves.

I don't need any other title than that. I don't have to try to do something big or accomplish something great in order to make a name for myself, because I already have the greatest name. I am the one Jesus loves, a child of Almighty God!

When you know that, you are free. The lies no longer have power over you. You no longer have to do anything to try to prove yourself to the world. You can cast off the heavy burdens of legalistic religion, saying 'no' to the gospel of fear and shame and 'yes' to the unfailing love of the Father through Jesus Christ. You can find healing from the painful experiences of your earthly father's house, and you can enter boldly into the joy and peace of your heavenly Father's house. Because you are the one Jesus loves. You are chosen. You are forgiven. You are alive. You are secure. You are free.

Not just free from personal bondage or pain, but free to love…free to serve…free to be used by the Father to set others free. When you are filled with the Father's love, you have a desire to do the Father's business. The Danish philosopher Soren Kierkegaard says that knowing the love of the Father causes the world to look much different than it did before, because now we see everything through a new set of lenses:

> When one has once fully entered the realm of love, the world–no matter how imperfect–becomes rich and beautiful, it consists solely of opportunities for love.[95]

When I am secure in my position as a child of the Father, the world is no longer a place of lust, where I see life primarily as an opportunity to meet my own needs and to satisfy my own desires. In my Father's love, I know that I already have everything I could ever need. That knowledge sets me free and transforms the world into a place of love, where I see life as a constant opportunity to share His heart with as many people as possible. That is what love does to a person. That is how free people live.

Understanding True Freedom

But many people today are teaching a different kind of freedom. They are taking the gospel that is clearly revealed in the New Testament and they are distorting it, creating a gospel that still makes plenty of room to live for their selfish and sinful desires. They are saying that since His love is freely given, since we're saved by grace and not because of any efforts of our own, then that means we have the freedom to live however we want to live. They are saying, "I can sleep with whoever I want to sleep with. I can go out and get drunk whenever I want to. I can say what I want to say. I can think what I want to think. I can do whatever I want to do with *my* time and with *my* resources. I am free, so I can just 'eat, drink, and be merry.' And when it's all over, I'll go to heaven. But in the meantime, it doesn't matter what I do. His grace is enough."

That is not the freedom that Christ came to give. Jesus didn't die so that you could be free to live a life of sin. He died and rose again so that you could be free *from* sin, free to live the life that God created you to live—a life in which you are continually transformed into His likeness and a life in which you increasingly reflect the beauty of who He is in everything that you say and do.

Does He love me no matter what? Absolutely. Could anything ever separate me from His love? Never. Is there anything I could do to make Him love me more? No way. Is there anything I could do to make Him love me less? Impossible!

But if I take the freedom that comes from His love and grace and use it to live a life of indulging my selfish desires, then it proves that I am actually not free at all. If I am living selfishly, immorally, or carelessly in the name of grace, it means that I didn't really understand His grace in the first place. True freedom in the Father's love doesn't lead me to sin. It leads me to holiness. It fills me with a hunger to know Him, and it gives me a burning desire to become more like Him.

Titus 2:11-12 says that the grace of God has appeared, not only bringing us salvation but "instructing us to deny ungodliness and worldly desires and to live sensibly, righteously and godly in the present age." Grace doesn't give me permission to be ungodly. It works in me to make me godly. Paul makes that point clear in Romans 6:

> Well then, should we keep on sinning so that God can show us more and more of His wonderful grace? Of course not! Since we have died to sin, how can we continue to live in it?...Do not let sin control the way you live; do not give in to sinful desires... Since God's grace has set us free from the law, does that mean we can go on sinning? Of course not!...When you were slaves to sin, you were free from the obligation to do right. And what was the result? You are now ashamed of the things you used to do, things that end in eternal doom. But now you are free from the power of sin and have become slaves of God. Now you do those things that lead to holiness and result in eternal life.
>
> Romans 6:1-2, 12, 15, 20-22 (NLT)

If we willfully continue in sin, it means we haven't really understood our freedom. Yes, His love is unfailing. And yes, His grace is amazing. But our freedom in Christ doesn't give us permission to live a life of disobedience. It's not a blanket that hides us while we do things that we don't want God to see us doing.

Our freedom in Christ is an understanding that we are now and forever beloved children of God...that nothing can separate us from His love...that we are free from the power of sin...that we don't have to work and strive to try to please God. Through the presence and power of the Holy Spirit, Jesus Himself works in us and through us. We have the ability to finally become everything that God intended us to be. That is true freedom!

> For you were called to freedom, brethren; only do not turn your freedom into an opportunity for the flesh, but through love serve one another.
>
> Galatians 5:13

> Live as people who are free, not using your freedom as a cover-up for evil, but living as servants of God.
>
> 1 Peter 2:16 (ESV)

Our freedom in Christ doesn't lead us away from God's purposes. It leads us right into the heart of God's purposes. When we are really free in His love, we become like the freed slave in Exodus 21 who said, "I love my master. I don't want to go away from Him. I want to stay and serve him forever." When we are truly free, we want nothing except to live in the Father's house and to give ourselves to be about His business in the world.

I will never forget the day when Jesus Christ walked into my heart and changed my whole understanding of what life was about. I had known the facts of the gospel since childhood, but the truth of the gospel came alive in me that day. On that day, I finally understood that God loved me perfectly, completely, and forever. I *knew* it. There was no doubt! I felt such an overwhelming sense of freedom. He did such a deep work of cleansing in my heart. It was so real and so powerful, very much like the conversion experience of the great evangelist Charles Finney, who said that the presence of the Holy Spirit "seemed to come in waves and waves of liquid love."[96]

At that moment, nobody had to tell me that I should desire holiness. I had such a hunger and thirst to be like Him that to desire anything else seemed absolutely ridiculous. At that moment, nobody had to tell me that I should seek first the kingdom of God. I knew exactly whose kingdom I wanted to seek. If God really loved me like that, if He could change my life so radically, then why would I ever want to seek any kingdom other than His? I knew that I had everything in Him. I didn't need anything else. I didn't want anything else. I was free!

Free people live like free people. When we really understand our freedom as children of the Father through Jesus Christ, it will transform the way that we live. John wrote, "Those who have been born into God's family do not make a practice of sinning, because God's life is in them. So they can't keep on sinning, because they are children of God" (1 John 3:9, NLT). Jesus said, "If you love Me, you will keep My commandments" (John 14:15). And Paul said, "Walk by the Spirit, and you will not carry out the desire of the flesh" (Galatians 5:16). When we are filled with the Father's love, we are free to be about the Father's business. Obeying is not something we try to *do*. It is the result of who we really *are*.

Doing What the Father Does

At His baptism, the Father spoke to Jesus clearly. Jesus knew that He was the beloved Son in whom the Father was well-pleased. He knew that the Father loved Him perfectly and completely. And the freedom that came with that certainty was the motivation behind everything that Jesus did: *"Whatever the Father does, the Son also does."* So what does the Father do? He loves. He pursues those who have strayed far from home, and He invites them to come and find their home in Him. He pours the fullness of His life into their lives. And then He sends them out to pursue others with that same relentless love.

That's what the Father does, and so that is exactly what Jesus did. The whole life of Jesus was a living billboard that put the compassionate love of the Father on display. He was called a "friend of sinners." He loved those who were despised. He pursued those who were condemned and rejected. He found those who were unwanted, and He invited them to come home to the love of the Father. Corrupt tax collectors. Prostitutes. Thieves. Adulterers. Lepers. The demon-possessed. The sick. The poor. He loved them. He pointed them to the Father. He poured His life into their lives, and then He sent them out to do the same for others.

Loving wasn't just something that Jesus did sometimes. It was the constant overflow of who He was. Jesus was filled with the Father's love, so He was free to be about the Father's business. A few years later, it was that same love that powerfully changed the life of a young man by the name of Saul.

Compelled by Love

Saul was the number one enemy of the church. He was dedicated to one thing—putting a stop to the preaching of the gospel. He traveled all over the place, arresting the followers of Jesus wherever he went. He had them beaten, put in prison, and sometimes even killed. One day, he was on his way to Damascus, where he intended to arrest many more believers. But instead, Saul himself was arrested...by the love of Jesus. He was blinded by a bright light and he heard the voice of Jesus speaking to him, saying that even though Saul had been persecuting Him, God still had a plan for Saul's life (Acts 9:1-6).

Saul had been passionately committed to what he believed to be the will of God. But on that day, Saul had a very real encounter with the love of God. Later, he described it like this: "Even though I was once a blasphemer and a persecutor and a violent man, I was shown mercy because I acted in ignorance and unbelief. The grace of our Lord was poured out on me abundantly, along with the faith and love that are in Christ Jesus" (1 Timothy 1:13-14, NIV). He was transformed by the love of God, and Saul, the biggest enemy of Jesus, soon became Paul, the most faithful servant of Jesus.

From that day on, Paul was motivated by only one thing: "We make it our goal to please Him" (2 Corinthians 5:9, NIV). Paul was beaten more times than he could count. He was thrown in prison, stoned, and shipwrecked. He was often in danger, hated, hungry, rejected, and threatened with death. But he kept going. He was consumed with the Father's business. Why did he endure all of that hardship for the sake of the gospel? Paul said it was very simple: "Christ's love compels us" to do it (2 Corinthians 5:14, NIV).

That word which we translate as "compel" or "control" literally means: "to press in on every side." It was used to describe a body that was consumed by a high fever, or a city that was under siege by an army, totally surrounded so that nobody could get in or out.[97]

What Paul was saying is, "The love of Christ is so wonderful, it has overwhelmed me so powerfully that I couldn't possibly do anything except to give my life to share His love with others. It has consumed my life, and it is the reason for everything that I do." Through Jesus, Paul had a very real encounter with the love of the Father. And that love changed his life forever. Paul was filled with the Father's love, so he was free to live for the Father's business.

But What About Normal People?

"Of course Paul lived like that," I can hear some of you saying. "He was the greatest missionary in the world. He was the greatest of all the apostles. He wrote almost half of the New Testament. He was a mighty man of God. But I am just a normal guy. I could never be like him."

But Paul said that Jesus died "for all," that when *anybody* really experiences the love of God, it radically transforms the purpose behind everything they do: "He died for all, so that those who live should no longer live for themselves, but for Him who died for them and was raised again" (2 Corinthians 5:15, NIV). The love that motivated Paul to live for Christ is the same love that lives in us.

And the power to live for Christ is in us as well. The power wasn't in Paul himself. The power was in the Spirit of God who lived in Paul...the same Spirit who lives in *every* person who has become a son or daughter of Almighty God through faith in Jesus Christ. Paul said it is for everybody, for "those who live" (if you are breathing as you read this, then that includes you).

We don't do the Father's business through our efforts or abilities. We do it by faith. We put our trust in His finished work on the cross that made it possible to become true children of God, and we surrender ourselves to the ongoing work of His Spirit that makes it possible to actually live like true children of God. The life of faith is a matter of believing and living in this awesome reality:

> I no longer live, but Christ lives in me. The life I now live in the body, I live by faith in the Son of God, who loved me and gave Himself for me.
>
> Galatians 2:20 (NIV)

And in the nearly two thousand years since Paul wrote those words, the Father has done His business through all kinds of normal people who believed and lived in that same awesome reality that Paul was talking about. God accomplishes His purposes through men, through women, and through children. He does it through those who are rich and through those who are poor. He does it through the educated and through the uneducated. He does it through those who are influential in society and through those who society thinks are worthless.

The power isn't in the people themselves, in their giftedness, influence, or resources. The power is in Him. "It is no longer I who live, but Christ lives in me." Christ, the Son of God. Christ, who loves me. Christ, who gave His life for me. When you really know that, you have everything. And that certainty makes you free to live completely for Him.

It's not only for great men and women of God who seem to have unusual gifts and resources. It's not only for people who have special advantages that most people don't have. It's not only for people who are in ministry as their full-time vocation.

Jackie Pullinger, a missionary to Hong Kong for more than 40 years, says that this is the normal experience for all true children of God, the expected fruit of the freedom that we have in Him. She says that a Christian is someone who has been touched by the love of God, someone who is completely convinced that Christ gave His life for him. Having been touched by the love of Christ, she says, that person then feels compelled to share His love with others.[98]

A New Dream

That's what happened to my friend Gloria. Like so many people in the world, she had lots of big dreams about what she wanted to do and become. But then she met Christ, and the Father began to reveal His heart to her. And as she began to see His heart, her dreams began to change. Listen to her story:

> I had a dream. I wanted to be famous and very rich. I had received
> a good education, and if everything worked out according to plan

I would be a famous and wealthy journalist by the age of thirty. The plan for my career was moving along well. I had been a news reporter with WBS. I was producing HIV/AIDS documentaries. I was even doing some media work for the First Lady's office. Things were going very well.

But not long after I had received Christ into my life, I went to a church where I first heard someone talk about the idea of missions. This term was very foreign to me, but its message touched me like no other. I couldn't explain it. I was being called. But I wondered if God could really use *me* as a missionary. And what about my career and my dreams?

A class was started at church, to train and mentor a group of us who were interested in serving God through missions. As the Lord worked in my heart, I was able to trust all of my cares to the Lord and surrender my dreams to Him. After more than two years of learning and mentoring, the Lord miraculously opened a door for my first missions experience in India, Sri Lanka, and Nepal. It was in Nepal that I began to discover for the first time that satisfaction in life wasn't found in making money and having others serve me. I realized that life wasn't about me at all. There was something much more. I found so much joy in showing love to others, through simple acts like serving the poor and taking care of people who were dying.

The Lord began to open my heart, and one night when I was alone in my room, He revealed His love to me in a powerful way. He brought to mind some things I had experienced in my life, and He showed me how it had kept me from really understanding His love, how it had filled me with so much doubt and fear. But then, in that moment, He opened my heart and filled me with His love. Everything He had been teaching me about His love suddenly became very real. And from that time on, I couldn't even think about living the kind of selfish life I had dreamed about before. I have another dream now – to be the hands and the feet through whom our Lord Jesus can shine His love to those who have never known that great love that only He can provide.

Filled with the Father's love. Free to live for the Father's business. That freedom led Gloria to leave everything that was familiar and serve for three years as a missionary in Nepal. When she came back from Nepal, the Lord gave her a burden for the children of Uganda, especially those who are vulnerable and hurting. And He gave her a special concern for the thousands of child-led families in Uganda, something she had learned about years earlier while working on a documentary in Rakai.

Through the work in Rakai and through some volunteer work at an orphanage in Kampala, the Lord opened her eyes to the vast number of children who don't have the ability to have even their most basic needs met. Gloria felt that the Lord was calling her to create a way to help meet those physical needs and also to provide the children with opportunities for mentoring and discipleship, "to encourage the kids to be everything that God has called them to be."

Out of this burden, Endiro Coffee was born. It has flourished from the beginning, becoming a popular place for friends and business associates to gather (it is my favorite "office" in Kampala). But don't be deceived. It's not just another successful restaurant. And even though Gloria is the owner, this is not really Gloria's business. This is the Father's business. She isn't getting rich and then throwing a few spare coins in the offering plate for God's work. God's work is the *whole purpose*.

Through the business, Gloria is able to support a variety of projects that minister to vulnerable children. She told me recently, "The truth is that Endiro wouldn't even be here if it weren't for the kids." That's because Endiro isn't the result of Gloria's desire to become a successful businesswoman. It is the result of the Father's work in Gloria and His desire to accomplish *His* business through her.

Touched by the Father's love. Compelled to do whatever she can to share that love with others. That's what loved people do. They love. And free people don't live for themselves. They live to set other people free.

Sharing the Father's Joy

Loving the unlovable. Pursuing those who have wandered far from Him. Making a home for the lonely and the fatherless. Giving life where life was not possible. Bringing healing to the broken. Bringing freedom to those who live in all kinds of bondage.

That's the Father's business. That was Jesus' business. And as beloved children of the Father, we are called to make it our business. If you think it sounds hard, that it seems like a heavy burden He is placing on us or a big sacrifice He is asking us to make, then you need to think again. It is not a burden at all. It is a privilege and an honor. David Livingstone once said, "If a commission by an earthly king is considered an honor, how can a commission by a Heavenly King be considered a sacrifice?"[99]

Dr. Livingstone was right. When the Lord calls us to give our lives for His purposes, it's not a demand from an unreasonable master. It's a gracious invitation from a loving Father. Let me explain.

It seems like I am always working on some kind of project at home, building something new or repairing something that was broken. I often ask my son Joshua to help me with what I am doing, something I did even when he was only five or six years old. He is older now, so these days he is actually very helpful to me. But when he was young, there was very little he could do to help in any way. To invite him to join me usually made the project take much longer, and finding a way for him to be involved didn't make it easier at all. It made it more difficult.

But if he wasn't actually helpful to me, then why did I ask him to help? There were three reasons, the same reasons why I still ask him to help me today. First of all, I love him. Working with him gives me an opportunity to be with my son, something that brings me great delight. Second, I want him to learn and grow. There are certain skills that will be valuable to him as he becomes a man, and I know that he will learn some of those skills just by watching me do my work. And third, I want him to experience the joy of finishing a task, to feel the satisfaction of a job well done.

That's the heart of the Father towards us. He has a plan. He can accomplish it any way He wants to. He certainly doesn't need us in order to get the job done. So why does He invite us to join Him in His work? He does it because He loves us, because He enjoys spending time with us. He does it because He wants us to learn and to grow to become just like Him. It gives Him great pleasure to teach us and to pour His life into our lives. And He does it because He wants us to experience the same joy and satisfaction that He Himself experiences when He does His work–when He invades broken lives with His love and makes them whole, when He fills empty lives with His life and gives them meaning and purpose, when He takes the worst of people and turns them into the best of people.

That's what brings God joy, so much that Jesus says in Luke 15 that they throw a party in heaven every time it happens. If that is what gets God excited, and if fullness of joy is found in Him, then bringing people to be fully at home in Him as His beloved sons and daughters must be the ultimate joy that could ever be experienced…by anyone. So when the Father calls us to give everything in order to join Him in what He is doing in the world, He is not taking anything from us. He is inviting us to experience the most abundant joy and the most complete satisfaction that it is possible to have. If that is the case, there is only one worthwhile reason to live–for His business!

That's what my friend Phil is beginning to see. Phil is a business-man who is growing in his understanding of the Father's heart. And it is changing the way he views everything in his life. His business is becoming the Father's business:

> I used to think that the reason for doing business was to be successful and make lots of money. But it seems to me that if our reason for living is to be about the Father's business, then the sole reason for the existence of *my* business ought to be to accomplish *His* business. In fact, *everything* we do ought to be a vehicle for that one purpose.

Phil is dead on with his assessment of life. But we will only live like that when our hearts have been transformed. We will only live with that kind of focus when our hearts are free. We need God to work in us, says Andrew Murray:

> We must have an inflowing of love in quite a new way. Our heart must be filled with life from above, from the Fountain of everlasting love, if it is going to overflow all the day. Then it will be just as natural for us to love our fellow men as it is natural for the lamb to be gentle or the wolf to be cruel.[100]

Following Jesus is not a call to duty. It is an invitation to joy. It isn't something you do. It is the overflow of who you are. And who are you? If you are a child of God through faith in Christ, then say it out loud: "I am the one Jesus loves." That means you already have everything in Him! And if you already have everything, you are free. Free to love. Free to lead others to life in the Father's heart. Free to point others to healing in the Father's love. Free to usher others into the freedom of life in the Father's house.

Loving. Giving life. Bringing healing and freedom. It's the Father's one and only business. It was the one and only business of Jesus. And as an adopted son or daughter of Almighty God, it is meant to be your one and only business as well. When you are filled with the Father's love, you are free to be about the Father's business. It gives the Father great pleasure to accomplish His business in you. It brings Him even greater joy to accomplish His business through you.

It's His delight...it's your destiny.

Key Thought:

In my Father's love, I know that I already have everything I could ever need. That knowledge sets me free and transforms the world into a place of love, where I see life as a constant opportunity to share His heart with as many people as possible. That is what love does to a person. That is how free people live.

Personal Reflection / Group Discussion:

True freedom in the Father's love doesn't lead me into sin…it leads me to holiness. It gives me a hunger for more of Him, a burning to desire to know Him more and to become more like Him. Our freedom in Christ doesn't lead us away from God's purposes…it leads us right into the heart of God's purposes. Jackie Pullinger said that someone who has really been touched by the love of God will feel compelled to share it with others.

- *Is this different from how you previously understood your freedom in Christ? How?*

- *Do you feel compelled? If not, the Lord needs to do some work in your heart. Take some time to seek Him and ask Him to fill you with a real understanding of His love.*

Scriptural Prescription:

For Christ's love compels us, because we are convinced that one died for all, and therefore all died. And He died for all, that those who live should no longer live for themselves but for Him who died for them and was raised again.

2 Corinthians 5:14-15 (NIV)

Further Study:

Read Romans 12:1-2. Up to this point, Paul has been talking for 11 chapters about the wonderful plan of God, including the powerful section in Romans 8 about the love of God and the certainty of our position as

His adopted children. Based on all of that, Paul says that our entire lives should be a sacrifice to Him. He says the way to do that is to order our lives, not according to the thinking of the world, but according to the will of God. Or, as my friend Phil said, that *everything*–including his business–is meant to be a vehicle for sharing the Father's love.

In light of what we have discussed in this book, think through some of the differences between the way the world has taught you to view life and God's will for your life.

If you lived with that kind of focus, what would be different in your life–in your goals, in your relationships, how you use your time, how you use your money, etc.?

Chapter 13

The Father's Table:

the Celebration of Freedom

How sweet is rest after fatigue! How sweet will heaven be when our journey is ended.[101]

George Whitefield

On that climactic day the heavens and the earth will be transformed into our Father's house. The renewed earth will become the place where we forever enjoy our Father's love as His sons and daughters.[102]

Dan Cruver

Almost There

There is nothing that compares with going home. We were all created with a hunger for home–a desire for acceptance, for love, for a place where we know that we belong. Home is that place where we can be ourselves. No need to wear make-up to try to impress anybody. Home is that place where everybody loves us for who we are, weaknesses and all. Home is where we are valuable...just because we are part of the family.

When I think about home, I think about my parents' house. It's a special place to me, especially since we only get to visit there when we go back to the States for a short time once every two years. During those times in America, we stay in a city that is about four hours from where my parents live. I have done a good bit of traveling over the years, but out of all my travels, that four-hour drive to Mom and Dad's house is my favorite journey of all...because it's the journey that leads me home.

As we travel, the most common question that we hear from our children (especially the youngest) is, "How much longer?" It begins early in the trip.

"Just relax," I tell them. "We still have some time. But don't worry. We'll make it."

Some time passes, and the question comes again: "Daddy, will we be there pretty soon?"

"Just be patient. It won't be too much longer," I assure them.

Eventually, the kids begin to get tired of riding in the car, and they become a little impatient: "Daddy, I'm tired. I'm hungry. I'm bored. Are we ever going to get to Grandpa's house?"

Finally, I tell them the words they have been waiting to hear: "Just a few more minutes. We're almost there."

Those words change everything. Suddenly everyone is free (including me). Boredom becomes excitement. Frustration becomes joyful anticipation. Fatigue turns into energy. Complaining turns into singing. Because we're almost there! We can feel it. When I turn onto Beckenham Road, the kids say with delight, "We're on Grandpa's road!!" I look up the street, and just ahead on the right hand side, I see my parents' house. Something in my heart leaps. *Home.*

We park in front of the house, and we see their door open before we even get out of the car. And there stands my dad. He's been waiting for us. He gives hugs to Jen and the kids, and then he comes and greets me. He says the same thing every time: "Hi Dave. It's good to see you." But it is much more than a routine greeting. He embraces me and says it in such a way that it tells me that he has been thinking about this moment...planning for this moment...longing for this moment. We couldn't wait to get there. And he couldn't wait to receive us.

After everybody greets Mom & Dad, we unpack the car and take our luggage inside. And then it is time to eat. We sit down together, and Dad prays a heartfelt prayer of thanks. Yes, he thanks the Lord for the food, but even if the plates and saucepans were empty, his prayer would still be the same. Because it's not just the prayer of a man who is glad that he has a nice meal in front of him. It's a prayer of profound gratitude, from the heart of a father whose children have come home. The father's table is full. That's how it is supposed to be.

Mom always asks, "How was your trip?" And we always tell her it was fine. But at this point, it really doesn't matter what happened on the journey. It doesn't matter if we got stuck in a traffic jam or if we drove straight through with no problems. It doesn't matter if the car ran well or if it broke down along the way. It doesn't matter how we felt on the trip, whether we were tired or strong, healthy or sick, bored or entertained. Whatever happened on the journey, whether good or bad, is finished. Only one thing matters now—we are home. It's time to celebrate.

It's not a celebration of someone's birthday or graduation, or any of the other occasions we normally celebrate in this world. It's a celebration of family, a celebration of the wonderful freedom to simply love and be loved. And as we sit around the table, eating, laughing, and talking together, I realize that this moment is what the whole journey was about. It was never about getting to a place. It was about getting to people. The only reason we traveled was to get home—where we are known, where we are treasured, where we are loved, and where we are free.

Thinking about this moment was what kept me going when I got tired, when I got frustrated with other drivers on the road, when I didn't feel like driving any longer and just wanted to be done with the whole thing. In the midst of it all, I looked ahead to what was coming, and I found encouragement in my own words to the children: "Don't worry… We'll make it…It won't be too much longer…We're almost there."

The Joy Set Before Us

Imagine if I had gotten lost in the details of the journey—getting so stressed about our provisions for the trip, constantly dealing with conflicts between our kids, and getting distracted by potholes and diversions. Imagine if I had focused my attention on making sure that we were well-dressed for the journey, that we traveled in the best car, and that we were properly entertained as we went. Imagine if all of my thoughts and energy were taken up with those details…but then I forgot where we were going. It wouldn't make much sense to be on the journey at all, would it? No, it wouldn't. Yet, sadly, it is how so many Christians live their lives.

You see, thinking about the joy of coming home to my earthly father's house makes me think about another homecoming, the day when we will finally all gather around our heavenly Father's table, to begin a celebration of His love that will last forever. That's where this journey is leading. That is the most beautiful motivation to keep going, and it's the only thing that makes any sense out of this confusing and painful world that we're traveling through each day.

But we don't talk much about heaven in our churches these days because we've become so obsessed with what we want God to do for us now. We have forgotten that our journey has a purpose, a final destination. We are satisfied with the Father's provision, but very few are longing for the Father's presence. We seek the Father's help, but not many really think much about the Father's house. We have forgotten where we are going. And that is tragic, because life in the Father's house is where we will experience the complete fulfillment of everything we were created for, the perfect satisfaction of everything our hearts have ever desired.

One of my favorite passages of Scripture is in Luke 22, when Jesus and His disciples were gathered for one final meal together. I love it because it is a beautiful picture of the heart of God, of His relentless desire to give life to His children. And I love it because it is a perfect example of how Jesus lived with His focus completely on the fulfillment of that desire.

It was the Passover meal, a once-a-year celebration of freedom when the children of Israel remembered how God had delivered their forefathers from slavery, executing judgment on every home in the land of Egypt, yet "passing over" the homes of the Israelites…as long as they had painted the blood of a perfect lamb on the doorposts. On that very night, God led them out of bondage and into freedom, the beginning of their journey to the home that He had prepared for them.

For the disciples, it was just another Passover celebration. They didn't understand what was about to happen. But Jesus knew that this particular night was much more than the annual remembrance of something that God had done a long time ago. He knew that as soon as this meal was finished, He was going to be betrayed and arrested. And on the following day, *He* was going to be the Passover lamb. It was *His* blood that was going to be spilled.

Knowing this, you would think that He would want to delay or even avoid this meal, that He would be saying to Himself, "I don't want suppertime to come, because I know what comes next." But He didn't dread it at all. He welcomed it. He was looking forward to it. Look at what He said:

I have eagerly desired to eat this Passover with you before I suffer. For I tell you, I will not eat it again until it finds fulfillment in the kingdom of God.

Luke 22:14-16 (NIV)

He knew that this meal was His last stop before heading down the path that would lead Him to the cross. And He *eagerly desired* it? Why? Well, when Jesus gathered with His disciples to look back and celebrate the freedom and homecoming of the children of Israel, it made Him look ahead to another gathering, another homecoming, another celebration of freedom.

This celebration, though, won't be with just a handful of people in a borrowed upstairs room. This one will be in the Father's house, at the

Father's table, where He will gather His sons and daughters from among every tribe, language, and nation, and from every time period in human history. It will be a celebration of the final homecoming of all of the Father's children, a celebration that will never end.

Jesus was eager for this meal with His disciples, because He was eager to do what was necessary to make this final homecoming possible, even though that meant a painful journey to the cross. He understood very well the depth of the pain and suffering that He was about to experience. His prayer in the Garden of Gethsemane shows us that. But the writer of Hebrews says that Jesus endured this pain because He was looking ahead to the joy that was on the other side of the pain. He had the strength to continue, because He could see the celebration that awaited Him when the journey was complete:

> Because of the joy awaiting Him, He endured the cross, disregarding its shame.
>
> Hebrews 12:2 (NLT)

Jesus wasn't concerned with making His journey pleasant. He was concerned with accomplishing the purpose of His journey. He was looking to the destination. He was thinking about the Father's table. He knew the love and the joy that would be shared around that table, and He was looking ahead with great anticipation to that wonderful day when all of the Father's children gather to celebrate the freedom that Jesus purchased for us at the cross, the freedom to live together in the beauty and the fullness of the Father's love…forever.

And if He would allow me to make an advance booking, I think I know who I would like to sit next to at that first meal – two young people who I used to teach about the Father's love. If I could talk to them now, though, they would be the ones teaching me. They would be able to explain all of these things to you much better than I could ever dream of doing…because now they see Him face to face.

A Real Man of God

Maurice was known by all as "M.O.G.", which stands for "Man of God." M.O.G. was from northern Uganda. He came to Kampala to go to university, but his heart was always for his people at home. This was during the time when Kony and his soldiers were still very active in the north, and whenever M.O.G. talked of the situation at home, tears would well up in his eyes. When he prayed for his people, he did it with such intense love that it felt as if we had left the room where we were praying and had stepped right into the heart of God.

He was a member of our missions class on campus for two years (the one that Gloria talked about in the last chapter). The last time that he was at our house, he took a long time to share with me how these two years together had fueled his passion to serve God and to share His love with as many people as possible. He said he had learned how to be a man of God, not only in name, but in reality. He said, "Pastor Dave, now I really understand. Now, I'm ready."

He had two desires. First, he said, "I just want to have the opportunity to tell my whole village about Christ." Then his eyes turned to a picture we had hanging on our wall, a West African version of Jesus surrounded by children in a village setting. M.O.G. pointed at Him and said the last words that I ever heard him speak: "I just want to be like that Guy."

Three weeks later, M.O.G. was killed in a car accident at the age of 25. But not before God gave him the desires of his heart. The previous weekend, he had gone home for his uncle's burial. And the report I received was that he shared the gospel all weekend. He shared Christ with his relatives. He shared the love of God with his neighbors. He even had the opportunity to preach to all the village leaders. "I just want to have the opportunity to tell my whole village about Christ." Mission accomplished.

As for his second request…well, let's just say that M.O.G. no longer looks at a likeness of Jesus on a wall. He sees Him face to face. And John promises, "We will be like Him, because we will see Him just as He is" (1 John 3:2).

Last time I saw M.O.G., we were talking in my sitting room. Next time I see him, we'll be rejoicing at the Father's table. I can't wait.

Finding Her Real Father

In chapter 7, I began to tell you about Justine, a girl who lived at the orphanage where we worked when we first came to Uganda. I promised I would tell you the rest of her story.

Justine was a great athlete, and she was always the top student in her class. But she was so bitter towards God because she had lost her parents at a very young age. She used to come to our house and play basketball with me, and she really loved our kids. Once in a while, it seemed like we were beginning to break through to her. But her heart was so hard.

When she was in her early 20s, we were all shocked to hear that Justine had been diagnosed with bone cancer in her leg. After surgery and months of treatment, though, the doctors said they were confident that they had dealt with the cancer completely. They expected her to be totally fine.

The following year, after we had moved on to establish a new ministry, Justine called me one day. She told me that she was going to law school soon, and she wanted to know if she could come and visit us over the Easter weekend. We said that would be great and that we looked forward to seeing her. But Easter came and went, and we didn't hear anything from her.

Then we received the news. Justine was in the hospital. The cancer had returned aggressively, and she only had a few weeks to live. I immediately got ready and drove to Kampala to see her. When I arrived, I hugged her and greeted her, and then I got straight to the point: "Justine, you're afraid to die aren't you?"

She looked down, and nodded her head slowly.

"Is it because you don't feel like God will forgive you?"

"Yes. He has put so many people in my life who love me, but I have rejected Him because I was angry at Him for taking my parents. It's too late now."

I talked to her about the love of Jesus, assuring her that He would forgive her, no matter what she had done. I told her that He had never stopped loving her, not even for a moment. I told her that He was there waiting, as He had always been, for her to open her heart so that He could fill it with His love. We prayed together, and then talked a bit about how she was feeling physically. I updated her on how Jen and the kids were doing, and then I left.

It was not at all the first time that Justine had heard about the love of God. She had heard it from me and from many other people at the children's home over the years. And she had always resisted it. I didn't leave the hospital with any indication that this time would be any different.

But when I came back two days later, I couldn't believe my eyes. As soon as I walked into the room, I knew that God had done something wonderful. I saw a Justine I had never seen before. Her eyes sparkled with joy, and for the first time ever, I saw Justine at peace. She confirmed with her words what I already knew by looking at her face—she had given her heart to Christ.

So now, unless God had a miracle planned that I didn't know about, I knew that it was time to prepare her to die. I said, "Justine, you know that you're never going to go to law school, don't you?" She said yes, she knew that.

I continued: "And you know that whether you live for another thirty years or thirty days, you have already entered fully into *everything* that God created you for…because He is your Father now."

She looked me in the eye with a big smile, and with complete assurance she said, "Yeah, I know that."

The next visit was my last one. I brought Jen and the kids with me so that they could say goodbye. Justine had always been so strong, but you could visibly see the effects of the cancer that was draining the life from her body.

I said, "You're ready, aren't you, Justine?"

She smiled, and just said, "Yeah."

I prayed with her, I hugged her, and I told her I loved her, knowing that I would never see her again on this side of eternity. We talked a few more times by phone, and two weeks later, at the age of 24, Justine passed into the arms of the only Father she was ever really meant to know.

On Our Way Home

In the eyes of the world, those are senseless tragedies, sad stories of promising lives that were cut short. But Justine and M.O.G. aren't missing anything. They are experiencing in reality what we can only imagine. Nothing on this earth can compare with what they have. And I can promise you that they aren't looking back with even one bit of regret, thinking about what could have been, if only they'd had a few more years here. They are in the presence of the Father, basking in the freedom of His love. That's all that they were ever meant to experience. It's the whole reason for the journey.

The apostle Paul says that when it comes to God's children, we should view death differently. He says that we need to understand where our journey is taking us, so that we will "not grieve like the rest of mankind, who have no hope" (1 Thessalonians 4:13, NIV). And where is our journey taking us? For all of God's children through Jesus Christ, the wonderful reality is this: "we will be with the Lord forever" (1 Thessalonians 4:17, NIV).

But in the meantime, I'll be very honest. I miss them. There is nothing I hate more than saying goodbye to people I love (whether due to death, or because somebody moves away). I have said so many of them over the past fifteen years that I think I should have enough credits to be awarded a PhD in goodbyes. But it is not a skill that can be mastered. It never gets any easier. In fact, as God expands my capacity to love, the goodbyes only become more difficult.

Goodbyes in the body of Christ are some of the most profoundly painful and deeply hopeful events that exist. Painful because it hurts to be separated from the depths of love that we shared together in Christ. Hopeful because we are promised that a day is coming when "goodbye" will no longer be part of our vocabulary. I will sit with Justine and M.O.G. at the Father's table, and we will celebrate the freedom of His love together forever. That is a promise, straight from the heart of the Father Himself:

> And I heard a loud voice from the throne saying, "Look! God's dwelling place is now among the people, and He will dwell with them. They will be His people, and God Himself will be with them and be their God. 'He will wipe every tear from their eyes. There will be no more death' or mourning or crying or pain, for the old order of things has passed away." He who was seated on the throne said, "I am making everything new!" Then he said, "Write this down, for these words are trustworthy and true." He said to me: "It is done. I am the Alpha and the Omega, the Beginning and the End. To the thirsty I will give water without cost from the spring of the water of life. Those who are victorious will inherit all this, and I will be their God and they will be my children.
>
> Revelation 21:3-7 (NIV)

It's mind-boggling to try to imagine what it could possibly be like to live a life that's free from death, sorrow, crying, and pain. After nearly fifty years of living in this world, though, I'm more than ready to give it a try. A world without suffering sounds unbelievably good to me right now.

But as wonderful as that will be, that's not the best part of it. Because life and freedom are not found in the absence of suffering…life and freedom are found in *Him*. The hope of heaven is that *He* is there. The real promise is the promise of His presence: "Look, God's home is now among His people! He will live with them and they will be His people.

God Himself will be with them…and I will be their God, and they will be My children."

There is nothing to celebrate unless God Himself is there, because the joy of the Father's table is the celebration of the Father's love. It's in His heart where we find freedom. It's in His presence where we find fullness of joy. What we experience now in part, we will experience then in full. That's what the journey is all about.

When we feast at His table, it won't matter if we were rich or poor during our years on this earth. It won't matter if we lived for many years or for few. It won't matter if we earned master's degrees or if we stopped studying after P1. It won't matter what anybody said about us, thought about us, or did to us. The things that seemed to be so important on the journey will fade away quickly like a distant dream, because we will be overwhelmed by His majesty, consumed by His love, and filled with His joy.

It's easy to lose sight of that, because this world is not always a very easy place to live. It can be confusing. It can be frustrating. It can be painful. And it can be so exhausting. Sometimes we get so distracted by the details of just trying to make it through this life, and we forget why we're here at all.

We need to be reminded that this world is not our final destination. We are on a journey. We need to be reminded that this world is not our home. We are on our way home. We need someone to point us to the Father's house, to remind us of the joy that is waiting just up the road: "Don't worry, we'll make it. It won't be too much longer." When we know that, it changes everything. It fills us with hope. It gives us strength. It makes us free to really live…because we're almost there.

The Joy of the Father's Table

And when we get there, our Father will be waiting for us. He will welcome us with an everlasting embrace that says, "I have been thinking about this moment…I've been planning for this moment…I've been longing for this moment."

On that day, when we gather around His table for the first time as His family, the Father's face will be radiant with the same love that has burned for His children from all eternity. As He looks around the room, His heart will burst with a joy that the whole universe could never contain.

"I have eagerly desired to eat this meal with you," He will say, as He laughs with infinite delight, "because this is the fulfillment of everything My heart has desired since before the beginning of time. This is why I created the world. This is why I called Abraham, Moses, David, and Elijah. This is why I gave the Law. This is why I sent My Son into the world. This is why the Church was born. This is why I put My Spirit within you. This is why I taught you to pray. This is the reason for everything."

The Father's table will be full. That's how it is supposed to be. The number of His children around the table will be so many that nobody but the Father would ever be able to count them all. Yet even though they are so many, He will turn up the palms of the biggest and strongest hands that anyone has ever seen, and He will reveal where He has engraved the name of every single son and daughter. And each name will be displayed in such a prominent place on His hand that it will seem as if it were the one that mattered the most.

Then He will look into the eyes of each child, one by one, and He will speak to them with the loving sincerity of One who has never wanted anything except to be their Father: "I have loved you with an everlasting love. Before you had ever done anything, either good or bad, I chose you to be My child. When you were born, I was more proud than any Father could ever be. I taught you how to walk, how to feed yourself, and how to talk. In every moment of your life, I have been there. When you slept, I rejoiced over you with songs of love. When you were happy, I celebrated with you. When you were hurting, I wept for you. When you went far from Me, I was always near. When you fell, it was I who caught you. When you were afraid, it was I who held you. When everyone else rejected you, I was right there beside you. I never stopped thinking about you. I never stopped watching you. I never stopped loving you.

When you became My child through faith in what My Son did for you at the cross, I threw a party in heaven like you have never seen on earth. It has been My joy to fill you with My Spirit and to invite you to walk with Me as I carried out My business on earth. All along, it was this day that I had in mind. I have eagerly desired this moment. And now here you are, with Me, where you have always belonged. You are My beloved child in whom I am well-pleased, and it is My delight to give you the fullness of everything that I am, now and for all eternity. Come, and share in My joy. Rest in My presence. Rejoice in My love."

Your room is prepared. The table is being set. Look ahead with joyful anticipation. Don't worry. We'll make it. It won't be too much longer. We're almost there.

Whatever happened to us on the journey, whether good or bad, will be finished. Only one thing will matter then—we will be home. And we will begin an eternal celebration of the wonderful freedom we have in Him, the freedom to simply love and be loved. At that moment, we will fully realize that this is what the whole journey was about.

It was never about getting to a place. It was always about getting home to Him: to dwell in the beauty of the Father's house…to feast on His love at the Father's table…to rest in the freedom of the Father's heart. It was His desire from the beginning. It will be your joy forever.

It's His delight…it's your destiny.

Key Thought:

The hope of heaven is that *He* is there. The real promise is the promise of His presence. When we feast at His table, the things that seemed to be so important on the journey will fade away quickly like a distant dream, because we will be overwhelmed by His majesty, consumed by His love, and filled with His joy. What we experience now in part, we will experience then in full.

Personal Reflection / Group Discussion:

Jesus wasn't concerned with making His journey pleasant. He was concerned with accomplishing the purpose of His journey. He was looking to the destination. He was thinking about the Father's table. He knew the love and the joy that would be shared around that table, and He was looking ahead with great anticipation to that wonderful day when all of the Father's children gather to celebrate the freedom that Jesus purchased for us at the cross, the freedom to live together in the beauty and the fullness of the Father's love…forever. "For the joy set before Him, He endured the cross, despising its shame."

- *How can looking ahead to the hope of heaven actually make us more focused on living for Christ NOW?*

- *With such a beautiful promise in front of us, how is it that we so easily and so often get distracted by temporary concerns which can never really satisfy what our souls are hungry for?*

Scriptural Prescription:

And if I go and prepare a place for you, I will come back and take you to be with Me that you also may be where I am.

John 14:3 (NIV)

And I heard a loud voice from the throne saying, "Look! God's dwelling place is now among the people, and He will dwell with them. They will be His people, and God Himself will be with them and be their

God. 'He will wipe every tear from their eyes. There will be no more death' or mourning or crying or pain, for the old order of things has passed away." He who was seated on the throne said, "I am making everything new!"

Revelation 21:3-5

Further Study:

Some people say that if we think too much about heaven, then we will ignore the good that God is calling us to do here and now. But is that what the Bible says?

Read Colossians 3:1-2; Romans 8:18-25; 2 Corinthians 4:16 - 5:9; 1 Thessalonians 4:13-18. What does Paul say is our motive for godly living, for enduring suffering, for serving Christ, for dealing with the death of loved ones?

NOTES

Before You Begin

[1]My dad used the "Scriptural Prescription" with thousands of people in counseling over the years. Hiding the Word in our hearts is a key to finding healing and freedom in Christ.

Introduction

[2]This phrasing comes from an interview with my good friend, Pastor David Zijjan.

[3]Floyd McClung, *Father Heart of God* (Eugene, OR: Harvest House Publishers, 1985), 11. This was one of the books that began to really shape my thinking years ago in terms of understanding God as Father, as well as giving me an eye-opening introduction into the ways that unresolved pain prevents people from knowing and experiencing the heart of God.

[4]Tony Evans, *Kingdom Man* (Carol Stream, IL: Tyndale House Publishers, 2012), 145.

[5]Brennan Manning, *The Furious Longing of God* (Colorado Springs: David C. Cook, 2009), 42-43. Anything you can find by Brennan Manning on the heart of God is more than worthwhile reading.

[6]Henri Nouwen, *Return of the Prodigal Son* (New York: Doubleday, 1992), 17. This is a beautiful look into the heart of the Father, based on Nouwen's reflections on a famous Rembrandt painting of the return of the younger son in Luke 15.

Chapter 1

[7]E. Stanley Jones, *A Song of Ascents: A Spiritual Autobiography* (Nashville: Abingdon Press, 1968), 135.

[8]Rick Warren: 'God Didn't Need Us, He Wanted Us,' interview by David (October 2005), www.beliefnet.com/Faiths/Christianity/2005/10/Rick-Warren-God-Didnt-Need-Us-He-Wanted-Us (accessed May 6, 2013).

[9]John Piper, "Dissatisfied Contentment: Toward an Ethic of Christian Hedonism," Desiringgod.org, January 2, 1989, www.desiringgod.org/resource-library/articles/dissatisfied-contentment (accessed May2, 2013).

Chapter 2

[10]Charles H. Spurgeon, "The Compassion of Jesus," (sermon, Metropolitan Tabernacle, London, England, December 24, 1914), www.spurgeon.org/sermons/3438.htm (accessed May 7, 2013)

[11]*Biblesuite.com*, "splagchnizomai,", http://biblesuite.com/greek/4697.htm (accessed April 30, 2013). Splagchnizomai is the Greek word that Matthew chose to use for "compassion" in Matthew 9:36. It is a compound word based on the root word splancha that refers to the inner organs in the human body—the bowels, the liver, the kidneys, etc. It came to be used as a term of extreme emotion, describing something stirring and even causing pain in the deepest part of your heart. It is defined here using Strong's definitions and other Greek resources.

[12]*Freedictionary.com*, "compassion," www.thefreedictionary.com/compassion (accessed April 28, 2013). Of course, Matthew didn't use the English word "compassion," nor did he know anything about the Latin roots of the word. But it is helpful for us to get a clearer understanding about what compassion really means, and it is perfectly consistent with how Matthew described what was happening in the heart of Jesus when He looked out over the crowds.

[13]Karl Barth, *Church Dogmatics: Volume 3, Part 2, The Doctrine of Creation* (London: T &T Ltd., 1960), 212.

[14]*Studylight.org*, "Matthew 9:36," http://classic.studylight.org/desk/view.cgi?number=4660
http://classic.studylight.org/desk/view.cgi?number=4496 (accessed May 5, 2013). Here, we examine the two words that Matthew used to describe what Jesus saw in the crowds: "harassed" and "helpless."

[15]Philip Keller, *A Shepherd Looks at Psalm 23* (Grand Rapids, MI: Zondervan, 1970), 61. This is such an insightful book, from the heart of a real shepherd whose experience gives us a unique look at the heart of the Good Shepherd towards us.

[16]Keller, *A Shepherd Looks at Psalm 23*, 55.

[17]"Icelandic Sheep Medical Common Problems," http://www.isfaxa.com/medical (accessed February 22, 2013).

[18]Keller, *A Shepherd Looks at Psalm 23*, 54.

[19]George MacDonald, *Creation In Christ: Unspoken Sermons* (Vancouver: Regent College Publishing, 2004; originally published as *Unspoken Sermons* in 3 volumes, in 1870, 1885, and 1891), 193.

Chapter 3

[20]Thomas Merton. *New Seeds of Contemplation* (New York: New Directions Publishing Corporation, 1962), 62, http://www.goodreads.com/quotes/234836-to-say-that-i-am-made-in-the-image-of (accessed March 14, 2013).

[21]J.I. Packer, *Knowing God* (Downers Grove, IL: InterVarsity Press, 1973), 182.

[22]*Jack Frost: Experiencing the Father's Embrace series*, Disc 1: "A Revelation of the Father's Love" (Shiloh Place Ministries), DVD. Jack used Matthew 22:37-40, 1 Corinthians 13:1-3, and 1 John 4:7-16, helping me to form some of the framework for this section.

[23]*Jack Frost: Experiencing the Father's Embrace series*, Disc 1: "A Revelation of the Father's Love" (Shiloh Place Ministries), DVD.

[24]Christian Research Institute, www.cri.com, "The Gnostic Jesus," http://www.equip.org/articles/the-gnostic-jesus/ (accessed May 10, 2013).

[25]Biblica.com, "1 John," http://www.biblica.com/niv/study-bible/1-john/ (accessed May 9, 2013).

[26]Biblica.com, "1 Corinthians," http://www.biblica.com/niv/study-bible/1-corinthians/ (accessed May 9, 2013).

[27]Tim Keller, *The Prodigal God* (Dutton: New York, 2008), 108. An excellent analysis of the very well-known Luke 15 parable of the prodigal son. Keller helps to define the heart of what sin really is, yet he puts the emphasis where it belongs—not on the sin of the sons but on the extravagant love and grace of the father.

Chapter 4

[28]Dan Cruver, *Reclaiming Adoption: Missional Living through the Rediscovery of Abba Father* (Cruciform Press, 2011), 14.

[29]Cruver, *Reclaiming Adoption*, 41.

[30]C.S. Lewis, *The Weight of Glory* (New York: Harper Collins, 2001; originally published 1949), 41, quoted in Keller, *The Prodigal God*, 94.

[31]Keller, *The Prodigal God*, 95-97.

[32]Packer, *Knowing God*, 207.

[33]C.J. Mahaney, "God as Father: Understanding the Doctrine of Adoption," (sermon, Covenant Life Church, Gaithersburg, MD, December 2, 2007), http://spurgeon.wordpress.com/2007/12/07/cj-mahaney-on-adoption/ (accessed February 20, 2013).

[34]Richard Phillips, "The Good News of Adoption," in *Reclaiming Adoption: Missional Living through the Rediscovery of Abba Father*, Dan Cruver et al. (Cruciform Press, 2011), 59-60.

[35]C.J. Mahaney, "God as Father"

[36]Max Lucado, *Six Hours One Friday* (Nashville: Thomas Nelson, 2013; originally published 1989), 11-12.

[37]Keller, *The Prodigal God*, 101-102.

Chapter 5

[38]Tim Keller, *The King's Cross* (New York: Dutton, 2011), 102.

[39]"How Can the Law on Defilement Be Made More Effective?" *New Vision*, October 20, 2010: http://www.newvision.co.ug/D/8/20/735618 (accessed February 16, 2013).

[40]David Boan and John Yates, Unpublished manuscript, quoted in Wayne Jacobsen, *He Loves Me* (Windblown Media, Newbury Park, CA, 2007), 150.

Chapter 6

[41]Tullian Tchividjian, *Jesus + Nothing = Everything* (Wheaton, IL: Crossway, 2011), 97.

[42]David Johnson and Jeff Van Vonderen, *The Subtle Power of Spiritual Abuse* (Minneapolis: Bethany House Publishers, 1991), 37. If you have lived under the weight of religious burdens and controlling pastoral leadership, this is a great resource to gain understanding and find healing and freedom.

[43]*The Zondervan NASB Study Bible* (Grand Rapids: Zondervan, 1999), 1402.

[44]Johnson and Van Vonderen, *The Subtle Power of Spiritual Abuse*, 141.

[45]Whitney J. Dough, ed., *Sayings of E. Stanley Jones: A Treasury of Wisdom and Wit* (Franklin, TN: Providence House Publishers,1994), 71.

[46]Festo Kivengere, *Revolutionary Love* (Fort Washington, PA: Christian Literature Crusade, 1983), 41. A great look at the heart of the East African Revival through the experience of one of its greatest leaders. An important book, as I think it gives us some insight into the heart of what we desperately need the Lord to do in Uganda…again.

[47]Jim Robbins, *Recover Your Good Heart* (Kindle Ink Press, 2008), 9. Jim is a good friend of mine from my days at Asbury Seminary.

Chapter 7

[48]John Eldredge, *Fathered by God* (Nashville: Thomas Nelson, 2009), 57-58, quoted in Mark Stibbe, *I Am Your Father*, 107.

[49]Ed Piorek, *The Central Event: Experiencing the Power of the Father's Love* (Cape Town, South Africa: Vineyard International Publishing, 2005), 26.

[50]McClung, *The Father Heart of God*, 19

[51]Robert S. McGee, *Father Hunger* (Ann Arbor, MI: Servant Publications, 1993), 18. This is great work by a counselor who has dealt with these issues of family pain in the lives of countless people.

[52]Richard Alan Krieger, *Civilizations Quotations: Life's Ideal* (Algora Publishing, 2002), 54, http://books.google.co.ug/books?id=zNQGk_fDYUIC&printsec=frontcover&dq=Civilizations+Quotations&hl=en&sa=X&ei=4kOSUZ6fCMqq4ASf-YDAAw&ved=0CEMQ6AEwBQ (accessed May 13, 2013).

[53]McGee, *Father Hunger*, 10.

[54]My understanding of the impact of different types of fathers on the way that their children come to view God has come from many different sources: teaching and writing from Floyd McClung, Jack Frost, Ed Piorek, Robert McGee, Mark Stibbe (authors already cited on these pages); learning from the counseling experiences of my dad and others; and what I have seen in my experiences both in Uganda and America in the past 15 years of ministry.

[55]Mark Stibbe, *I Am Your Father* (Oxford: Monarch Books, 2010), 50.

[56]Stibbe, *I Am Your Father*, 52.

[57]McGee, *Father Hunger*, Servant Publications, Ann Arbor, MI, 1993, 58

[58]McGee, *Father Hunger*, 58.

[59]George Herbert was a Welsh born orator, Anglican priest and poet in the early 17th century. He served in Parliament for 2 years under King James (who authorized the translation of the King James Version of the Bible), and his poems had widespread influence on many throughout England. Quote retrieved from http://christian-quotes.ochristian.com/George-Herbert-Quotes/page-2.shtml (accessed March 2, 2013).

[60]Mark Stibbe, *I Am Your Father*, 158.

[61]Stibbe, *I Am Your Father*, 158.

[62]Corrie Ten Boom, *The Hiding Place: 35th Anniversary Edition* (Grand Rapids: Chosen Books, 2006), 8, www.books.google.co.ug (accessed March 2, 2013). Corrie Ten Boom endured the horrors of a German World War II

prisoner of war camp for nearly a year in 1945, witnessing unspeakable suffering and losing her dear sister as well. It is a powerful story of forgiveness and healing, and of God's love shining in the darkest of places, leading her to her famous statement, "There is no pit so deep that His love is not deeper still."

Chapter 8

[63]Phillip Yancey, *What's So Amazing About Grace: Visual Edition* (Grand Rapids, MI: Zondervan, 2003; original edition published 1997), 22.

[64]Nouwen, *Return of the Prodigal Son* (New York: Doubleday, 1992), 42.

[65]Robbins, *Recover Your Good Heart*, 106.

[66]Robbins, *Recover Your Good Heart*, 106.

[67]*Studylight.org*, "Colossians 2:13," http://classic.studylight.org/desk/view.cgi?number=1813 (accessed April 23, 2013).

[68]*The Zondervan NASB Study Bible*, 1742.

[69]Martin Luther, *Luther: Letters of Spiritual Counsel*, trans. and ed., Theodore G. Tappert, 1960, (Vancouver, BC: Regent College Publishing, 2003), 85, http://www.desiringgod.org/blog/posts/luther-on-five-actions-for-struggling-believers (accessed March 7, 2013).

[70]Andrew Murray, *God's Best Kept Secrets, An Inspirational Daily Devotional* (Grand Rapids: Kregel Publications, 1994; originally published 1923), 196.

[71]Floyd McClung, *Loving the God Who Loves You* (Eastbourne: Kingsway Publications, 1993), 109.

[72]McClung, *Loving the God Who Loves You*, 109.

[73]These are taken from a longer list in McClung, *Loving the God Who Loves You*, 117-118.

[74]Murray, *God's Best Kept Secrets*, 196.

Chapter 9

[75]Lewis, *The Weight of Glory*, 182.

[76]F.B. Meyer Our Daily Homily, Volume 2, 1 Samuel to Job (New York Revell, 1898), 1, www.pleasantplaces.org (accessed March 19, 2013).

[77]Anne Lamott, *Travelling Mercies: Some Thoughts on Faith* (New York: Doubleday / Anchor, 2000), 128, 134.

[78]Lee Strobel, *God's Outrageous Claims: Thirteen Discoveries That Can Revolutionize Your Life* (Grand Rapids: Zondervan, 1997), 13.

[79]Lamott, *Travelling Mercies*, 217.

[80]Lewis Smedes, *Forgive and Forget: Healing the Hurts We Don't Deserve* (New York: Pocket Books, 1996), 170.

[81]Ken Sande, *The Peacemaker: A Biblical Guide to Resolving Personal Conflict* (Grand Rapids: Baker Books, 2004; originally published 1991), 204.

[82]Jean Vanier is the founder of the international movement of L'Arche communities, where people who have developmental disabilities and the friends who assist them create homes and share life together. Quote retrieved from http://www.beliefnet.com/Quotes/Christian/J/Jean-Vanier/Love-Is-An-Act-Of-Endless-Forgiveness.aspx (accessed March 27, 2013).

[83]*Jack Frost: Experiencing the Father's Embrace series*, Disc 5: "Dealing with Father Issues" (Shiloh Place Ministries), DVD.

[84]*Jack Frost: Experiencing the Father's Embrace series*, Disc 5: "Dealing with Father Issues" (Shiloh Place Ministries), DVD.

[85]Jack Frost, *Experiencing Father's Embrace* (Shippensburg, PA: Destiny Image Publishers, 2002), 124.

Chapter 10

[86]Dr. David Jeremiah, *God Loves You: He Always Has – He Always Will* (New York: FaithWords, 2012), xii.

[87]Alan Watson, *Roman Law and Comparative Law* (Athens, GA: University of Georgia Press, 1991), 34, www.books.google.co.ug (accessed March 25, 2013).

[88]William Barclay, *The Letter to the Romans* (Louisville, KY: Westminster John Knox Press, 1975; originally published 1955), 125-26, www.books.google.co.ug (accessed March 22, 2013).

[89]W.M. Ramsay, *A Historical Commentary on St. Paul's Epistle to the Galatians* (Grand Rapids, MI: Baker Book House, 1979; originally published 1900), 353, www.truthortradition.com (accessed March 22, 2013).

[90]Martin Lloyd-Jones, *Howell Harris and Revival* (Edinburgh, Scotland: Banner of Truth, 1973), 290, quoted in Mark Stibbe, *I Am Your Father*, p. 250.

Chapter 11

[91]Nouwen, *Return of the Prodigal Son*, 16.

[92]*Studylight.org*, "Matthew 3:17," http://classic.studylight.org/desk/view.cgi?number=2106 (accessed May 16, 2013).

Chapter 12

[93] Kivengere, *Revolutionary Love*, 7.

[94] D.L. Moody, "Christian Love," (sermon, Moody Church, Chicago), http://www.biblebelievers.com/moody_sermons/m20.html (accessed May 8, 2013).

[95] Soren Kierkegaard, *Works of Love* (Princeton, NJ: Princeton University Press, 1998; originally published 1847), http://www.egs.edu/library/soeren-kierkegaard/quotes/ (accessed May 6, 2013).

[96] "My Heart Was So Full of Love That It Overflowed: Charles Grandison Finney Experiences Conversion," in *Memoirs of Rev. Charles G. Finney*, (New York: A.S. Barnes & Company, 1876), http://historymatters.gmu.edu/d/6374/ (accessed May 5, 2013).

[97] *BibleStudyTools.com*, "Sunecho," http://www.biblestudytools.com/lexicons/greek/nas/sunecho.html (accessed May 14, 2013).

[98] *The Law of Love: The Story of Jackie Pullinger*, (Contracts International/Vision Video, 1989), VHS.

[99] *History Makers: The Fuel of Missions Flame*, "Inspirational Quotes: World Missions," http://www.historymakers.info/stuff/inspirational-quotes.html (accessed May 7, 2013). David Livingstone was a great explorer, but more than anything he was a humble servant of God whose quiet devotion to Jesus is a big reason that the gospel came to Uganda. His Christlike way of living led to the conversion of a British journalist named Henry Morton Stanley (though there is a lot of disagreement as to how genuine that conversion actually was). It was Stanley who sent the appeal to the UK that led to the coming of Alexander Mackay and others in 1877. The simple life of one man who gave his all for Christ opened the way for millions in Uganda to come to know Him!

[100] Andrew Murray, *Absolute Surrender* (Chicago: Moody Press, 1895), 36, http://www.ccel.org/ccel/murray/surrender.pdf (accessed May 5, 2013).

Chapter 13

[101] George Whitefield, *The Works of the Reverend George Whitefield, Volume 1* (Edward and Charles Dilly, 1771), 451, www.books.google.co.ug (accessed May 4, 2013).

[102] Cruver, *Reclaiming Adoption*, 14.

CPSIA information can be obtained at www.ICGtesting.com
Printed in the USA
LVOW12s0547190913

353048LV00005B/7/P